THEODORE PARKER:
American Transcendentalist

A Critical Essay and a Collection
of his Writings

by

Robert E. Collins

The Scarecrow Press, Inc.
Metuchen, N.J.   1973

Library of Congress Cataloging in Publication Data

Parker, Theodore, 1810-1860.
   Theodore Parker: American transcendentalist.

   CONTENTS: Essay: A forgotten American.--Selections
from Theodore Parker: Transcendentalism. The transient
and permanent in Christianity. The position and duties of
the American scholar. [etc.]
   1. Parker, Theodore, 1810-1860. 2. Emerson,
Ralph Waldo, 1803-1882. I. Collins, Robert E., ed.
BX9869. P3A25 1973   288'. 092'4 [B]   73-9593
ISBN 0-8108-0641-X

PREFACE

There is good reason for a book on Theodore Parker. First of all, there are a number of indications, perhaps the clearest of which is the increasing popularity of Henry David Thoreau, that our day might fairly be called an age of neo-transcendentalism. Another indication is the more than passing echo of transcendental-type thought in such writings as the recent best-selling Greening of America by Theodore Reich and in much of the currently popular later writings of Herbert Marcuse. But in a general way, as the original transcendentalists--Thoreau, Emerson, Fuller, Ripley, and others--emphasized the individual over the institutional and humane values over materialistic price tags, so, in our present time, any number of writers, thinkers, and people emphasize the same priorities. Parker was a transcendentalist.

Parker, further, was one of the most outstanding transcendentalists. In fact, in my view he was the most outstanding member of the pre-Civil War group. Parker has the most orderly and vigorous mind of any of the group and is the equal of any in forcefulness of expression. A case in point is Parker's study of the movement itself, "Transcendentalism." Over 100 years later this essay is still the most exact and comprehensive presentation of this somewhat elusive trend of thought. One scholar states that this essay "has been recognized by recent scholarship as one of the best contemporary accounts of the movement," and another makes an even more sweeping evaluation, declaring it "one of the clearest expressions we have of the American rejection of the empirical philosophy of the Enlightenment."[1] The clarity, comprehensiveness, and forcefulness of this essay are typical of any number of other pieces of Parker's writings.[2]

However, despite the timeliness of transcendental thought and the outstanding position of Parker among this

iii

group, it is difficult to get his works. With the exception
of a few of his essays and sermons, for the most part
severely abridged, Parker's works are unavailable even in
many larger libraries. The reader must search out the
1910 "Centenary Edition" or the Civil War-vintage Cobbe
one. A notable exception is Commager's Theodore Parker:
An Anthology but even in this fine work Parker's writings
are considerably abridged and it is presently out of print.

Hence this book on Parker. The latter part consists
of unabridged selections from the best of Parker, thus making at least some of his writings currently available. The
first part consists of a careful comparison with the much
better known transcendentalist, Ralph Waldo Emerson, a
comparison which serves both to introduce Parker and to
demonstrate that he rates a superior position among the
transcendentalists. The aim is not to downgrade Emerson
but to help Parker get the reputation he richly deserves.

Few prophets get honor in their own time and lands.
Such was the case with Parker's fellow transcendentalist,
Henry David Thoreau. Thoreau's popularity came a good
while after his death and, to an extent embarrassing to
Americans, came from across the Atlantic. Something of
the same kind has apparently happened to Parker. He is,
and has been since his death, comparatively little known.
But I am confident that, if given half a chance, Parker will,
like his fellow transcendentalist Thoreau, gain the position
to which he is entitled as one of our country's greatest
thinkers, writers, and social activists.

Notes

1. Whicher, G.F.(ed.), The Transcendentalist Revolt Against
    Materialism (Boston: Heath, 1949), p. vi; Bartlett,
    I. H., "Theodore Parker," Encyclopedia of Philoso-
    phy, ed. Paul Edwards (8 vols.; New York:
    Macmillan, 1967), VI, 46.

2. I would especially recommend "Sermon of Merchants,"
    Collected Works, ed. F. Cobbe (London: Trubner,
    1863-79), VII, 1-33; "Letter to the People of the
    United States Touching the Matter of Slavery," V,
    17-84; "The True Idea of a Christian Church," III,
    36-60; "The Character of Prescott as an Historian,"
    X, 81-116; and, finally, Parker's book, Discourse of
    Matters Pertaining to Religion, I, 1-335.

TABLE OF CONTENTS

Page

Theodore Parker, aged 42, in 1852

A FORGOTTEN AMERICAN

When people think of American transcendentalism they tend to think of Ralph Waldo Emerson. Both the general public and professional scholars see this early American essayist, lecturer, philosopher, and poet as the preeminent representative of the pre-Civil War American thinkers labeled "transcendentalists."[1] The number of paperback editions of Emerson indicates his continuing popularity among the general public and the judgments of Ralph H. Gabriel, John Dewey, and Perry Miller indicate the estimation of some noted scholars.[2] However, there is another transcendentalist[3] who deserves to take at least equal rank with Emerson. Today, this man's writings are almost unavailable and his name is comparatively unknown. He is a "forgotten American." But he deserves to be remembered.

This forgotten man is the Rev. Theodore Parker. Parker was born in 1810 and died on the eve of the Civil War. He was a Unitarian minister who spent the major portion of his ministry at the 28th Congregational Church in Boston, a congregation formed specifically that the voice of this radical have a chance to be heard in Boston. His original bent and life-long hope was that he might lead a life of research and writing but a Christian concern impelled him to become deeply involved in the problems of his day and place. On all he commented incisively, courageously, and clearly. The wonder of his career is how he could get away with the scathing and particular charges he made. For example, when one realizes that Boston was as hostile to abolitionists as Charlestown, S. C., his early, constant, and ringing denunciations of slavery, not just as an institution peculiar to the South but of the large part that Boston merchants, shippers, and politicians played in the "American sin," are a marvel. Though he was never able to devote himself to the quiet scholarship he so longed and hoped for, perhaps he combined the best of two worlds, the theoretical and the practical, for he brought to the analysis of the practical problems of the time the incisiveness, vigor and clarity of a scholarly mind.[4]

1

Parker lived out his view of the task of the scholar, "to represent the higher modes of human consciousness."[5] He saw the land beset with numerous evils, poverty, exploitation, unjust war, mistreatment of the Indians, and especially slavery, and saw it as his task to move people to lessen or erase these evils. This was his chosen vocation. This was how he viewed his Christian ministry. Since the prejudice against him made publication often impossible and nearly always difficult, he turned from the more usual scholarly approach of writing to the less congenial one of lecturing. As he put it, "I appointed myself a home missionary for lectures."[6] He was unbelievably energetic in carrying out this mission. For 10 years and more before his final illness, he spoke from 80 to 100 times a year in every northern state east of Mississippi, in this way reaching from 60,000 to 100,000 people each year![7] And all this lecturing was in addition to his regular sermons to his Boston congregation.

Besides his lectures and sermons Parker engaged in other ways in the fight against societal evils, especially against slavery. He was one of the most active supporters of John Brown and had even hoped at one time to join him in Kansas. He was indicted as one of the leaders of an ill-fated attempt to liberate a slave caught in the meshes of the Fugitive Slave Law. He sheltered a number of fugitive slaves in his own home. He lobbied many politicians, from Seward to Sumner to Chase, to move them to prosecute the fight against this great "American sin."

The best way to meet Theodore Parker is through his writings. For that reason selected quotations on various subjects are presented here, both as a general introduction to this great transcendentalist thinker and as a preparation for a more exact comparison of Parker with Ralph Waldo Emerson. Since Parker is so little known by comparison with Emerson, an extended sampling is necessary. The samples are grouped in four areas: political affairs, social matters, religion, and scholarship and education.

In the area of politics Parker's most memorable phrase is the oft-repeated definition of democracy as government of the people, by the people, and for the people, which he voices in many slightly different forms on many occasions. One such statement of this definition is probably what inspired Lincoln's famous phrase in his Gettysburg Address. Lincoln read one of Parker's sermons and penciled the phrase, "democracy is direct self-government, over all the people,

by all the people, for all the people."[8] There are many
other memorable phrases, for example, Parker's characteri-
zation of Boston: "Boston is now a shop, with the aim of a
shop, and the morals of a shop, and the politics of a shop."[9]
Another is his assertion that if either President Tyler or
President Polk had died in office and their deaths had been
kept quiet with a factotum to sign papers that came to the
presidential desk, none would have been aware of the death
of either president. His most caustic words were for the
former hero of most of New England, Daniel Webster: "I
knew he was a bankrupt politician, in desperate political circumstances, gaming for the Presidency.... I knew he was
not rich: his past history showed that he would do almost
anything for money...."[10]

But Parker does not merely criticize. He praises the
good in American politics and politicians. For instance, "I
think Mass. is a State to be thankful for."[11] He is grateful
for the absence of war and standing armies in the land and
for a past history suffused with religious and moral ideals.
He has high praise for former President John Quincy Adams'
staunch stand for justice in the House of Representatives
from 1831 to his death in 1848.[12] He has kind words for
Charles Sumner as well as for a number of traditional American heroes: Washington, Jefferson, Hancock. Though he
criticizes him sharply, Parker points out that President
Taylor, a man of mediocre ability, was at least honest and
tried hard to be a good president. He even respects John
Calhoun, the great Southern senator who defended what to
Parker was the great American sin, slavery. Parker says
that Calhoun fought "manfully in an unmanly cause."

Finally, Parker speaks movingly of the wonderful future of America:

> What a noble destination is before us if we are but
> faithful. Shall politicians come between the people
> and the eternal right--between the American and
> his history! When you remember what our fathers
> have done; what we have done--substituted a new
> industrial for a military state, the self-rule of this
> day for the vicarious government of the middle
> ages; when you remember what a momentum the
> human race has got during its long run--it is plain
> that slavery is on the way to end.

As soon as the North awakes to its ideas, and uses

> its vast strength of money, its vast strength of
> numbers, and still more gigantic strength of edu-
> cated intellect, we shall tread this monster under-
> neath our feet.... One day the North will rise in
> her majesty, and put slavery under our feet, and
> then we shall extend the area of freedom. The
> blessing of almighty God will come down upon the
> noblest people the world ever saw--who have tri-
> umphed over Theocracy, Monarchy, Aristocracy,
> Despotocracy, and have got a Democracy--a govern-
> ment of all, for all, and by all--a Church without
> a bishop, a State without a king, a community with-
> out a lord, and a family without a slave. [13]

In the area of social problems, Parker takes a number of noteworthy stands. He was an adamant foe of slavery,
so it is no surprise that some of his most forceful language
is in his attacks on that institution. Commenting on the
argument that there are passages in the Bible which defend
slavery, he says, "if the Bible defends slavery, it is not so
much the better for slavery, but so much the worse for the
Bible."[14] In parallel words he says that "if Christianity
support American slavery, so much the worse for Christianity, that is all."[15] In his remarkable "Letter on Slavery"
Parker asks, "can the Christian relations of human brotherhood, the Christian duty of love to men, be practically
preached in the slave States? I only publish an open secret
in saying that it is impossible. The forms of Christianity
may be preached, not its piety, not its morality, not even
its philosophy, or its history."[16] After citing such despots
as the Bey of Tunis and the Czar of Russia who, while not
acknowledging the inalienable rights of man had yet freed the
slaves in their lands, and contrasting this with American
which is founded on these inalienable rights yet maintains
slavery, Parker concludes:

> Take all the slave-laws of the United States to-
> gether, consider the race that has made them,
> their religion, the political ideas of their govern-
> ment, that it is in the nineteenth century after
> Christ, and they form the most revolting work of
> legislation to be found in the annals of any pacific
> people. [17]

Parker is just as strong in his comments on a number of other social matters. In regard to the Meixcan War,
in many respects the Viet Nam of that day, Parker recounts

with bitter sarcasm the naval bombardment of the Mexican
City of Vera Cruz. Both sides are Christians and as such
devoted to precepts of the Sermon on the Mount. Both see
all men as sons of God and so their brothers. The Americans in particular, according to Parker, have sent more
missionaries to the heathen than any other nation. Yet its
naval forces stand off this Mexican port and shell it. To cap
the irony, the translation of the town's name is "True
Cross." Parker comments acidly, "see how these Christians
love one another."[18] Parker was one of the first to criticize the shabby treatment of the Indians. "We have extermi-
nated the Indians; we keep no treaties made with the red
men; they keep all."[19]

Parker was an outspoken foe of northern slavery, the
exploitation of the poor and downtrodden by the wealthy and
powerful: "Is it Christian or manly to reduce wages in hard
times, and not raise them in fair times? and not raise them
again in extraordinary times? Is it God's will that large
dividends and small wages be paid at the same time?"[20] As
a result of such exploitation more and more wealth and power
accumulates in fewer and fewer hands until "the comfortless
hutch of the poor, who works, though with shiftless hands
and foolish head, is a dark back-ground to the costly stable
of the rich man, who does nothing for the world but gather
its treasures, and whose horses are better fed, housed,
trained up, and cared for, than his brother."[21]

Further, Parker answers the typical American argument that such conditions foster the development of man.
"I know that misery has called out heroic virtue in some men
and women.... We have noble examples of that in the midst
of us; but how many men has poverty trod down into the mire;
how many has the sight of misery hardened into cold world-
liness, the man frozen into mere respectability, its thin
smile on his lips, its ungodly contempt in his heart."[22]
Such ruthless competition not only crushes the manliness and
Christianity of the masses but rots that of the economically
successful. The successful gain the entire world but end up
soulless.

Ever a man to make his points with specific instances,
Parker tells how the poor and downtrodden suffer. They
suffer in buying their daily bread:

Having neither capital nor store-room, they must
purchase articles of daily need in the smallest

quantities. They buy, therefore, at the greatest
disadvantage, and yet at the dearest rates. I am
told it is not a rare thing for them to buy inferior
qualities of flour at six cents a pound, or $11. 88
a barrel, while another man buys a month's supply
at a time for $4 or $5 a barrel.... So it is
with all kinds of food; they are bought in the smallest quantities, and at a rate which a rich man
would think ruinous. [23]

This sounds like something out of one of the recent studies
of ghetto conditions. Parker cites an actual case to illustrate how differently the downtrodden suffer at the hands of
the law:

Let the son of a distinguished man beat a watchman, knowing him to be such, and be brought before a
justice (it would be 'levying war' if a mulatto had
done so to a marshal); he is bailed off for two
hundred dollars. But let a black man have in his
pockets a weapon, which the Constitution and the
laws of Mass. provide that any man may have, if
he pleases, and he is brought to trial and bound
over for--two hundred dollars, think you? No!
but for six hundred dollars! three times as much
as is required of the son of the secretary of State
for assaulting a magistrate![24]

On the other hand the powerful use the state to aug-
ment their power. In fact, they look on the state as "a
machine to help them make money."[25] The end result, the
making of money, is what counts; the means are unimportant.
"No matter how you get money. You may rent houses for
rumshops and for brothels; you may make rum, import rum,
sell rum to the ruin of thousands whom you thereby bring
down to the kennel and the almshouse and the gaol. If you
get money by that, no matter: it is 'clean money,' however
dirtily got."[26] All the while the law stands by unconcerned.
"Much of our common law, it seems to me, is based on
might, not right."[27]

But Parker sees a better day coming

when the few shall not be advanced at the expense
of the many; when ten pairs of female hands shall
not be deformed to nurse a single pair into preter-
natural delicacy, but when all men shall eat bread

in the sweat of their face, and yet find leisure to
cultivate what is best and divinest in their souls,
to a degree we do not dream of as yet; when the
strong man who wishes to be a mouth and not a
hand, or to gain the treasures of society by violence
or cunning, and not by paying their honest price,
will be looked upon with the same horror we feel
for pirates and robbers, and the guardians who
steal the inheritance of their wards, and leave them
to want and die. [28]

And America has demonstrated the energy that can bring such
a better day. In the election of 1848, Parker notes, pro-
digious work was done to bring about a change in administration. If such an effort were directed to reforming the ills
of society, "What evil can stand against mankind?"[29] If the
work expended on building the railroads radiating out from
Boston, the work expended on damming up the New England
rivers and on constructing the factory towns of Lowell and
Lawrence were so directed, that better day would be a reality.

In the third area, that of religion, Parker has much
of worth to say. He is full of anger at the clergy and
churches who ignore the sin which blacks the American soul,
slavery.

Eight and twenty thousand Protestant ministers!
The foremost sect of them all debated, a little
while ago, whether it would have a Litany, and on
what terms it should admit young men to the communion table--allow them to drink 'grocer's wine, '
and eat 'baker's bread, ' on the 'Lord's day, ' in the
'Lord's house'; and never dared lift that palsied
hand, in which was once the fire and blood of Channing, against the world's mightiest sin. Eight and
twenty thousand Protestant ministers, and not a sect
that is opposed to slavery! Oh, the Church! the
Church of America! False to the great prophets of
the Old Testament, the great world's Prophet of the
New; false to the fathers whose bloody knees once
kissed the Rock of Plymouth![30]

Once the clergy were the leaders of the people. Now they
remain silent, or even defend the plight of the people they
ought to lead. "Once the clergy were the masters of the
people, and authors of public opinion to a great degree; now
they are chiefly the servants of the people, and follow public

opinion, and but seldom aspire to lead it, except in matters of their own craft, such as the technicalities of a sect, or the form of a ritual."[31] If anything, the practice of the churches is more wretched than its preaching. Parker illustrates by describing the congregation planning to build a church. Having raised a fund of $50,000 the congregation does not even consider devoting a fifth of that fund to the poor and putting up the building with the rest, but instead borrows an additional $30,000 to build a lavish temple and "then shuts the poor out of its bankrupt aisles."[32] Christ shouldered his cross to save men, his followers shoulder their ornate temples to impress men.

But as in his comments on political affairs and social matters, Parker is not all negative criticism. His inaugural sermon at the Boston 28th Congregational Church presents a noble view of what true Christianity ought to be. For example, the true Christianity ought to treasure freedom, not insist on unity of dogma. "The greater the variety of individualities in church or state, the better it is.... If a church cannot allow freedom it were better not to allow itself, but cease to be.... It is a poor thing to purchase unity of church-action at the cost of individual freedom."[33] Then Parker describes the true church's role:

> We expect the sins of commerce to be winked at in the street; the sins of the state to be applauded on election days and in a Congress.... Here they are to be measured by Conscience and Reason, which look to permanent results and universal ends; to be looked at with reference to the Laws of God, the everlasting ideas on which alone is based the welfare of the world.... If there be a public sin in the land, if a lie invade the state, it is for the church to give the alarm.... We are all brothers before God. Mutually needful we must be; mutually helpful we should be.... Every beggar, every pauper, born and bred among us, is a reproach to us, and condemns our civilization.... Every jail is a monument, on which it is writ in letters of iron that we are still heathens, and the gallows ... the last argument a 'Christian' state offers to the poor wretches it trained up to be criminals, stands there, a sign of our infamy ... as an index of our shame.... It seems to me that a church which dares name itself Christian, the Church of the Redeemer, which aspires to be a true church, must

set itself about all this business, and be not merely
a church of theology, but of religion; not of faith
only, but of works; a just church by its faith bringing works into life. It should not be a church
termagant, which only peevishly scolds at sin, in
its anile way; but a church militant against every
form of evil, which not only censures, but writes
out on the walls of the world the brave example of
a Christian life, that all may take pattern therefrom. Thus only can it become the church trium-
phant. If a church were to waste less time in
building its palaces of theological speculation,
palaces mainly of straw, and based on chaff, erect-
ing air-castles and fighting battles to defend those
palaces of straw, it surely would have more time
to use in the practical good works of the day....
Now if men were to engage in religion as in politics, commerce, arts; if the absolute religion, the
Christianity of Christ, were applied to life with all
the might of this age ... what a result should we
not behold! We should build up a great state with
unity in the nation, and freedom in the people; a
state where there was honourable work for every
hand, bread for all mouths, clothing for all backs,
culture for every mind, and love and faith in every
heart. [34]

Finally, in the area of scholarship and education,
Parker has many memorable things to say. A good example
is his review of Prescott's History of the Reign of Ferdinand
and Isabella, in which he demonstrates his breadth of view,
his mastery of detail, and his critical balance. Beginning
with a discussion of the task of an historian, Parker points
out that the historian does not chronicle but explains. In
Parker's view, history is philosophy teaching by experience.
He criticizes Prescott for a lack of such a philosophy.
Prescott, says Parker, contents himself with strings of facts.
"He tells the facts for the facts' sake."[35] This lack fatally
mars the work. "It would be difficult to find a history in
the English language, of any note, so entirely destitute of
philosophy. Accordingly, the work is dull and in-animate;
the reading thereof tiresome and not profitable." He shows
his mastery of detail in criticizing Prescott for leaving out
pertinent matters, e. g. , not giving an adequate account of
the conditions at the beginning of this reign. Without this
knowledge as a background, he says, it is difficult if not
impossible to evaluate the changes Ferdinand and Isabella

made. Parker himself then describes the conditions, indicat-
ing that he must have done at least as serious research in
writing his review as Prescott did in writing his book.
Finally, Parker shows his critical balance when he taxes
Prescott with whitewashing the persecution of the Spanish
Arabs by identifying it with God's will: "in this impotent condition, it was wisely ordered that their territory should be
occupied by a people whose religion and more liberal form
of government ... qualifies them for advancing still higher
the interest of humanity. "36

        Parker makes some interesting observations on edu-
cation in America. He points out that each child has a
special right to education, for here government is "government of all the citizens for the sake of all the citizens, and
by means of all. " With such a form of government universal
education is indispensible. "Democracy is the ideal of
America. But it is an ideal which can never be realized except on the condition that the people, the whole people, are
well educated, in the large sense of that word. "37 Percep-
tively, he points out the shifting nature of just how much education is the right amount: "in a progressive people the
zero-point of education is continually rising: what was once
the maximum of hope, one day becomes the minimum of suf-
ferance. "38

        He scores the niggardly attitude towards spending
money on this essential support of democracy. Teachers are
underpaid, a policy which has disastrous results.

>   Some men are born with a genius for teaching;
> many with a talent for it. Offer a sufficient pay
> and they will come, and the results will appear in
> the character of the next generation.... It is easy
> to be penny-wise and pound-foolish, and it seems
> to us that the system of small salaries for school-
> masters hitherto pursued, even in New England, is
> like sacrificing a whole cloak of velvet to save the
> end of a farthing candle. 39

In contrast with this niggardliness in regard to education is
the generosity in regard to much less deserving expenditures.
Parker points out that the Boston people haggle over a $30
appropriation for the library but raise no question about the
$50 spent on the West Point cadets for a single session on
the rifle range.

But in this area also Parker does not just criticize.
He praises Horace Mann who, to help develop education in
Massachusetts, gave up a promising career in law and took
a salary half what he had been making, with the prospect
that even that pittance would be further reduced. In this
area, too, Parker presents a larger view of possibilities.
After describing the popular view of education--"education is
valued, as it helps to make men able to serve as tools in
the great workshop of society, "40--as narrow, Parker presents his own enlarged vision:

> We take mean views of life, of man and his pos-
> sibility, thinking the future can never be better
> than the past. We think the end of man is to live
> for this: wealth, fame, social rank. Genius, wis-
> dom, power of mind, of heart and soul, are
> counted only as means to such an end. So in the
> hot haste to be ' rich, famous, respectable, many
> let manhood slip through their fingers, retaining
> only the riches, fame and respectability. Never
> till manliness is thought the end of man, never till
> education is valued for itself, can we have a wide,
> generous culture, even among the wealthiest class.
> Not til then in the mass of men shall we find a
> scheme of education worthy of the American people
> and the great ideas given them unfold in life. But
> day teaches day, and experience offers wisdom if
> she does not give it. 41

This extended sampling of Parker's views in the areas
of political affairs, social matters, religion, and scholarship
and education will serve as an introduction to Parker's vigor
of thought and expression. More important, it will serve as
preparation for a more exact comparison with Ralph Waldo
Emerson, with whom Parker deserves at least equal rank.

Parker and Emerson

This comparison must, of course, be fair, exact, and
representative; that is, it cannot put the best of Parker
against some of Emerson's less effective pieces in order to
support the thesis of this essay. The works selected must
be really comparable. For instance, since there is no
counterpart to Emerson's Nature in Parker's writings, nor
any counterpart to Parker's "Letter to the People of the
United States Touching the Matter of Slavery" in Emerson's

writings, no comparison is possible in either case.   Finally, the comparison must cover as varied a range of subjects as possible.   Thus it would be unrepresentative to limit the comparison to the subject of politics, for while Parker is particularly strong in this area Emerson pretty much ignores it.

A comparison based on four selected lectures by each man meets the above criteria.   Such a basis of comparison is defensible, for though he was deeply interested in and wrote much poetry, Emerson was primarily a lecturer[42] and, as we have seen, so was Parker.   The comparison is fair in that the four Emerson lectures are among his best; it is exact in that the respective lectures treat the same subjects from the same viewpoint and make the same main points. Finally, the comparison is representative, for it covers each man's views on four main areas of American life and times; philosophy, religion, literary and scientific endeavor, and politics.   The first comparison will measure Parker's "Transcendentalism" against Emerson's "The Transcendental- ist"; the second, Parker's "Transient and Permanent in Christianity" against Emerson's "Divinity School Address"; the third, Parker's "Position and Duties of the American Scholar" against Emerson's "The American Scholar"; and the fourth, Parker's "Political Destination of America and Signs of the Times" against Emerson's "Politics. "[43]

Philosophy

The first comparison, between Parker's "Transcenden- talism" and Emerson's "The Transcendentalist, " will meet all our requirements.   It is fair in that Emerson's lecture is among his better and more famous works; it is representative in that it brings out both mens' views in one important area, philosophy; and it is an exact comparison in that each man treats the same subject from the same viewpoint and makes the same general points.   Only this last factor needs any ex- tended study.   I intend to establish that Parker deserves at least equal rank with Emerson because, while each man makes the same general points, Parker does so with much greater order, detail, and comprehensiveness.

Each lecturer describes in the same way both trans- cendentalism and the kind of thought against which trans- cendentalism is reacting.   Each describes transcendentalism as an insistence on the preeminence of the mind, and for each this preeminence is the central tenet of this kind of philosophy. Parker expresses the view of each when he states:

> Transcendentalism is distinguished by its chief metaphysical doctrine, that there is in the intellect (or consciousness), something that never was in the senses, to wit, the intellect (or consciousness) itself; that man has faculties which transcend the senses; faculties which give him ideas and intuitions that transcend sensational experience; ideas whose origin is not from sensation, nor their proof from sensation. [44]

Each man sees the mind preeminent not just in knowing but also in acting. Whether he describes the mind in this office as will or conscience, each sees it as the source of guidance in human activities. Finally, each holds that the mind not only transcends sense experience but is enlightened by its union with God. For each man these three points, the preeminence of the mind in knowing, its preeminence in providing guidance for acting, and its union with God which is the source of its enlightenment and inspiration, constitute the heart of the transcendental philosophy.

Both Parker and Emerson also describe in the same way the kind of thought against which transcendentalism objects. Where transcendentalism emphasizes the superiority of the mind, the counterpart way of thinking emphasizes the superiority of experience. Again Parker speaks the view of both when he asserts that this other school's "most important metaphysical doctrine is this: there is nothing in the intellect which was not first in the senses.... They say that experience by one or more of the senses is the ultimate appeal in philosophy: all that I know is of sensational origin; the senses are the windows which let in all the light I have...."[45] In addition, each sees this other philosophy as holding that experience is the source of guidance in human activities and, finally, since this is the case in both knowing and acting, this philosophy neither needs nor allows any mysterious union with God.

But although both Parker and Emerson make the same general points about the nature of transcendentalism and its opposite type of thought, they differ greatly in the detail, order, and comprehensiveness with which they make these points. In all three respects Parker excels. In his expla-

nation of transcendentalism and of that other way of thought
Parker is far more detailed and orderly.   Further--and this
is an important point and not true of Emerson's lecture--
Parker considers both the good in the other philosophy and
the potential for abuse in the transcendental philosophy.
Parker's lecture, then, has a comprehensiveness, in this
case a critical balance, entirely lacking in Emerson's.
Emerson's lecture might fairly be characterized as more impressionistic and Parker's as more truly philosophic.

Emerson is more concerned with setting forth and
urging an individualistic freedom from the old restrictions
and institutions, whether they be political, religious, eco-
nomic, or philosophic.   His theme is "let the soul be erect,
and all things will go well."[46]   Man ought to be himself.
He ought to be true to himself or to the highest part of himself, his soul.   He must make his own circumstance.
Emerson describes and urges such independence with a light
and deft hand but he says little on exactly how one might be
true to himself and how one might make his own circumstance.

After giving a general description of transcendentalism
and its opposite, Emerson devotes the heart of his lecture to
describing the subject of his essay, the transcendentalist
person.   But first he points out that such a way of thinking
does not lend itself to constituting a party or school.   All
that is possible is to characterize various movements as
more or less transcendentalist.   Thus the Stoic philosophers,
the prophets, the Quakers and, in Emerson's time, the group
of New England people loosely labeled "transcendentalists"
are general groups which are more rather than less transcendental.   For the individuals in each group are attempting
to break from a mould which threatens to render them creatures of an institution or school.   The prophets rebelled
against a limiting superstition, the Quakers against priest-
ridden religion, and the New England transcendentalists are
rebelling against a tradition-bound and commercially managed
life.

Then Emerson proceeds to the central part of his
lecture, in which he characterizes the transcendentalist individual.   The transcendentalist is lonely, critical, disdains to
shape himself to fit society's structure, loves beauty.   He
has a vision and attempts to live up to it.   He refuses to
cooperate in work which might give the lie to his vision.
The transcendentalist may not seem to accomplish much when

compared with the captains of industry and commerce or the
politicians in high positions or the preachers famous for their
oratory, but the transcendentalist sees such accomplishments
as divergent from his vision and so refuses to compromise
himself by getting involved in such activities. The transcendentalist, Emerson says, has

> made the experiment and found that from the liberal
> professions to the coarsest manual labor, and from
> the courtesies of the academy and college to the
> conventions of the cotillion-room and the morning
> call, there is a spirit of cowardly compromise and
> seeming which intimates a frightful skepticism, a
> life without love, and an activity without an aim. [47]

Refusing such a life or activity, the transcendentalist strives
to "let the soul be erect," to remain true to his vision and
thus to himself. "If I cannot work," he says to himself, "at
least I need not lie. All that is clearly due today is not to
lie. "[48]

Though his description is suggestive, it contains so
little detail and order that it would fit any individual who differs in any degree from any established society or school or
institution. For instance, Emerson's description would seem
to fit such a zealot as Joseph Smith who, not content with
seeing himself as possessing special access to God or even
as holding the position of God's right-hand man, elevated
himself to the position where God was his right-hand man![49]

Parker's description, on the other hand, is detailed
and orderly. While Emerson's is impressionistic, Parker's
is characteristic of a philosophic treatise. Not only does
Parker connect this way of thinking by way of either contrast
or comparison with a number of philosophers such as Hobbes,
Hume, Locke, Bentham, Berkeley, and Rousseau;[50] he also
carefully outlines its major tenets in the four areas of
physics, politics, ethics, and religion. A brief consideration
of the first two will show the order and detail of his discussion.

In the area of physics, Parker points out, transcendentalism holds that while the senses acquaint us with the
body, the mind "gives us the idea of substance, answering to
an objective reality. "[51] Further, we know in an a priori
fashion that the action and laws of nature are universal and
certain. All the first truths of mathematics, e. g. , that the

whole is greater than the part, are independent of sensation and, in fact, "the whole matter of geometry is transcendental."[52] Finally, a number of physical theories have come to be seen in this light, i. e., as true and universal accounts of nature, because they proceed from "ideas and intuitions that transcend sensational experience; ideas whose origin is not from sensation, nor their proof from sensation."[53]

> ... /P/hilosophy is often in advance of observation; e. g. Newton's law of gravitation, Kepler's third law, the theory that a diamond might be burned, and Berkeley's theory of vision--these are interpretations of nature, but also anticipations of nature, as all true philosophy must be.[54]

In the area of politics, Parker points out, transcendentalism holds that history, precedents, experience are not the basic guide but only serve to illustrate. Human nature, or more exactly, the facts of consciousness, provide the absolute basis for natural right and justice, and allow men to anticipate experience and history. The faculty by which men get this guidance is conscience. In a sentence which could serve as a compact but comprehensive resumé of the core of transcendentalism, Parker states his view of conscience: "Now the source and original of this justice and right it finds in God--the conscience of God; the channel through which we receive this justice and right is our own moral sense, our conscience, which is our consciousness of the conscience of God."[55]

Given this to be the situation, the transcendental politician, by listening to his conscience which is the voice of God, can anticipate experience and transcend history. To show that this claim is not just sentimental religiosity, Parker cites the instance of our own Declaration of Independence. Two of the three truths the authors expressed in that document are, according to Parker, not derived from experience or history, but are an anticipation of the one and a transcendence of the other. These two truths, that each man is endowed with certain inalienable rights and that in respect to these all men are equal, are facts of consciousness, "ideas and intuitions that transcend sensational experience." Via a reasoning process which also transcended experience, the authors moved from these two truths to a third: that the task of government is to protect and promote the enjoyment of these rights.

In the other two areas, ethics and religion, Parker is just as orderly and detailed in his exposition of the transcendental position. The four areas together give an exact and comprehensive exposition of this position. This same quality holds true of his description of the kind of thought against which the transcendentalists are reacting. Emerson's treatment lacks the detail and order of Parker's. As with their respective expositions of transcendentalism itself, so in their characterizations of the opposite kind of thought: Emerson's is more impressionistic, Parker's more truly philosophic.

At the beginning of his lecture Emerson gives a general critique of the other way of thinking, which he labels materialism. Emerson describes this position as one which embodies a respectful attitude towards the facts and an "I'm from Missouri" attitude toward theorizing beyond the facts. Emerson cleverly objects that while the facts seem to be solid and secure, upon further investigation they seem as tenuous and insecure as theorizing. With a few deft questions Emerson shows how illusory the facts are, for their very "factualness," their permanence, rests upon the "belief" that experience is uniform.

Parker, on the other hand, gives a comparatively lengthy treatise on this other kind of thought, which he labels sensational philosophy. As in the case of his exposition of transcendentalism, Parker divides his treatment of the sensationalist philosophy into the same four areas--physics, politics, ethics, and religion--and provides a critique of the main tenets of this philosophy in each. A brief consideration of the first two will show Parker's order and detail of treatment.

In the area of physics, Parker criticizes the sensationalist philosophy for offering no secure basis for universal laws of nature, for the very existence of the natural world, nor even for the existence of the world of consciousness. Since the senses can give only limited evidence, such a philosophy can never provide a basis for natural laws. For instance, the law of gravity would lose its universality, for sense testimony will never warrant the judgment that this law has, does, and always will hold in every place. As a result, human science, including even mathematics, loses its scientific character and becomes instead a kind of elegant farmers' almanac.

Even worse, the sensationalist philosophy casts doubt
upon the very existence of the world of nature.   Echoing the
words of Descartes, Parker argues that if when we dream
of an apparently natural world we are mistaken, we cannot
be sure that we are not likewise mistaken when awake.
Berkeley, Parker argues, goes further to undermine our
confidence that we live with other people, while Priestley
goes to the ultimate absurdity of casting doubt on the existence of the very realm of consciousness itself.   Thus, by
undermining any proof for the universality of natural laws,
for the very existence of the world, for the existence of
other people, and, finally, for the existence of the realm of
consciousness, the sensationalist philosophy bars any surety
in our thinking and living.

In the area of politics Parker attacks the sensationalist philosophy for obliterating absolute right and absolute
justice.   Again, since experience is limited, it cannot provide the basis for such universal guides to human action.
The sensationalists divide into two groups, those who hold
that the elite should have and exercise political rule and
those who hold that the people should themselves do so.
Both reflect historical trends and both have led to terrible
tyranny, either of the few over the many or of the many
over the few, for there is and can be no such thing as inalienable rights of individual men under such a philosophy.
Hobbes is a representative of the first group, Thomas Paine
of the second.   At its worst this sensationalist position
fosters the crudest kind of exploitation and even at its best,
for example in the guise of "the greatest good of the greatest
number, " can justify "sacrificing the greatest good of the
lesser number. "   As Parker points out, this philosophy leads
to and justifies a whole society being used for the sake of
the nobility and gentry as in England, of the landed proprietors and rich burghers in Switzerland, and of the slaveholders in North Carolina.   If by its fruits we can judge the
tree, Parker argues, the abuses which stem from the sensationalist philosophy justify the judgment that there is something rotten about it.

As was the case with his exposition of transcendentalism, so in his exposition of the sensationalist philosophy
Parker continues with the same detailed and orderly treatment in the other two areas of ethics and religion.   And
again, his discussion in the four areas taken together gives
an exact and comprehensive exposition of the transcendentalist view of the sensationalist position.   But there is a

further important mark which sets off Parker's exposition,
and which is totally lacking in Emerson's presentation.

This important factor is comprehensiveness; in this
particular case, critical balance.   Parker does not consider
transcendentalism as all good and its opposite all bad but
acknowledges the good that has come from the sensationalist
philosophy and the bad that can arise out of the transcendental one.   Such a critical balance is especially important
because transcendentalism, being primarily an intuitionist
kind of philosophy, is open to much abuse.   We have already
seen the example of Joseph Smith.   Smith might be an extreme case but surely many fanatics and zealots have, with
complete sincerity, thought they saw the truth and acted according to the right.   But their sincerity has not saved them
from doing terrible harm both to themselves and to those
around them.   Emerson's contemporary, John Brown, might
be a good example.   Surely he sincerely felt he lived Emerson's "let the soul be erect and all things will go well" and
in that sincerity one Kansas night he supervised the brutal
massacre of eight men dragged from their beds, wives and
children, in a couple of cases because they had talked in
favor of slavery in the area saloons.   Brown sincerely felt
a drastic example had to be made.   While Emerson does not
say anything about such abuses Parker is careful to warn
about such injudicious transcendentalism by pointing out the
dangers of the "transcendental-mad" in each of his four
areas, physics, politics, ethics and religion.   As before,
we shall consider only the first two.

In the area of physics Parker points out that many
generalizations of the "transcendental-mad" have proven to
be embarrassing.   He cites the example of Schelling who decreed that there are only seven primary planets in the solar
system.

> He had intelligence in advance of the mail; but the
> mail did not confirm, for six months afterwards
> Dr. Piazzi discovered one of the asteroids; and in
> a few years three more were found, and now
> several more have been discovered, not to mention
> the new planet Neptune. [56]

Such embarrassments are the result, Parker points out, of
a failure on the part of transcendentalist philosophers to give
due weight to sense experience.   The true transcendentalist
does not scorn such experience and observation but holds it

essential to provide the materials for the mind's judgment.
Parker's view is that of Kant, that thought without content is
empty and sense experience without the forms of thought,
blind. [57] Further, the true transcendentalist must guard
against hasty generalizations from this essential data.   He
must not attempt to spin physics out of his own head or
create it by decree.

In the area of politics Parker warns against the politician who takes "his own personal whims as oracles of
human nature. "[58]   Such a man is unable or refuses to learn
from either history or his own experience.   Parker describes
the resultant situation:

> Men that are transcendental-mad we have all seen
> ... to be transcendental-wise, sober, is another
> thing.   The notion that every impulse is to be
> followed, every instinct totally obeyed, will put
> man among the beasts, not angels. [59]

When such men have power the situation is fraught with
danger, for it is a case of the "blind leading the blind."

But Parker not only points out the dangers inherent
in the transcendentalist position; he again also praises the
good that the sensationalist philosophy has accomplished.
For instance, this philosophy has successfully protested
against the exaggerated spiritualism of the middle ages which
saw the body and all bodily desires and functions as evil.
Further, Parker notes, this position has brought about or
greatly helped to bring about marvelous advances in physics
and mechanics.   Parker also praises some of the great men
who belong to this school, such men as Bacon, Locke, and
Newton.   Such magnanimity on the part of so staunch a sup-
porter of one philosophic position towards those holding the
opposite view is uncommon and certainly noteworthy.

In summarizing our comparison of Emerson's "The
Transcendentalist" with Parker's "Transcendentalism, "
Parker's critical balance is an especially important characteristic and, together with his greater detail and order,
makes Parker's essay a truly philosophic treatise; the deficiency in detail and order and especially the lack of critical
balance makes Emerson's lecture only a suggestive, impressionistic, literary essay.   Parker's essay provides much the
better exposition of the transcendental philosophy, both in itself and in its view of its opposite.   This judgment is not

new; at least three scholars have made it.   One calls
Parker's essay "one of the clearest expressions we have of
the American rejection of the empirical philosophy of the
Enlightenment" and another says that it "has been recognized
by recent scholarship as one of the best contemporary accounts of the movement."[60]

Religion

The next comparison is between Parker's "A Discourse of the Transient and Permanent in Christianity" and
Emerson's famous "Divinity School Address."   It was hearing
the Emerson "Address" which inspired Parker to write along
similar lines, resulting in his "Transient and Permanent in
Christianity."[61]   As in the case of the first comparison,
this one is intended further to establish my thesis, that
Parker deserves at least equal rank with Emerson, by showing that while each makes the same general points, Parker
does so with greater order, detail, and comprehensiveness.
And the judgment is the same, that while Emerson's "Address" is the more poetic, Parker's "Discourse" is the more
substantial.[62]

Both Parker and Emerson characterize true religion
as having two basic traits, the first of which is the immediacy of the man-God relationship.   Parker states that
true religion is "a method of attaining oneness with God,"[63]
while Emerson says that "if a man is at heart just, then in
so far is he God."[64]   True religion is not a matter of com-
plex rites, a network of dogmas, nor an authoritarian institution.   A church, the Bible, even Christ are not essential
to this immediate relationship and, as a matter of historical fact, often intrude into and even disrupt it.   The
second trait, which follows directly from the first, is that
a man's own heart and conscience are his inspiration and
guide.   Given the intimate at-oneness with God which is the
first trait, both Parker and Emerson emphasize that man
needs no external management but, by means of his own in-
terior God-centered enlightenment and inspiration, can guide
and judge for himself.

Both Parker and Emerson characterize false religion
as any that disrupts the intimacy of the man-God relationship and undermines man's reliance on his own heart and
conscience.   All such religion is, as Emerson puts it, "hollow, dry, creaking formality."[65]   Both men center their

criticism on two specific abuses which turn true religion
into such a formality: the first, the personality cult of
Christ, and the second, adulation of the Bible or ancient
revelation, which Parker dubs "bibliolatry." In the case of
the first abuse, Christ, by coming to stand as mediator between God and man, disrupts the immediacy of that union,
the immediacy which is the heart and soul of true religion.
Christ's life, his example, his word, come to be the source
of guidance for man rather than man's own heart and conscience. Man's aim comes to be, not to be himself, but to
be an imitation-Christ.

The same happens in the case of the second abuse,
"bibliolatry." The writings of a few men who lived in a far
distant age and land come to stand between man and his God
and, further, to entice him from relying on his own heart.
God is to be found only through the scripture and the way
thereto is marked by the maxims, stories and examples recorded in these writings. It is a case of the Bible becoming
"the way, the truth, and the life." Both Emerson and
Parker feel that the personality cult of Christ and the idolatry of the Bible are the two golden calves man has set up
in the place of God. Or, to put the matter in another
scriptural way, these are two messes of pottage for which
man has sold his precious religious heritage.

Finally, both Parker and Emerson offer the same
solution for the "hollow, dry, creaking formality" of religion.
That solution is a matter of a living ministry, preaching
chiefly, to which Emerson adds the observance of the Sabbath. Parker pleads with the young, just-ordained minister,
at whose ordination he delivered his "Discourse", to speak
the truth to his congregation, and urges the congregation to
listen with open minds and hearts. Emerson warns that
preaching must not be the "sounding brass and tinkling cym-
bals" of a minister he once heard, but must be the natural
outflowing of a life inspired by God.

But though Parker and Emerson make the same general points about the character of true religion, criticize the
same abuses, and propose the same solution, they differ, as
before, in detail, order, and comprehensiveness; and again
it is Parker who excels. Thus Emerson describes true religion as essentially a reverence for divine law. The good
actions which follow from this reverence foster a union in
which man comes to be at one with God. Both the reverence
and the union are a matter of intuition, that is, of direct and

immediate experience.

Parker, on the other hand, provides an outline of the
structure of true religion. Its morality is the love of man
and the love of God shown by actions. Its creed is that
there is an all-perfect God; its aim, that men be as perfect
as the heavenly father. Its source of guidance is the voice
of God in the heart of man. Then Parker describes the
most important result of true religion, freedom. Since man
is at one with God he needs no external management but can
guide himself. Parker echoes John's "you shall know the
truth and the truth shall make you free," when he says that
"Christianity gives us the largest liberty of the sons of
God."66

Finally, Parker illustrates how a true religion uses
both Christ and the Bible. Christ serves not as an iron
pattern for any and all religious life but rather as an in-
spiring example of one man's free and intimate communion
with God. In Parker's view true religion aims not at making us other Christs but other Christs, that is, not carbon
copies but individual persons who live their own individual
lives as Christ lived his. Further, man was not made for
the Bible but the Bible for man. The Bible can help us live
the divine life by means of example and guidance. Like the
example of Christ, the Bible can inspire us to live our own,
individual, free, God-like lives. And since God is infinite,
there are an infinite number of variants of the divine life.
Neither the examples and guidance in the Bible nor even the
life of Christ comes close to beginning to cover all these
variants. The divine life offers, then, infinite freedom.
Men are saved, not by carbon-copying Christ or some particular example in the Bible, but by taking advantage of this
freedom and living their own lives.

The basic points are the same, but while Emerson
only suggests the freedom that comes with the God-life,
Parker describes it in some detail. And while Emerson
scatters his points, Parker's thoughts on true religion are
grouped in such a way that the reader can readily catch
their essence. Further, while Emerson says very little
about the role of Christ's example and nothing about the role
of ancient revelation in true religion, Parker takes pains to
show this legitimate and helpful role.

There are further differences in the way the two men
describe the abuses of true religion, the idolatry of Christ

and of the Bible. Emerson describes in a general way the
personality cult of Christ as akin to the slavish adoration
which his subjects offer an Oriental potentate. He points
out how demeaning such adoration is. Men become minions.
Similarly, Emerson bemoans the view of the Bible which
relegates all inspiration to a distant past, land, and people.
Inspiration is finished; modern man can but look longingly
back to the great days when God inspired his people and,
though he lives in a far distant place and time, try to imitate the lives of those people. The result is cultural
schizophrenia.

Parker's criticism has far more substance. He criticizes the idolatry of Christ from reason and from history.
He argues that it is unparalleled that any great truths rest
on the authority of any man. No more is it the case that
the great truths of Christianity rest on the authority of
Christ than that those of geometry rest on the character of
Euclid or those of science rest on that of Archimedes.
Parker also outlines the history of the different views on the
position of Christ. To some early Christians he was God;
to others, man; to still others, a mixture of both. Each
view was the orthodox one at different times. An excellent
instance, Parker points out, is that of the views of Arius
and of Athanasius. At one time the view of Arius was orthodox, for many high Church officials, synods and, very
possibly, even Pope Liberius held to it. [67] But since then
the view of Athanasius has surplanted what is now considered
the heretical view of Arius. Parker concludes that, rather
than being the rock upon which Christianity is founded, Christ
is the subject of a history of such varying views that he is
more like the shifting sands of which the New Testament
warns.

Parker criticizes the abuses of scripture with the
same substance, again on the basis of both reason and history. There was a time when each word in the scripture
was seen as infallibly inspired; Christians had to accept
legends as truth, conflicting views as somehow unified or at
least unifiable, "a collection of amatory idyls for a serious
discourse 'touching the mutual love of Christ and Church, ' "[68]
and even that the all-good and all-loving God ordered his
servant Abraham to sacrifice his son--"a thought at which, "
as Parker puts it, "the flesh creeps with horror. "[69] Such
acceptance requires a cessation of thinking. Parker avers
that the views of scripture, like those of Christ, are as
shifting sands. Christ himself criticizes adulation of the

letter of the Old Testament, and Paul does the same. There
has been a history of diverse interpretations of these writings, culminating in the biblical criticism so prominent in
Germany at that time and in which Parker was deeply interested, and which was, as he put it, "fast breaking to
pieces this idol which men have made out of the Scriptures. "[70]

While Emerson at most only hints at it, Parker puts
his finger directly on the root source of the debasement of
true religion, a matter which adds an important balance to
Parker's criticism.   It is important to know the source of
any abuse, and this source, Parker points out, is the human
contribution to religion, the "transient" part thereof.   The
eternal truth of God is the "permanent" part.   The first
varies as the times vary.   It varies as the abilities of different men vary.   It varies as man's experience varies.
Since man must interpret and apply the eternal truth of God
there is necessarily and always present this "transient" factor.
Parker cites the parallel of the "true system of nature. "
This true system is always the same but man's knowledge
and description of it varies with his outlook, experience, and
times.   Since the situation is necessarily a transactional
one, as Dewey would put it, the human factor is a necessary
and constant one.   Such is the case with religion.   This too
is a transactional situation, with the human contribution being theology or philosophy of religion, and the divine being
religion itself.   The debasement of true religion comes when
man takes his own contribution as tantamount to true religion.   He begins by shaping his golden calf to represent
and suggest God and ends up bowing before it as God.

Parker's criticisms of the abuses of religion clearly
excel over the suggestive but general observations of Emerson.   The most important difference is that Parker illustrates by historical examples, such as the telling one of
Arius and Athanasius on the nature of Christ, and also by
such persuasive argument as the parallel of geometry not
being based on Euclid's character.   Emerson's lecture may
be the more impressive in its delicate beauty, but Parker's
is the more convincing in its robust strength.   For an exact
and comprehensive grasp of the transcendentalist view of religion, Parker's "Discourse" is by far the better study.

Intellectual Endeavor

   The third comparison is between Parker's "Position
and Duties of the American Scholar" and Emerson's "The
American Scholar. "

   Both men point out that American scholarship of that
time does not amount to much.   Emerson begins his talk by
stating rather briefly that to talk of American scholarship is
more an exercise in hope than a description.   In 1838
Americans seemed content to let Europeans do their scholarship for them.   But Emerson had hope that "the sluggard
intellect of this continent will look from under its iron lids
and fill the postponed expectation of the world with something
better than the exertions of mechanical skill. "[71]   Parker
goes into great detail in criticizing the American scholarship
of the period.   He considers science as well as literature,
which he divides into several categories, considering each
in some detail.   Although, unlike Emerson, Parker acknowledges some "exceptional" literature, he agrees in general
with Emerson's judgment.   Typical of Parker's view is his
observation that the evaluation of American literary criticism
is inversely proportional to the lowly status of its literature.

> I have known three American Sir Walter Scotts,
> half a dozen Addisons, one or two Macaulays--a
> historian that was Hume and Gibbon both in one,
> several Burnses, and Miltons by the quantity, not
> 'mute' the more is the pity, but 'inglorious'
> enough; nay, even vain-glorious at the praise which
> some penny-a-liner or dollar-a-pager foolishly gave
> their cheap extemporary stuff.   In sacred litera-
> ture it is the same: in a single winter at Boston
> we had two American Saint Johns, in full blast for
> several months.   Though no Felix trembles, there
> are now extant in the United States not less than
> six American Saint Pauls, in no manner of peril
> except the most dangerous--of idle praise. [72]

Like Emerson, Parker thinks that Americans are so diffident
towards European and especially English literature that in
this respect, as he puts it, America is still a colony of
England.   However, Parker does have a hope for better
things, a hope based on the "exceptional literature" he notes.

   Next, both men give similar accounts of the cultural
setting of American scholarship.   Each makes much of the

bond of fraternity which binds a culture together.   At the
beginning of his lecture Emerson illustrates this bond by re-
counting a fable of how in the beginning the gods divided
Man into men in order that he might be more helpful to himself in the way a hand divided into fingers is a more effective instrument.   This humanity which all men have in common is the very center or heart of any culture, including the
American.   When this common bond, which is a matter of
common heritage, common ideals, and common goals, is
lost sight of, the society crumbles.   Emerson presents his
view in a somewhat mystical way, reminiscent of the early
philosopher Plotinus who described the relationship between
the center of his cosmos and its outer levels in terms of the
spokes and hub of a wheel and of the essence of a perfume
and the fragrance given off by it.

Parker makes the same point much more con-
cretely.   He tells a story which must have been typical of
the country in his day.   The New England family does not
have enough money to send all of its children on for higher
education.   It decides on one, the one who appears to have
the best chance of succeeding.   The father, mother, sisters,
and brothers all pinch and scrimp in order to maintain the
young scholar.   He learns while they earn.   When the
scholar graduates it is his task to repay that support not in
terms of money but of service, and service not just to the
immediate family but to the surrounding society.   The story
illustrates the brotherhood of man in a most concrete way.
Parker's illustration is homey, specific; Emerson's somewhat remote and mystical.

Both men proceed beyond general description of any
and all cultures to point out aspects peculiar to the American
culture.   These aspects reduce to one central one, democracy.   Emerson states that the revolution which has lifted
the common man to a position of dignity has also lifted his
interests, affairs, and plans.   These are now seen as valuable, just as valuable as the remote and romantic.   They
are now beautiful and wonderful.   The common man's dignity
and value are thus enhanced.   In fact, it is a reciprocal
situation, for the more the affairs, interests, and plans of
the common man become the center of interest, the more
does the common man himself become so, and vice versa.
That center of interest is no longer limited to the great
affairs of kings and nobles and princes but now extends to
the lives of all people.

Parker makes much of this same central aspect of
the American culture. In contrast with European countries
there is not the constraining pressure of a noble class on
the one hand nor the general ignorance of the common people
on the other to hem in the work and influence of the scholar.
For example, in Germany, the land of scholars, the king
will allow scholars freedom of ideas among themselves but
not the implementation or spreading of ideas to the common
people; as a result of this long oppression the common
people are not interested in nor able to comprehend the ideas
of the scholars. German scholars write profound works but
only for each other. Their ideas are thus sterile, or, as
Parker puts it, they go into a nunnery. But here in America
the scholar is free from the positive limitation of government censorship and the negative one of comparative ignorance and indifference of the common people. Here ideas
stand on their own two feet and make their own way to the
extent that their intrinsic worth will allow. Here the common people are interested in ideas, for they are not bound
by traditions and customs but are self-reliant. [73] Here,
since they are making their own way and building a new land,
the common people are not only open to new ideas but are
keenly interested in any that might be helpful to that work.
Here each man is convinced that he judges and decides what
the state shall do and not do, not the other way around.
Any kind of censorship is thus unthinkable.

After assessing the general state of American scholarship and describing the American cultural setting in the same
way, both Parker and Emerson characterize true scholarship
in the same way. For both, such scholarship is a matter of
studying and making known the higher modes of human consciousness and its mark of success is raising men to live
out these higher modes. As Emerson puts it, the scholar
is "the world's eye" and "the world's heart."[74] His office
is to defer not one jot to the popular and the superficial but
ever to study the true and the just and to make them known
without fear or modification. His task is that of differenti-
ating the substance of man from the midst of the shadows of
institutions, parties, and customs. His goal is to bring men
to his substance of life, and this substance of life to men,
for all men are Man, and the scholar is "Man thinking."
Parker describes this task as the duty of the scholar, duty
because his scholarship was obtained at the expense of society, which earned while he learned, so that he might lead
the way, might break open the paths, might provide the new
perspectives so needed if men are to progress to a better

life. "He is ... to represent truth, justice, beauty, philanthropy, and religion--the highest facts of human experience,"
Parker says, and thereby "pay mankind for their advance to
him.... "75

Finally, both men see great opportunity for the
scholar in the American setting. Emerson hints at this tre-
mendous opportunity, Parker describes it more fully.
America is young and so without the iron weight of tradition
that loads down other lands. America is eager for new
ideas. This is the opportunity of the scholar. For new
ideas come not from the politician nor from the business
man, but from him. His pen is potentially more powerful
than the power of the political office and even than the might
of accumulated wealth. Further, since the land is new the
scholar does not have to move mountains, for as yet only
molehills stand there. "... /W/hile the State is young, a
single great and noble man can deeply influence the nation's
mind. "76 Even the abuses which have cropped up in this
country, notably the idolatry of money, can be corrected by
such efforts. "A few great souls can correct ... the mean
economy of the State, and amend the vulgarity of the American church, now the poor prostitute of every wealthy sin. "77
The land is in its springtime. The way things grow hangs
in the balance, and that balance can be tipped by a tiny
number of great-minded and great-souled men, by the men
of vision, the scholars. The scholar, as Emerson points
out, "take/s/ up into himself all the ability of the time, all
the contributions of the past, all the hopes of the future. "78
When he thus lives and works he alters not only the country
but the whole world. "... /I/f the single man plant himself
indomitably on his instincts, and there abide, the huge world
will come round to him. "79

Both Emerson and Parker give basically the same
critique of American scholarship but Parker's, as in the
other two comparisons we made, is the more substantial.
For Parker's critique is far more detailed, orderly, and
comprehensive. These differences are present in varying
degrees in each of the four basic considerations of the respective lectures: the status of American scholarship; the
cultural setting, both general and particular; the description
of true scholarship; and the opportunities for such scholarship, but they are especially apparent in the first area, the
status of American scholarship.

Emerson's appraisal of the status of American

scholarship is quite brief. He is content to offer the conclusion that it is in a poor state.   Parker's divides scholarship into science and literature.   He points out that though
science which has practical application is strong in America,
pure or theoretical science is not.   Franklin is famous not
because of his experiments with electricity but because his
lightning rod protects barns and homes.   Emerson does not
consider science at all.   Parker also divides literature into
two main headings: the "instantial" or typical, and the "exceptional"; and further subdivides the "instantial" into "permanent"--for instance philosophical and theological works--and
"transient", such as political speeches, state papers, and
pamphlets.   There is nothing to match this order in Emerson nor to match Parker's detailed assessment of each of
these divisions.

The "transient" literature shows some of the independence and vigor characteristic of a people building a new
nation in a new land.   Some authors have broken out of the
accustomed patterns and are attempting new ways.   But
there is in most works under this heading an appalling nar-
rowness and superficiality.   For in most such works it is
not a matter of the right and the just but of the almighty rule
of the majority and, worse, the power of money.   The
preacher bows to the power of the rum interests.   A fear of
this and other such interests constrains him to write sermons which are as little pertinent to his people's lives as "an
almanack calculated for the meridian of no place in particular, for no time in special. "[80] Even the artist sells out.
As Parker caustically remarks: "the artist prostitutes his
pencil and his skill, and takes the law of beauty from the
fat clown, whose barns and pigs, and wife, he paints for
daily bread. "[81]   Parker does not mince words.   In regard
to "permanent" literature Parker thinks that the American
states are "still colonies of England. " Eighty percent of
American works are the common thoughts of common men.
As evidence of this unself-reliant poverty Parker makes a
comparison between the four chief periodicals in America
and a like number of leading periodicals in England.   Emerson offers nothing approaching such detail.

Parker completes his comprehensive critique by considering the "exceptional" literature, the literature which has
the depth and originality one would hope for and expect of a
people building a new society in a new land.   He acknowledges
implicitly such works as those of Jonathan Edwards, the
Federalist Papers, the writings of Hawthorne, of Thoreau,

and of Emerson himself, whom Parker considered the greatest American author. [82] Emerson leaves no room for such
great works.

As regards the cultural setting in general, again
Parker presents the more compelling case. Each man offers
a story to illustrate the basic relationship of the community
and the scholar. The community supports the scholar and
in return for that support looks for the scholar to be its
"eye" and "heart." Emerson offers the tale about the oneness of man. Parker offers the account of the New England
family which scrimps to send one son through college, and
strengthens his account by reference to the still wide-spread
idea of "service," especially among a significant number of
professional men, for example, the doctor who works in a
free clinic on his afternoon off. While Parker's account is
homey and typical, as American as the proverbial apple pie,
one is tempted to tax Emerson with sinning against his own
rule that Americans ought not to follow the European lead.
For his fable is out of "unknown antiquity" and so foreign to
a new people in a new land. Given this context and aim,
this point is not as minor as it otherwise would be.

In regard to that aspect which both regard as peculiar
to the American culture, democracy, Emerson's general description lacks the concrete forcefulness of Parker's.
Parker's forcefulness derives largely from his comparison
with Germany, where the positive limitations set by the
government and the negative ones set by the indifference of
the people severely circumscribe the influence of scholarly
endeavor. Though Germany is the land of scholars, their
ideas are "often as idle as shells in a lady's cabinet."[83]
In contrast, in America ideas can go as far as their worth
will carry them. The people are eagerly interested in them;
the government does not dare censor them. True, wealth is
an obstacle, but it is a "movable" one, one that can be overcome. Parker brings out the character of democracy in
America much more effectively than Emerson's general statements, such as a mention of the "new importance given to
the single person" and "help must come from the bosom
alone," statements unsupported by evidence or detail. [84]

In regard to the nature of true scholarship, Emerson
speaks in general terms of the true scholar being the eye and
the heart of the world, of his being self-dependent, taking
the good of the past and joining it to the good of the present
in order to help build a better future. Parker describes the

fledgling embodiment of such scholarship in the "exceptional"
literature of the United States.   This literature, though rough
and crude in many respects, shows the vigor and freshness
one would expect of a people building a new society in a new
land.   Historical works are written from the standpoint of
democracy, poetry looks at nature face to face rather than
repeating what is found in European poetry.   It sings of
Monadnock and not of Parnassus.   Religious works treat of
a loving and friendly God, not of a grim, gimlet-eyed, tyrannical God.   Parker's description of true scholarship is thus
more compelling than Emerson's because he provides concrete examples, American examples, of what he is talking
about.

Finally, while Emerson is content to hint at the influential role the scholar can play in America, Parker goes
into the reason why his role can be so influential.   As we
have seen, Parker's reasoning is that this new society in a
new land is not bound to the old but is open to and eagerly
interested in new ideas.   There is no external limitation to
ideas, no government censorship such as in Germany.   The
populace is more learned and more interested in ideas.
Parker claims, for instance, that Macaulay has had more
readers here in America in three months than Thucydides
and Tacitus in twelve centuries in Europe.   He also points
out that people crowd to hear such learned events as Emerson's lectures.   With such an intensely interested audience
and no external constraint, the American scholar has before
him a unique opportunity to accomplish through his leadership
immense good, and to redress widespread injustice.

> This is a new country, the great ideas of a noble-
> man are easily spread abroad; soon they will ap-
> pear in the life of the people, and be a blessing in
> our future history to ages yet unborn.   A few great
> souls can correct the licentiousness of the Ameri-
> can press, which is now but the type of covetous-
> ness and low ambition; correct the mean economy
> of the State, and amend the vulgarity of the Ameri-
> can church, now the poor prostitute of every
> wealthy sin. [85]

The impact of the novel Uncle Tom's Cabin, a few years
later, may exemplify what Parker was talking about.

Politics

Our final comparison is between Parker's "Political Destination of America and the Signs of the Times" and Emerson's "Politics. " This comparison also meets our three previous criteria. Though not as well known as "The Divinity School Address" or "The American Scholar, " Emerson's "Politics" is one of the lectures in the Second Series and is certainly not unrepresentative. Again, also, this comparison studies the views of these two men in another important area, that of politics, where each man treats the same subject from the same viewpoint and makes the same basic points. As before, I propose to demonstrate that Parker presents his points with greater detail, order, and comprehensiveness.

There may be some objection in this case that Emerson and Parker are not dealing with the same subject from the same viewpoint, since Emerson considers politics in general and Parker considers American politics in particular. However, there are sufficient references in Emerson to American politics, especially his brief but keen analysis of the two chief American political parties, and sufficient references in Parker to politics in general, especially his opening consideration of the political destinations of a number of other nations, to say that both men present a view of politics in America, if a long range one. Emerson delves into such basic issues of politics as whether government is founded on the law or on men, whether the primary interest of the state should be the rights of men or of property, and whether the more perfect state ought to rest its authority on force or on what he calls love but what another age might call community spirit. Parker's very title, "The Political Destination ... ," suggests a like approach, and does so accurately. Parker spends the first part of his lecture describing the central spirit and attendant qualities of several nations. Both men then apply these general considerations to American politics, their aim being to help their listeners see the moving forces, the attendant circumstances, and the probable destination of this nation. To do so required just the approach they took. Both men, then, really do approach essentially the same subject from the same viewpoint.

Each man considers the goal of politics, the means to that goal, and an appraisal of the American political situation at the time. In regard to the first point, each sees the ideal of politics as to secure the welfare of each indi-

vidual. Emerson sees it as a matter of a community founded
on love, a community in which all will be employed, loved,
and trusted. When he says that this ideal community in-
volves the demise of the State, it is clear that he means the
state based on fear and the bayonet.

> The power of love, as the basis of a State, has
> never been tried. We must not imagine that
> all things are lapsing into confusion if every tender
> protestant be not compelled to bear his part in
> certain social conventions; nor doubt that roads can
> be built, letters carried, and the fruit of labor
> secured, when the government of force is at an
> end. Are our methods now so excellent that all
> competiton is hopeless? could not a nation of
> friends even devise better ways?[86]

Emerson's ideal is not one which demands an end of all
governmental organization, but of all such which is founded
on fear or force. There is to be organization, but organization founded on love, not imposed from without by legal
code, by police surveillance, by the pressures of a wealthy
elite, but a communal arrangement arising from the minds
and hearts of the people. This is the government of the
people, by the people, and for the people, of which Parker
spoke so often.

Parker eloquently describes the same kind of ideal.
Shortly, we Americans "shall go forth," Parker says, "to
realize our great national idea, and accomplish the great
work of organizing into institutions the unalienable rights of
man."[87] Then shall the rights of the hand, the rights of the
head, and the rights of the heart hold sway. All will then
have a chance to work, to get an education, and to live with
respect and honor. Then there will be no need of jails or
workhouses for the poor, devices which bear bitter testimony to the failure of a society. This ideal society will be
"free from the antagonism of races, classes, men--repre-
senting the American idea in its length, depth, and height,
its beauty and its truth, and then the old civilization of our
time shall seem barbarous and even savage."[88] Both men
present a noble and moving picture of the ideal towards
which men strive, or ought to strive, in their political
activity.

Both men agree, again, on the means necessary to
reach this ideal community: the education of people to see,

acknowledge, and live by first principles. Emerson points
out that many people think that governments are founded on
law but they fail to see that the law in turn is "only a mem-
orandum"[89] of what men agreed to yesterday but now see,
because of their further experience and insight, to be faulty,
and plan to change tomorrow. In fact, government is founded
on the moral identity of man. Men of a like moral nature
dealing with the same problems devise a governmental structure to help them solve those problems and so live full and
happy lives. This moral identity expresses itself in a
"common conscience" which could be arrived at by closely
studying the various codes of law of various peoples. All
government is founded on this identity and conscience and,
as such, is quasi-divine, for man is united with God. "Yet
absolute right is the first governor; or, every government is
an impure theocracy."[90] While laws make the city or state,
men make the laws, so at bottom we find that the "State
must follow and not lead the character and progress of the
citizen."[91] The ideal community will come about, then, not
by external manipulation or imposition, but will grow out of
the natures of the individuals who make up the community
when those natures have been educated in the first principles.
Thus "the highest end of government is the culture of men;
and ... if men can be educated, the institutions will share
their improvement and the moral sentiment will write the
law of the land."[92]

Parker emphatically agrees on the means necessary
to bring about the ideal community. He states that "the
positive things which we chiefly need for this work are first,
education, next, education, and then education, a vigorous
development of the mind, conscience, affections, religious
power of the whole nation."[93] The aim of this education is
to make the first principles set forth in the Declaration of
Independence the very basis of American life. The aim is
to realize the American ideal which, as we have seen, is
the "organization of the rights of man", rights which God
has imprinted on the very nature of man.

In appraising the American political situation both
Emerson and Parker agree that American politics of their
day leave much room for improvement but that there is
ground for hope for such improvement. Emerson says, "we
think our civilization near its meridian, but we are yet only
at the cock-crowing and the morning star."[94] Political
affairs may be in a bad way but there is steady improvement.

Many men may have their eyes fixed to the ground but the
saving remnant has its gaze on the stars. Men have consciences and those consciences ever light the way to better
things. "We are haunted by a conscience of this right to
grandeur of character.... "95 Such thoughts work as a grace
from within which will eventually turn a crowd of barbarous
individuals into a heavenly community.

     Parker echoes the same profound hope. "To me it
seems almost treason to doubt that a glorious future awaits
us. "96 True it is, Parker continues, that Americans have
many faults, but they have also an all-compensating love of
and increasing adherence to the first principles so nobly put
forth in the Declaration of Independence. They have an in-
veterate idealism which no money-grubbing, or power seeking, has been able to root out. This idealism once so en-
raptured the American soul and heart and mind that where-
ever Americans turn they are haunted by their first and true
love. This love of freedom and human rights is the outstanding trait of the American spirit and, in fact, this love
expresses America's providentially ordained role, to organize
the "unalienable rights of man. " However, this bright hope
does not blind Parker, or Emerson, to the defects which
mark the course and character of American politics.

     Emerson is particularly acute in sketching the defects
of American politics. He goes to the heart of the matter
when he describes the tension between men and property in
politics in general, and in American politics in particular.
If all men have equal rights, not all have equal ability. The
result is that those of superior ability amass property while
those of inferior ability grow poor.

> Personal rights, universally the same, demand a
> government framed on the ratio of census; property
> demands a government framed on the ratio of
> owners and of owning. 97

Thence arises the ever-increasing stress which besets
America. It was so in Emerson's day; it is much more so
today. This stress is so damaging to a state that Emerson
flatly asserts that "every actual State is corrupt. "98 Utter
ruin is prevented only by the laws of persons and things,
which will not be trifled with. For Emerson, the great laws
of the course of history, both natural and human, are beyond
human tampering.

The political parties, according to Emerson, take advantage of this stress for their own purposes. For they are
interested in patronage and not in principles; in office and
power and not in justice and truth. For the parties, politics
is entirely a matter of "image" and not of conviction, of
shadow and not of substance. Of the two chief political
parties of that day, one has the better cause while the other
has the better men, but neither offers hope of real improvement. "From neither party, when in power, has the world
any benefit to expect in science, art, or humanity, at all
commensurate with the resources of the nation. "[99]

Parker, too, finds defects in American politics. In
regard to principle, Americans, in Parker's judgment, have
put aside the traditional mores but have not yet fully founded
their lives on first principles. They talk much of such principles but there is still "a lamentable want of first principles, well known and established; we have rejected the
authority of tradition, but not yet accepted the authority of
truth and justice. "[100] Specifically, Parker charges that the
rights of man take a lower place than the rights of property.
"Manliness is postponed and wealth preferred. "[101] Americans have cast aside the aristocracy of birth but have sub-
stituted that of gold. Americans act in an ethical way when
it is to their advantage, obey the law when it is to their
gain. Thus the bankrupt speculator feels justified in paying
off ten cents on the dollar because the law has legally freed
him of his old debt, but once he is wealthy again he arro-
gantly charges interest on loans at a rate forbidden as usur-
ious by the law. In regard to political parties and politicians, Parker is particularly caustic. The measure of expediency's success in American politics is demonstrated by
the strong support both the two major parties give to that
great "American sin, " slavery. So changeable is the course
of scheming politicians, Parker remarks, that "it would be
emblematic to inaugurate American politicians by swearing
them on a weathercock. "[102] Even the great men of American politics have made as many turns in their careers as
the Missouri in its course. Parker caustically mentions the
twists and turns of Webster's career: against the Mexican
War, then for it, against slavery but then for the Fugitive
Slave Law. He comments on the amazing absurdity of men
demonstrating a man's fitness for the presidency by arguing
that he has no definite convictions or ideas! He compares
politicians in general to the blank page between the Old and
New Testaments.

> Mr. Facing-both-ways is a popular politician in
> America just now, sitting on the fence between
> honesty and dishonesty, and, like the blank leaf
> between the Old and New Testaments, belonging
> to neither dispensation. [103]

Parker's appraisal of the American political situation
at the time is more comprehensive than Emerson's in that
he not only criticizes the bad that mars American politics
but takes pains to balance that criticism by emphasizing the
good. Every land, Parker maintains, has a "peculiar
character." America's "peculiar character" is its love of
freedom and the rights of man, and the extent of this com-
pliment is clear when he adds that "this is a problem hitherto
unattempted on a national scale, in human history." [104] True
it is that the nation has not always and everywhere lived out
this noble ideal--its course is, as Parker says, as full of
twists and turns as the Rio Grande--yet this ideal and its
partial application stand out in the overall view. Further,
this balance of good and bad extends throughout most of
Parker's description of what he calls the "subordinate qualities" of the nation. For example, there is one such quality,
a disdain for authority, which is good to an extent and bad
to an extent. The good is nicely illustrated by the tart reply
of the American Protestant to the sly Jesuit's argument that
"the rites and customs and doctrines of the Catholic church
go back to the second century, the age after the apostles!"

> 'No doubt of it,' said the American who had also
> read his Fathers, 'they go back to the times of
> the apostles themselves; but that proves nothing,
> for there were as great fools in the first century
> as the last. A fool or a folly is no better because
> it is an old folly or an old fool. There are
> fools enough now, in all conscience. Pray don't
> go back to prove their apostolical succession.' [105]

There is no such comprehensive balance in Emerson.

Parker's appraisal is also far more detailed and orderly, while Emerson's loses much of its power because of
a lack of detail. For, instance, Emerson deftly presents
what is perhaps the basic problem of the politics of that day,
and of ours also; the clash between the rights of men and
those of wealth. His point is well made and most important.
Parker not only makes the same point but makes it doubly
by firmly attaching it to the American situation. First of

all, it was not unimportant, Parker points out, that the pioneers concentrated on property, the clearing of land and putting up homes. Such concentration was absolutely essential for their very survival. But now this interest has become a fetish. "Manliness is postponed and wealth preferred." Parker illustrates this inversion of values by the typical American estimation of scholarly and artistic endeavor in terms of how much money it has or will get. For example, a painter is noteworthy because his paintings have sold for twenty thousand dollars. Another example is that America's foremost mathematician, Bowditch, has to support himself by work in an insurance office. So much is this inversion of values the case that the wealthy are now ashamed of the work that got their wealth. It might be objected, Parker concludes, that it goes thus in every land. That well may be true, he admits, but in other lands such a situation does not clash with ideals. "In America it is a contradiction."[106]

Likewise, Emerson's pointed remarks about party politics in America do not have the full force they might have had. They are too generalized. In contrast, while Emerson contents himself with the conclusion that the parties are not really interested in principle but only in office, Parker illustrates his case with sad examples:

> The whig party of the North loves slavery; the Democratic Party does not even seek to conceal its affection therefor. A great politician declares the Mexican War wicked, and then urges men to go and fight in it; he thinks a famous general not fit to be nominated for President, but then invites men to elect him.... It is a little amusing to ... hear a man's fitness for the Presidency defended on the ground that he has no definite convictions or ideas! ... It must strike a stranger as a little odd that a republic should have a slaveholder for President five-sixths of the time, and most of the important offices be monopolized by other slaveholders.... [107]

Such instances lend pointed support to Parker's judgment that "there are two capital maxims which prevail amongst our hucksters of politics: to love your party better than your country, and yourself better than your party."[108]

Finally, Parker's appraisal of the American political

situation is much more ordered. Parker offers a tidy
schema of the traits which distinguish American politics.
In addition to the fundamental one--a deep and abiding love
of freedom and the rights of man--Parker catalogs no less
that five subordinate traits: an impatience of authority, a
philosophic tendency which shows itself in a desire for the
ultimate facts, a lamentable want of first principles, an intensity of life, and materialism. A few words about the
second of these traits serves to illustrate Parker's orderly
presentation and also illustrates his acuteness, for at least
initially, this seems to be an unusual trait to predicate of
American political life. However, Parker substantiates his
predication by citing the deep, pervading interest of Americans of that age, and not just those living in larger cities
such as Boston, in the ultimate facts, first principles, and
universal ideas. One indication of this interest is the
astounding numbers of people, city people and farmers, business men and woodsmen, who attended scholarly lectures
such as those of Emerson. 109 Though American scholars
did not compare with the European ones, the bulk of the
population is interested in and competent about philosophic
ideas. An instance to show this fact is the wider interest
in such writers as Bacon and Newton in this country than in
Europe. Further, there is even what Parker calls a "philosophical party" in politics, the Free Soil Party, whose plat-
form is based on first principles and universal laws.

     Parker proceeds in the same way with the other
traits. He goes into considerable detail, offers actual instances to illustrate his point, and does so in a balanced
way, showing both sides. For example, he demonstrates
how the American impatience towards authority can be both
good and bad. Each of these traits, including the fundamental one, love of freedom and the rights of man, Parker
describes in terms of American history and the American
situation of that day.

     To a lesser degree Parker's description of the ideal
community and the means thereto excels Emerson's. Neither
man says much about the means necessary to bring about
that society. Emerson speaks in a general way of the ideals
which haunt the consciences of men and of the need for education in those principles. Parker illustrates those principles
in American life. Thus, for example, the "philosophical
party, " the Free Soil Party, pleads and works for the care
and education of orphans, the reformation of wrong-doers,
the curtailment of war. Further, the country is founded on

these principles; they are the principles of the Declaration
of Independence. "The political ideas of the nation are
transcendent, not empirical. Human history could not justify
the Declaration of Independence and its large statements of
the new idea: the nation went behind human history and
appealed to human nature."[110] Finally, Parker introduces
an all-important factor in speaking of the improvement of
America, one which Emerson does not mention. This is the
great obstacle in the way of improvement--slavery. When,
and only when it is removed, can real improvement come
about, for slavery is a cancer which is stifling the moral
life of America. When it is cut out lesser evils can be dealt
with.

Finally, while Emerson offers only a brief, general
description of the ideal or goal of politics, Parker ties his
description to the Declaration of Independence and the Pre-
amble to the Constitution, and applies it not just to society
in a general way but also to the more important parts of
that society: to art, to literature, to education, to the
church. In American literature, for instance, Parker states
that there will be democratic freedom, thought and power,
"a literature with all of German philosophic depth, with English solid sense, with French vivacity and wit, Italian fire of
sentiment and soul, with all of Grecian elegance of form,
and more than Hebrew piety and faith in God."[111] Granted
that Parker does not go to great lengths in this argument,
still, since ideals are so crucial in guiding practical affairs,
even a little more description of them is important.

Again, as in the other comparisons, we may fairly
conclude, after examining the evidence, that for the more
substantial critique of American politics of that day, Parker's
lecture is by far the better place to go.

Though our four comparisons do not include Emerson's Nature or such works of Parker as his "Letter on
Slavery" and his speeches on Webster and John Quincy Adams,
the four comparisons together provide a representative, fair,
and exact basis for the judgment that Parker deserves at
least equal rank with the Concord Sage as one of the most
outstanding members of that somewhat varying grouping of
pre-Civil War American thinkers called "transcendentalists."
In fact, we may perhaps use the evaluation Emerson made
of himself in relation to his friend, Henry David Thoreau.
Emerson speaks of Thoreau's "oaken strength" in performing
tasks beyond his own strength, and continues:

He has muscle, and ventures on and performs
feats which I am forced to decline.   In reading
him, I find the same thought, the same spirit that
is in me, but he takes it a step beyond, and illustrates by excellent images that which I should have
conveyed in a sleepy generality.   'Tis as if I went
into a gymnasium, and saw youths leap, climb,
and swing with a force unapproachable, --though
their feats are only continuations of my initial grap-
plings and jumps. 112

This same evaluation is pertinent to the relationship between
Parker and Emerson.

But the only way to really get to know Parker and his
views is not through another person's eyes, but face to face
in his own writings.   The rest of this book provides that
opportunity.   The first four readings are the lectures used
in this essay in comparing Parker with Emerson.   The next
selection is Parker's appraisal of Emerson, and the last is
one of his sermons which is particularly appropriate to our
present time.

Notes

1.   Some helpful studies of transcendentalism are Frothing-
      ham, Octavius, Transcendentalism in New England:
      A History (New York: Harper, 1959), esp. pp. 136 ff. ;
      Tyler, Alice, Freedom's Ferment (New York: Harper,
      1962), pp. 47ff. ; Parrington, V. L. , Main Currents
      in American Thought (New York: Harcourt, Brace &
      World, 1954), II, 371ff. ; Whicher, Geo. F. , (ed),
      Transcendentalist Revolt Against Materialism (Boston:
      Heath, 1949); Schneider, H. , A History of American
      Philosophy (New York: Columbia U. Press, 1962),
      pp. 223ff. ; and Miller, Perry, The Transcendentalists
      (Cambridge: Harvard U. Press, 1960).   Miller's book
      contains an extensive bibliography.
2.   Gabriel, Ralph H. , The Course of American Democratic
      Thought (New York: Ronald Press, 1956), pp. 40ff. ;
      Dewey, John, "Ralph Waldo Emerson, " Emerson, ed.
      Milton Konvitz and Stephen E. Whicher (Englewood
      Cliffs, N. J. : Prentice-Hall, 1962), pp. 24-30; Miller,
      pp. 3-4.   For an example of a contrary judgment see
      Adams, James T. , "Emerson Reread, " Transcenden-
      talist Revolt, pp. 31-39.

3. Schneider doubts that Parker was much of a transcendentalist. But on the other side, see Parker on himself as such in Weiss, Life and Correspondence of Theodore Parker (New York: Bergman, 1969), I, 155, and also Parker's "Transcendentalism. " For others who so view him, see Parrington, Tyler, Frothingham. For a reasoned defense of such a view see Newbrough, Geo. F. , "Reason and Understanding in the Works of Theodore Parker, " South Atlantic Quarterly (Jan., 1948), 64-75, and Smith, H. Shelton, "Was Theodore Parker a Transcendentalist?" New England Quarterly, XXIII (1950), 351-64. Finally, for an interpretation which makes Emerson not so much a transcendentalist, at least in his later years, see Whicher, Stephen E. , Freedom and Fate (Philadelphia: U. of Pennsylvania Press, 1953).

4. Cf. Weiss, I, 99, 144, but esp. II, 115; 191; 239; Schneider, p. 227; Frothingham, p. 317. Mead, Edwin D. , The Influence of Emerson (Boston: American Unitarian Association, 1903), p. 121.

5. Parker, Theodore, "Position and Duties of the American Scholar, " Collected Works, ed. F. Cobbe (London: Trübner, 1863-79), VII, 223. Unless otherwise noted all Parker references are to the Cobbe edition.

6. Parker, "Theodore Parker's Experience as a Minister, " XII, 307.

7. Parker, "Theodore Parker's Experience as a Minister, " XII, 308; cf. also Weiss, I, 260, 304, where, old and worn out and ill, he resolves, evidently without effect, to reduce his lecturing to 40 times a year. See also Weiss II, 115, 239.

8. Chadwick, John W. , Theodore Parker (Boston: Houghton, Mifflin and Co. , 1900), pp. 322f.

9. Parker, "The Boston Kidnapping, " (1852), V, 212.

10. Parker, "The Boston Kidnapping, " V, 215.

11. Parker, "State of the Nation, Considered in a Sermon Preached on Thanksgiving Day, " (1850), IV, 237.

12. Parker, "Discourse Occasioned by the Death of John Quincy Adams, " (March 5, 1848), IV, 135.

13. Parker, "Nebraska Question, " (1854), V, 296.

14. Parker, "Slave Power in America, " (1850), V, 122.

15. Parker, "Slave Power in America, " V, 128.

16. Parker, "Letter on Slavery, " (1848), V, 55.

17. Parker, "Letter on Slavery, " V, 69.

18. Parker, "A Sermon of the Mexican War, " (1848), IV, 55f.

19. Parker, "Nebraska Question, " (1854), V, 270.

20. Parker, "Sermon of the Perishing Classes in Boston, " (1846), VII, 54.

21. Parker, "Thoughts on Labor, " (1848), IX, 136.
22. Parker, "Sermon of the Moral Condition of Boston, "
     (1849), VII, 124.
23. Parker, "Sermon of the Perishing Classes in Boston, "
     (1846), VII, 42.
24. Parker, "The Chief Sins of the People, " (1851), VII,
     267.
25. Parker, "The Chief Sins, " VII, 270.
26. Parker, "The Chief Sins, " VII, 264-65.
27. Parker, "The Perishing Classes of Boston, " (1846),
     VII, 38.
28. Parker, "Thoughts on Labour, " (1848), IX, 137.
29. Parker, "Sermon on the Moral Condition of Boston, "
     (1849), VII, 145.
30. Parker, "The Nebraska Question, " (1854), V, 290-91.
31. Parker, "Slave Power in America, " (1850), V, 127.
32. Parker, "Perishing Classes in Boston, " (1846), VII, 44.
33. Parker, "The True Idea of a Christian Church, " (1846),
     III, 38, 40.
34. Parker, "True Idea, " III, 44-55.
35. Parker, "Review of Prescott's Reign, " (1849), X, 116.
36. Parker, "Review, " (1849), X, 102.
37. Parker, "Education of the People, " (1848), IX, 267.
38. Parker, "Education of the People, " IX, 266.
39. Parker, "Education, " IX, 273.
40. Parker, "Education, " IX, 291.
41. Parker, "Education, " IX, 292.
42. Matthiessen, F. O. , American Renaissance (New York:
     Oxford U. Press, 1941), p. 23.
43. In regard to a comparison between Parker and Emer-
     son, see Chadwick, pp. 175ff. ; Newbrough, "Reason
     and Understanding . . . "; Dirks, John E. , The Critical
     Theology of Theodore Parker (New York: Columbia U.
     Press, 1948), esp. pp. 98f. , 110; Mead, p. 111; and
     Bartlett, I. H. , "Parker, Theodore, " Encyclopedia
     of Philosophy ed. Paul Edwards (New York: Macmil-
     lan, 1967), VI, 46.
44. Parker, "Transcendentalism, " (see p. 64 in this
     volume).
45. Parker, "Transcendentalism, " (see p. 53)
46. Emerson, R. W. , "The Transcendentalist, " Selected
     Essays, Lectures, and Poems of Ralph Waldo Emer-
     son, ed. Robert E. Spiller (New York: Washington
     Square Press, 1967), p. 101. Subsequent references
     to Emerson, unless otherwise noted, will be to
     Spiller's edition.
47. Emerson, p. 108.

48. Emerson, p. 109.
49. Tyler, p. 100; cf. the following pages for a number of other such examples.
50. On Parker's understanding of such philosophers see Newbrough, p. 67 and Wellek, Rene, "The Minor Transcendentalists and German Philosophy, " New England Quarterly XV, 4 (1942), 668.
51. Parker, "Transcendentalism, " p. 65.
52. Parker, "Transcendentalism, " p. 65.
53. Parker, "Transcendentalism, " p. 64.
54. Parker, "Transcendentalism, " p. 65.
55. Parker, "Transcendentalism, " p. 66.   On conscience in Parker, see his "Experience as a Minister, " XII, 272f.;   Weiss, I, 108, 381; Dirks, p. 133; Newbrough, esp. 64-67; "The Law of God and the Statutes of Men, " (1854), V, 227f. ; "The True Idea of the Christian Church, " p. 44; Wellek, 669.
56. Parker, "Transcendentalism, " p. 66.
57. Parker, "Transcendentalism, " p. 66.
58. Parker, "Transcendentalism," p.68; cf.Newbrough 65-66.
59. Parker, "Transcendentalism, " p. 70.
60. Bartlett, p. 46; Whicher, Transcendentalist Revolt, vi; cf. also Commager, H. S. , Theodore Parker (Boston: Little, Brown, 1936), p. 81.   An indication of Parker's fate is that when Gail Kennedy revised Whicher's book in 1968, he left in Whicher's introduction which contains the quoted statement about Parker's "Transcendentalism" but left out the essay itself!
61. Weiss, I, 113; Chadwick, pp. 87ff.
62. Chadwick, p. 96.
63. Parker, "Discourse, " p. 96.
64. Emerson, "Address, " p. 83.
65. Emerson, "Address, " p. 92.
66. Parker, "Discourse, " p. 96.
67. Newman, John Henry, On Consulting the Faithful in Matters, of Doctrine (New York: Sheed and Ward, 1961), pp. 75ff.
68. Parker, "Discourse, " p. 85.
69. Parker, "Discourse, " p. 86.
70. Parker, "Discourse, " p. 86.
71. Emerson, "The American Scholar, " p. 63.
72. Parker, "Position and Duties of the American Scholar," p. 124.
73. Cf. Tyler, pp. 196ff. , esp. 262-64.
74. Emerson, "The American Scholar, " p. 73.
75. Parker, "Position and Duties, " p. 109.
76. Parker, "Position and Duties, " p. 136.
77. Parker, "Position and Duties, " p. 138.

78. Emerson, "The American Scholar, " pp. 79f.
79. Emerson, "The American Scholar, " p. 80.
80. Parker, "Position and Duties, " p. 127.
81. Parker, "Position and Duties, " p. 131.
82. Cf. Parker, "The Writings of Ralph Waldo Emerson," pp. 170-231.
83. Parker, "Position and Duties, " p. 111.
84. Emerson, "The American Scholar, " p. 79.
85. Parker, "Position and Duties, " p. 138
86. Emerson, "Politics, " p. 327; on Emerson's anarchism, see Tyler, p. 58 and Parrington, II, 385ff. For a similar view, see Parker, "The Nebraska Question, " V, 296.
87. Parker, "The Political Destination, " p. 167.
88. Parker, "The Political Destination, " p. 168.
89. Emerson, "Politics, " p. 318.
90. Emerson, "Politics, " p. 324.
91. Emerson, "Politics, " p. 317.
92. Emerson, "Politics, " pp. 319f. Cf. Gandhi, M. Non-violence in Peace and War (Ahmedabad: Navajivan, 1949), II, 101.
93. Parker, "Political Destination, " p. 167.
94. Emerson, "Politics, " p. 326.
95. Emerson, "Politics, " p. 326.
96. Parker, "Political Destination, " p. 167.
97. Emerson, "Politics, " p. 318.
98. Emerson, "Politics, " p. 321.
99. Emerson, "Politics, " p. 323.
100. Parker, "Political Destination, " p. 151.
101. Parker, "Political Destination, " p. 163.
102. Parker, "Political Destination, " p. 151.
103. Parker, "Political Destination, " p. 153.
104. Parker, "Political Destination, " p. 143.
105. Parker, "Political Destination, " p. 147.   This remark sounds as if it were taken from an actual discussion which Parker did have with a priest on his visit to Rome.
106. Parker, "Political Destination, " p. 162.
107. Parker, "Political Destination, " p. 153f.
108. Parker, "Political Destination, " p. 154.
109. Tyler, p. 262f.
110. Parker, "Political Destination, " p. 155.
111. Parker, "Political Destination, " p. 168.
112. Perry, Bliss (ed.), The Heart of Emerson's Journals (New York: Houghton Mifflin Co. , 1926), pp. 298f.

SELECTIONS

FROM

THEODORE PARKER

Theodore Parker at age 48, in 1858

1.   TRANSCENDENTALISM*

The will is father to the deed, but the thought and
sentiment are father and mother of the will.   Nothing seems
more impotent than a thought, it has neither hands nor feet,
--but nothing proves so powerful.   The thought turns out a
thing; its vice or virtue becomes manners, habits, laws, institutions; the abstraction becomes concrete; the most universal proposition is the most particular; and in the end it
is the abstract thinker who is the most practical man and
sets mills a-running and ships to sail.

A change of ideas made all the difference between
Catholic and Protestant, monarchical and democratic.   You
see that all things are first an idea in the mind, then a fact
out of the mind.   The architect, the farmer, the railroad-
calculator, the founder of empires, has his temple, his
farm, his railroad, or his empire, in his head as an idea
before it is a fact in the world.   As the thought is the thing
becomes.   Every idea bears fruit after its kind, --the good,
good; the bad, bad.   Some few hundred years ago John Huss,
Luther, Lord Bacon, Descartes said, We will not be ruled
by authority in the church or the school, but by common
sense and reason.   That was nothing but an idea; but out of
it has come the Protestant Reformation, the English Revolution, the American Revolution, the French Revolution, the
cycle of Revolutions that fill up the year 1848.   Yes, all the
learned societies of Europe, all the Protestant churches, all
the liberal governments, --of Holland, England, France,
Germany, America,--have come of that idea.   The old fellows in Galileo's time would not look through his telescope
lest it should destroy the authorized theory of vision; they
knew what they were about.   So have all the old fellows
known ever since who refuse to look through a new telescope,
or even at it, but only talk against it.   Once the Egyptian
sculptors copied men into stone with their feet joined and
their hands fixed to their sides.   The copy indicated the im-
mutableness of things in Egypt, where a mummy was the

*Parker, Theodore.   The Works of Theodore Parker ("Cen-
tenary Edition, " 15 vols.; Boston: American Unitarian Association, 1907-13), VI, 1-38.

type of a man.   A Greek sculptor separated the feet, as in
life, illegally taking a live man for his type.   The sculptor
lost his head, for the government saw a revolution of the
empire in this departure from the authorized type of man.
Such is the power of ideas.   The first question to ask of a
civilized nation is.   How do they think?   what is their philosophy ?

Now it is the design of philosophy to explain the phenomena of the universe by showing their order, connection,
cause, law, use and meaning.   These phenomena are of two
kinds or forms, as they belong to the material world--facts
of observation; and as they belong to the spiritual world--
facts of consciousness: facts without, and facts within.   From
these two forms of phenomena or facts there came two grand
divisions of philosophy: the philosophy of outward things, --
physics; the philosophy of inward things, --metaphysics.

In the material world, to us, there are only facts.
Man carries something thither, to wit, ideas.   Thus the
world has quite a different look; for he finds the facts without have a certain relation to the ideas within.   The world
is one thing to Newton's dog Diamond, quite another to Newton himself.   The dog saw only the facts and some of their
uses; the philosopher saw therein the reflected image of his
own ideas, --saw order, connection, cause, law and meaning,
as well as use.

Now in the pursuit of philosophy there are two methods
which may be followed, namely, the deductive and the inductive.

I.   By the deductive the philosopher takes a certain
maxim or principle, assumes it as a fact and therefrom de-
duces certain other maxims or principles as conclusions, as
facts.   But in the conclusions there must be nothing which
is not in the primary fact else the conclusion does not conclude.   All pure science is of this character--geometry,
algebra, arithmetic. $1 + 1 = 2$ is a maxim, let us suppose: $1000 + 1000 = 2000$ is one deduction from it; 25 x
$25 = 625$, another deduction.   Thus the philosopher must
be certain of the fact he starts from, of the method he goes
by, and the conclusion he stops at is made sure of beforehand.

The difficulty is that the philosopher often assumes
his first fact, takes a fancy for a fact; then, though the

method be right, the conclusion is wrong.   For instance,
Aristotle assumed this proposition, --the matter of the sun is
incorruptible; thence he deduced this fact, that the sun does
not change, that its light and heat are constant quantities.
The conclusion did not agree with observation, the theory
with the facts.   His first fact was not proved, could not be,
was disproved.   But when Galileo looked at the sun with a
telescope he saw spots on the sun, movable spots.   Aristotle's first fact turned out a fancy, so all conclusion from
it.   The Koran is written by the infallible inspiration of God,
the Pope is infallible, the King can do no wrong, the People
are always right, --these are assumptions.   If taken as
truths, you see the conclusions which may be deduced therefrom, --which have been.   There is in God somewhat not
wholly good, is an assumption which lies at the bottom of a
good deal of theology, whence conclusions quite obvious are
logically deduced, --1, Manicheism, God and the devil; 2,
God and an evil never to be overcome.   God is absolute
good is another assumption from which the opposite deductions are to be made.   The method of deduction is of the
greatest value and cannot be dispensed with.

II.   By the inductive method the philosopher takes
facts, puts them together after a certain order, seen in nature or devised in his own mind, and tries to find a more
comprehensive fact common to many facts, i. e. , what is
called a law, which applies to many facts and so is a general law, or to all facts and so is a universal law.   In the
deductive method you pass from a universal fact to a particular fact; in the inductive, from the particular to the general.   In the deductive process there is nothing in the conclusion which was not first in the premises; by the inductive
something new is added at every step.   The philosopher is
sifting in his own conjecture or thought in order to get at a
general idea which takes in all the particular facts in the
case and explains them.   When this general idea and the
facts correspond the induction is correct.   But it is as easy
to arrive at a false conclusion by the inductive process as to
assume a false maxim from which to make deductions.   A
physician's apprentice once visited his master's patient and
found him dead, and reported the case accordingly.   "What
killed him?" said the old doctor.   "He died of eating a
horse. "   "Eating a horse!" expostulated the man of experience; "impossible! how do you know that?"   "He did, " said
the inductive son of Aesculapius, "for I saw the saddle and
bridle under the bed. "   Another, but a grown-up doctor, once
gave a sick blacksmith a certain medicine; he recovered.

"Post hoc, ergo propter hoc, " said the doctor, and tried the
same drug on the next sick man, who was a shoemaker. The
shoemaker died, and the doctor wrote down his induction:
"This drug will cure all sick blacksmiths, but kill all sick
shoemakers (Rule for phosphorus). "

The inductive method is also indispensable in all the
sciences which depend on observation or experiment. The
process of induction is as follows: After a number of facts
is collected, the philosopher looks for some one fact common to all and explanatory thereof. To obtain this he assumes a fact as a law, and applies it to the facts before
him. This is an hypothesis. If it corresponds to the facts,
the hypothesis is true. Two great forms of error are noticeable in the history of philosophy: 1, the assumption of
false maxims, whence deductions are to be made, --the assumption of no-fact for a fact; 2, the making of false inductions from actual facts. In the first, a falsehood is assumed, and then falsehood deduced from it; in the second,
from a truth falsehood is induced, and this new falsehood is
taken as the basis whence other falsehoods are deduced.

Pythagoras declared the sun was the centre of the
planets which revolved about it; that was an hypothesis, --
guesswork, and no more. He could not compare the hypothesis with facts, so his hypothesis could not be proved or
disproved. But long afterwards others made the comparison
and confirmed the hypothesis. Kepler wished to find out what
ratio the time of a planet's revolution bears to its distance
from the sun. He formed an hypothesis, --"The time is pro-
portionable to the distance. " No, that did not agree with the
facts. "To the square of the distance?" No. "To the cube
of the distance?" No. "The square of the time to the cube
of the distance?" This he found to be the case, and so he
established his celebrated law, --Kepler's third law. But he
examined only a few planets: how should he know the law was
universal? He could not learn that by induction. That
would only follow from this postulate, "The action of nature
is always uniform, " which is not an induction, nor a deduction, but an assumption. The inductive method alone never
establishes a universal law, for it cannot transcend the particular facts in the hands of the philosopher. The axioms of
mathematics are not learned by inductions, but assumed out-
right as self-evident. "Kepler's third law is universal of all
bodies moving about a centre, "--now there are three processes by which that conclusion is arrived at: 1. The process of induction, by which the law is proved general and to

apply to all the cases investigated. 2. A process of deduction from the doctrine or axiom, that the action of nature is
always uniform. 3. That maxim is obtained by a previous
process of assumption from some source or another.

Such is the problem of philosophy, to explain the facts
of the universe; such the two departments of philosophy,
physics and metaphysics; such the two methods of inquiry,
deductive and inductive; such are the two forms of error, --
the assumption of a false fact as the starting-point of deduction, the induction of a false fact by the inductive process.
Now these methods are of use in each department of philosophy, indispensable in each, in physics and in metaphysics.

This is the problem of metaphysics, --to explain the
facts of human consciousness. In metaphysics there are and
have long been two schools of philosophers. The first is the
sensational school. Its most important metaphysical doctrine
is this: There is nothing in the intellect which was not first
in the senses. Here "intellect" means the whole intellectual,
moral, affectional and religious consciousness of man. The
philosophers of this school claim to have reached this conclusion legitimately by the inductive method. It was at first
an hypothesis; but after analyzing the facts of consciousness,
interrogating all the ideas and sentiments and sensations of
man, they say the hypothesis is proved by the most careful
induction. They appeal to it as a principle, as a maxim,
from which other things are deduced. They say that experience by one or more of the senses is the ultimate appeal in
philosophy: all that I know is of sensational origin; the
senses are the windows which let in all the light I have; the
senses afford a sensation. I reflect upon this, and by reflection transform a sensation into an idea. An idea, therefore, is a transformed sensation.

A school in metaphysics soon becomes a school in
physics, in politics, ethics, religion. The sensational school
has been long enough in existence to assert itself in each of
the four great forms of human action. Let us see what it
amounts to.

I. In physics. 1. It does not afford us a certainty
of the existence of the outward world. The sensationalist believes it, not on account of his sensational philosophy, but in
spite of it; not by his philosophy, but by his common sense:
he does not philosophically know it. While I am awake the
senses give me various sensations, and I refer the sensations

to an object out of me, and so perceive its existence.   But
while I am asleep the senses give me various sensations,
and for the time I refer the sensations to an object out of
me, and so perceive its existence, --but when I awake it
seems a dream.   Now, if the senses deceive me in sleep,
why not when awake?   How can I <u>know</u> philosophically the
existence of the material world?   <u>With</u> only the sensational
philosophy I cannot!   I can only <u>know</u> the facts of consciousness.   I cannot pass from ideas to things, from psychology
to ontology.   Indeed there is no ontology, and I am certain
only of my own consciousness.   Bishop Berkeley, a thorough
sensationalist, comes up with the inductive method in his
hand, and annihilates the outward material world, annihilates
mankind, leaves me nothing but my own consciousness, and
no consciousness of any certainty there.   Dr. Priestley, a
thorough sensationalist, comes up with the same inductive
method in his hand, and annihilates the spiritual world, annihilates the soul.   Berkeley, with illogical charity, left me
the soul as an existence, but stripped me of matter; I was
certain I had a soul, not at all sure of my body.   Priestley,
as illogically, left me the body as an existence, but stripped
me of the soul.   Both of these gentlemen I see were entirely
in the right, if their general maxim be granted; and so, between the two, I am left pretty much without soul or sense!
Soul and body are philosophically hurled out of existence!

From its hypothetical world sensationalism proceeds
to the laws of matter; but it cannot logically get beyond its
facts.   Newton says, "Gravitation prevails, --its power di-
minishing as the square of the distance increases between two
bodies, so far as I have seen. " "Is it so where you have
not seen?" Newton doesn't know; he cannot pass from a general law to a universal law.   As the existence of the world
is hypothetical, so the universality of laws of the world is
only hypothetical universality.   The Jesuits who edited the
Principia were wise men when they published them as an
hypothesis.

The sensational philosophy has prevailed chiefly in
England; that is the home of its ablest representatives, --
Bacon, Locke.   See the effect.   England turns her attention
to sciences that depend chiefly on observation, on experiment, --botany, chemistry, the descriptive part of astronomy,
zoology, geology.   England makes observations on the tides,
on variations of the magnetic needle on the stars; fits out ex-
ploring expeditions; learns the facts; looks after the sources
of the Nile, the Niger; hunts up the North Pole; tests the

strength of iron, wood, gunpowder; makes improvements in
all the arts, in mechanics.   But in metaphysics she does
nothing; in the higher departments of physics--making comprehensive generalizations--she does little.   Even in mathematics, after Newton, for a hundred years England fell behind the rest of Europe.   She is great at experiment, little
at pure thinking.

The sensational philosophy has no idea of cause, except that of empirical connection in time and place; no idea
of substance; no ontology, but phenomenology.   It refers all
questions--say of the planets about the sun--to an outward
force: when they were made, God, standing outside, gave
them a push and set them a-going; or else their motion is
the result of a fortuitous concourse of atoms, a blind fate.
Neither conclusion is a philosophical conclusion, each an hypothesis.   Its physics are mere materialism; hence it de-
lights in the atomistic theory of nature and repels the dynamic
theory of matter.   The sensationalist's physics appear well
in a celebrated book, The Vestiges of the Natural History of
Creation.   The book has many valuable things in it, but the
philosophy of its physics is an unavoidable result of sensationalism.   There is nothing but materialism in his world.
All is material, effects material, causes material, his God
material, --not surpassing the physical universe, but co-ex-
tensive therewith.   In zoology life is the result of organization, but is an immanent life.   In anthropology the mind is
the result of organization, but is an immanent mind; in
theology God is the result of organization, but is an immanent God.   Life does not transcend organization, nor does
mind, nor God.   All is matter.

II.   In politics.   Sensationalism knows nothing of absolute right, absolute justice; only of historical right, historical justice.   "There is nothing in the intellect which was
not first in the senses. "   The senses by which we learn of
justice and right are hearing and seeing.   Do I reflect, and
so get a righter right and juster justice than I have seen or
heard of, it does me no good, for "nothing is in the intellect
which was not in the senses. "   Thus absolute justice is only
a whim, a no-thing, a dream.   Men that talk of absolute
justice, absolute right, are visionary men.

In politics, sensationalism knows nothing of ideas,
only of facts; "the only lamp by which its feet are guided is
the lamp of experience. "   All its facts are truths of observation, not of necessity.   "There is no right but might, " is

the political philosophy of sensationalism.   It may be the
might of a king, of an aristocracy, of a democracy, the might
of passions, the might of intellect, the might of muscle, --it
has a right to what it will.   It appeals always to human history, not human nature.   Now human history shows what has
been, not what should be or will be.   To reason about war it
looks not to the natural justice, only to the cost and present
consequences.   To reason about free trade or protection, it
looks not to the natural justice or right of mankind, but only
to the present expediency of the thing.   Political expediency
is the only right or justice it knows in its politics.   So it always looks back, and says, "it worked well at Barcelona or
Venice," or "did not work well."   It loves to cite precedents
out of history, not laws out of nature.   It claims a thing not
as a human right, but as an historical privilege received by
Magna Charta or the Constitution; as if a right were more of
a right because time-honored and written on parchment; or
less, because just claimed and for the first time and by a
single man.   The sensationalist has no confidence in ideas,
so asks for facts to hold on to and to guide him in his blindness.   Said a governor in America, "The right of suffrage is
universal."   "How can that be," said a sensationalist, "when
the Constitution of the state declares that certain persons
shall not vote?"   He knew no rights before they became con-
stitutional, no rights but vested rights, --perhaps none but
"invested."

    The sensationalists in politics divide into two parties,
each with the doctrine that in politics "might makes right."
One party favors the despotism of the few, --is an oligarchy;
or of the one, --is a monarchy.   Hence the doctrine is, "The
king can do no wrong."   All power is his; he may delegate it
to the people as a privilege; it is not theirs by right, by nature, and his as a trust.   He has a right to make any laws
he will, not merely any just laws.   The people must pay
passive obedience to the king, he has eminent domain over
them.   The celebrated Thomas Hobbes is the best representative of this party, and has one great merit, --of telling what
he thought.

    The other party favors the despotism of the many, --is
a democracy.   The doctrine is, "The people can do no
wrong."   The majority of the people have the right to make
any laws they will, not merely any just laws; and the minority
must obey, right or wrong.   You must not censure the measures of the majority, you afford "aid and comfort to the
enemy."   The state has absolute domain over the citizen, the

majority over the minority; this holds good of the voters,
and of any political party in the nation.   For the majority
has power of its own right, for its own behoof; not in trust,
and for the good of all and each!   The aim of sensational
politics is the greatest good of the greatest number; this may
be obtained by sacrificing the greatest good of the lesser
number, --by sacrificing any individual, --or sacrificing absolute good.   In No-man's-land this party prevails: the dark-
haired men, over forty million, --the red-haired, only three
million five hundred thousand, --the dark-haired enslave the
red-haired, for the greatest good of the greatest number.
But in a hundred years the red-haired men are most numerous, and turn round and enslave the black-haired.

Thomas Paine is a good representative of this party;
so is Marat, Robespierre, the author of the Système de la
Nature.   In the old French Revolution you see the legitimate
consequence of this doctrine, that might makes right, that
there is no absolute justice, in the violence, the murder, the
wholesale assassination.   The nation did to masses, and in
the name of democracy, what all kings had done to the nation and in the name of monarchy, --sought the greatest good
of the controlling power at the sacrifice of an opponent.   It
is the same maxim which in cold blood hangs a single culprit, enslaves three million negroes, and butchers thousands
of men as in the September massacres.   The sensational
philosophy established the theory that might makes right,--
and the mad passions of a solitary despot, or a million-
headed mob, made it a fact.   Commonly the two parties unite
by a compromise, and then it consults not the greatest good
of its king alone, as in a brutal, pure monarchy; not of the
greatest number, as in a pure and brutal democracy; but the
greatest good of a class, --the nobility and gentry in England,
the landed proprietors and rich burghers in Switzerland, the
slaveholders in South Carolina.   Voltaire is a good representative of this type of sensational politics, not to come
nearer home.   In peaceful times England shares the defect
of the sensational school in politics.   Her legislation is empirical; great ideas do not run through her laws; she loves a
precedent better than a principle; appeals to an accidental
fact of human history, not an essential fact of human nature
which is prophetic.   Hence legislative politics is not a great
science which puts the facts of human consciousness into a
state, making natural justice common law; nothing but a poor
dealing with precedents, a sort of national housekeeping and
not very thrifty housekeeping.   In our own nation you see
another example of the same, --result of the same sensational

philosophy. There is no right, says Mr. Calhoun, but
might; the white man has that, so the black man is his political prey. And Mr. Polk tells us that Vermont, under the
Constitution, has the same right to establish slavery as
Georgia to abolish it.

      III. In ethics. Ethics are the morals of the indi-
vidual; politics of the mass. The sensationalist knows no
first truths in morals; the source of maxims in morals is
experience; in experience there is no absolute right. Absolute justice, absolute right, were never in the senses, so
not in the intellect; only whimsies, words in the mouth. The
will is not free, but wholly conditioned, in bondage; character made always for you, not by you. The intellect is a
smooth table; the moral power a smooth table; and experience
writes there what she will, and what she writes is law of
morality. Morality is expediency, nothing more; nothing is
good of itself, right of itself, just of itself, --but only because it produces agreeable consequences, which are agreeable sensations. Dr. Paley is a good example of the sensational moralist. I ask him "What is right, just?" He says,
"There are no such things; they are the names to stand for
what works well in the long run. " "How shall I know what
to do in a matter of morals? by referring to a moral sense?"
"Not at all: only by common sense, by observation, by experience, by learning what works well in the long run; by
human history, not human nature. To make a complete code
of morals by sensationalism you must take the history of
mankind, and find what has worked well, and follow that because it worked well. " "But human history only tells what
has been and worked well, not what is right I want what is
right!" He answers, "It is pretty much the same thing. "
"But suppose the first men endowed with faculties perfectly
developed, would they know what to do?" Not at all. Instinct would tell the beast antecedent to experience, but man
has no moral instinct, must learn only by actual trial. "
"Well, " say I, "let alone that matter, let us come to details.
What is honesty?" "It is the best policy. " "Why must I
tell the truth, keep my word, be chaste, temperate?" "For
the sake of the reward, the respect of your fellows, the
happiness of a long life and heaven at last. On the whole
God pays well for virtue; though slow pay, he is sure. "
"But suppose the devil paid the better pay?" "Then serve
him, for the end is not the service, but the pay. Virtue,
and by virtue I mean all moral excellence, is not a good in
itself, but good as producing some other good. " "Why should
I be virtuous?" "For the sake of the reward. " "But vice

has its rewards, they are present and not future, immediate
and certain, not merely contingent and mediate. I should
think them greater than the reward of virtue. " Then vice to
you is virtue, for it pays best. The sensational philosophy
knows no conscience to sound in the man's ears the stern
word, Thou oughtest so to do, come what will come!

In politics might makes right, so in morals. Success is the touchstone; the might of obtaining the reward the
right of doing the deed. Bentham represents the sensational
morals of politics; Paley of ethics. Both are Epicureans.
The sensationalist and the Epicurean agree in this, --enjoy-
ment is the touchstone of virtue and determines what is good,
what bad, what indifferent: this is the generic agreement.
Heathen Epicurus spoke only of enjoyment in this life;
Christian Archdeacon Paley--and a very archdeacon--spoke
of enjoyment also in the next: this is the specific difference.
In either case virtue ceases to be virtue, for it is only a
bargain.

There is a school of sensationalists who turn off and
say, "Oh, you cannot answer the moral questions and tell
what is right, just fair, good. We must settle that by revelation. " That, of course, only adjourns the question and
puts the decision on men who received the revelation or God
who made it. They do not meet the philosopher's question;
they assume that the difference between right and wrong is
not knowable by human faculties, and, if there be any difference between right and wrong, there is no faculty in man
which naturally loves right and abhors wrong, still less any
faculty which can find out what is right, what wrong. So all
moral questions are to be decided by authority, because
somebody said so; not by reference to facts of consciousness, but to phenomena of history. Of course the moral
law is not a law which is of me, rules in me and by me;
only one put on me, which rules over me! Can any lofty
virtue grow out of this theory? any heroism? Verily not.
Regulus did not ask a reward for his virtue; if so, he made
but a bargain, and who would honor him more than a desperate trader who made a good speculation? There is something in man which scoffs at expediency; which will do right,
justice, truth, though hell itself should gape and bid him
hold his peace; the morality which anticipates history, loves
the right for itself. Of this Epicurus knew nothing, Paley
nothing, Bentham nothing, sensationalism nothing. Sensationalism takes its standard of political virtue from the House
of Commons; of right from the Constitution and common law;

of commercial virtue from the board of brokers at their best,
and the old bankrupt law; or virtue in general from the most
comfortable classes of society, from human history, not human nature; and knows nothing more.   The virtue of a Regulus, of a Socrates, of a Christ, it knows not.

See the practical effect of this.   "A young man goes
into trade.   Experience meets him with the sensationalist
morals in its hand, and says, " 'Caveat emptor, Let the
buyer look to it, not you'; you must be righteous, young man,
but not righteous overmuch; you must tell the truth to all
who have the right to ask you, and when and where they have
a right to ask you, --otherwise you may lie.   The mistake is
not in lying, or deceit; but in lying and deceiving to your own
disadvantage.   You must not set up a private conscience of
your own in your trade, you will lose the confidence of respectable people.   You must have a code of morals which
works well and produces agreeable sensations in the long run.
To learn the true morals of business you must not ask conscience, that is a whim and very unphilosophical.   You must
ask, How did Mr. Smith make his money?   He cheated, and
so did Mr. Brown and Mr. Jones, and they cheat all round.
Then you must do the same, only be careful not to cheat so
as to 'hurt your usefulness' and 'injure your reputation. ' "

Shall I show the practical effects of this, not on very
young men, in politics?   It would hurt men's feelings, and I
have no time for that.

IV.   In religion.   Sensationalism must have a philosophy of religion, a theology; let us see what theology.
There are two parties; one goes by philosophy, the other mis-
trusts philosophy.

1.   The first thing in theology is to know God.   The
idea of God is the touchstone of a theologian.   Now to know
the existence of God is to be certain thereof as of my own
existence.   "Nothing in the intellect which was not first in
the senses, " says sensationalism; "all comes by sensational
experience and reflection thereon. "   Sensationalism--does that
give us the idea of God?   I ask the sensationalist, "Does the
sensational eye see God?"   "No. "   "The ear hear him?"
"No. "   "Do the organs of sense touch or taste him?"   "No."
"How then do you get the idea of God?"   "By induction from
facts of observation a posteriori.   The senses deal with finite
things; I reflect on them, put them all together I assume that
they have cause; then by the inductive method I find out the

character of that cause: that is God." Then I say, "But the
senses deal with only finite things, so you must infer only a
finite maker, else the induction is imperfect. So you have
but a finite God.   Then these finite things, measured only by
my experience, are imperfect things.   Look at disorders in
the frame of nature; the sufferings of animals, the miseries
of men; here are seeming imperfections which the sensational
philosopher staggers at.   But to go on with this induction:
from an imperfect work you must infer an imperfect author.
So the God of sensationalism is not only finite, but imperfect
even at that.   But am I certain of the existence of the finite
and imperfect God?   The existence of the outward world is
only an hypothesis, its laws hypothetical; all that depends on
that or them is but an hypothesis, --the truth of your faculties, the forms of matter only on hypothesis: so the existence
of God is not a certainty; he is but our hypothetical God.
But a hypothetical God is no God at all, not the living God:
an imperfect God is no God at all, not the true God: a finite
God is no God at all, not the absolute God.   But this hypothetical, finite, imperfect God, where is he?   In matter?
No.   In spirit?   No.   Does he act in matter or spirit?   No,
only now and then he did act by miracle; he is outside of the
world of matter and spirit.   Then he is a nonresident, an
absentee.   A non-resident God is no God at all, not the all-
present God. "

   The above is the theory on which Mr. Hume constructs
his notion of God with the sensational philosophy, the inductive method; and he arrives at the hypothesis of a God, of a
finite God, of an imperfect God, of a non-resident God. Beyond that the sensational philosophy as philosophy cannot go.

   But another party comes out of the same school to
treat of religious matters; they give their philosophy a vacation, and to prove the existence of God they go back to tradition, and say, "Once God revealed himself to the senses of
men; they heard him, they saw him, they felt him; so to
them the existence of God was not an induction, but a fact of
observation; they told it to others, through whom it comes to
us; we can say it is not a fact of observation but a fact of
testimony. "

   "Well, " I ask, "are you certain then?" "Yes. "
"Quite sure? Let me look. The man to whom God revealed
himself may have been mistaken; it may have been a dream,
or a whim of his own, perhaps a fib; at any rate, he was
not philosophically certain of the existence of the outward

world in general; how could he be of anything that took place
in it?   Next, the evidence which relates the transaction is
not wholly reliable: how do I know the books which tell of it
tell the truth, that they were not fabricated to deceive me?
All that rests on testimony is a little uncertain if it took
place one or two thousand years ago; especially if I know
nothing about the persons who testify or of that whereof they
testify; still more so if it be a thing, as you say, unphilosophical and even supernatural. "

So, then, the men who give a vacation to their philosophy have slurred the philosophical argument for a historical, the theological for the mythological, and have gained
nothing except the tradition of God.   By this process we are
as far from the infinite God as before, and have only arrived
at the same point where the philosophy left us.

The English Deists and the Socinians and others have
approached religion with the sensational philosophy in their
hands; we are to learn of God philosophically only by induction.   And such is their God.   They tell us that God is not
knowable; the existence of God is not a certainty to us; it is
a probability, a credibility, a possibility, --a certainty to
none.   You ask of sensationalism, the greatest question, "Is
there a God?"   Answer: "Probably. "   "What is his character?"   "Finite, imperfect. "   "Can I trust him?"   "If we
consult tradition it is creditable; if philosophy, possible. "

2.   The next great question in theology is that of the
immortality of the soul.   That is a universal hope of mankind; what does it rest on?   Can I know my immortality?
Here are two wings of the sensational school.   The first
says, "No, you cannot know it; it is not true.   Mind, soul,
are two words to designate the result of organization.   Man
is not a mind, not a soul, not a free will.   Man is a body,
with blood, brains, nerves--nothing more; the organization
gone, all is gone. "   Now that is sound, logical, consistent;
that was the conclusion of Hume, of many of the English
Deists, and of many French philosophers in the last century;
they looked the fact in the face.   But mortality, annihilation,
is rather an ugly fact to look fairly in the face; but Mr.
Hume and others have done it, and died brave with the sensational philosophy.

The other wing of the sensational school gives its
philosophy another vacation, rests the matter not on philosophy but history; not on the theological but the mythological

argument; on authority of tradition asserting a phenomenon of
human history, they try to establish the immortality of man
by a single precedent, a universal law by the tradition of a
single, empirical, contingent phenomenon.

But I ask the sensational philosopher, "Is immortality
certain?" "No." "Probable?" "No." "Credible?" "No."
"Possible?" "Barely." I ask the traditional division, "Is it
probable?" "Yes, there is one witness in six thousand years,
one out of ten million times ten million." "Well, suppose it
is probable; is immortality, if it be, sure to be a good
thing, for me, for mankind?" "Not at all! There is nothing
in the nature of man, nothing in the nature of the world,
nothing in the nature of God to make you sure immortality
will prove a blessing to mankind in general, to yourself in
special!"

3. That is not quite all. Sensationalism does not
allow freedom of the will; I say not absolute freedom--that
belongs only to God, --but it allows no freedom of the will.
See the result: all will is God's, all willing therefore is
equally divine, and the worst vice of Pantheism follows. "But
what is the will of God, is that free?" "Not at all; man is
limited by the organization of his body, God by the organization of the universe." So God is not absolute God, not absolutely free; and as man's will is necessitated by God's, so
God's will by the universe of matter; and only a boundless
fate and pitiless encircles man and God.

This is the philosophy of sensationalism; such its doctrine in physics, politics, ethics, religion. It leads to
boundless uncertainty. Berkeley resolves the universe into
subjective ideas; no sensationalist knows a law in physics to
be universal. Hobbes and Bentham and Condillac in politics
know of no right but might; Priestley denies the spirituality
of man, Collins and Edwards his liberty; Dodwell affirms the
materiality of the soul, and the mortality of all men not
baptized; Mandeville directly, and others indirectly, deny all
natural distinction between virtue and vice; Archdeacon Paley
knows no motive but expediency.

The materialist is puzzled with the existence of matter; finds its laws general, not universal. The sensational
philosophy meets the politician and tells him through Rousseau
and others, "Society has no divine original, only the social
compact; there is no natural justice, natural right; no right,
but might; no greater good than the greatest good of the

greatest number, and for that you may sacrifice all you will;
to defend a constitution is better than to defend justice. " In
morals the sensational philosophy meets the young man and
tells him all is uncertain; he had better be content with things
as they are, himself as he is; to protest against a popular
wrong is foolish, to make money by it, or ease, or power,
is a part of wisdom; only the fool is wise above what is
written.   It meets the young minister with its proposition that
the existence of God is not a certainty, nor the immortality
of the soul; that religion is only traditions of the elders and
the keeping of a form.   It says to him, "Look there, Dr.
Humdrum has got the tallest pulpit and the quietest pews, the
fattest living and the cosiest nook in the land; how do you
think he won it?   Why, by letting well enough alone; he never
meddles with sin; it would break his heart to hurt a sinner's
feelings, --he might lose a parishioner, he never dreams to
make the world better, or better off.   Go thou and do likewise. "

        I come now to the other school.   This is distinguished
by its chief metaphysical doctrine, that there is in the intellect (or consciousness), something that never was in the
senses, to wit, the intellect (or consciousness) itself; that
man has faculties which transcend the senses; faculties which
give him ideas and intuitions that transcend sensational experience; ideas whose origin is not from sensation, nor their
proof from sensation.   This is the transcendental school.
They maintain that the mind (meaning thereby all which is
not sense) is not a smooth tablet on which sensation writes
its experience, but is a living principle which of itself origi-
nates ideas when the senses present the occasion; that, as
there is a body with certain senses, so there is a soul or
mind with certain powers which give the man sentiments and
ideas.   This school maintains that it is a fact of consciousness itself that there is in the intellect somewhat that was
not first in the senses; and also that they have analyzed consciousness, and by the inductive method established the conclusion that there is a consciousness that never was sensation, never could be; that our knowledge is in part a priori;
that we know, 1, certain truths of necessity; 2, certain
truths of intuition, or spontaneous consciousness; 3, certain
truths of demonstration, a voluntary consciousness; all of
these truths, not dependent on sensation for cause, origin,
or proof.   Facts of observation, sensational experience, it
has in common with the other school.

        Transcendentalism, also, reports itself in the four

great departments of human activity--in physics, politics, ethics, religion.

I.   In physics it starts with the maxim that the senses acquaint us actually with body, and therefrom the mind gives us the idea of substance, answering to an objective reality. Thus is the certainty of the material world made sure of. Then a priori it admits the uniformity of the action of nature; and its laws are a priori known to be universal, and not general alone.   These two doctrines it finds as maxims resulting from the nature of man, facts given.   Then it sets out with other maxims, first truths, which are facts of necessity, known to be such without experience.   All the first truths of mathematics are of this character, e. g., that the whole is greater than a part.   From these, by the deductive method, it comes at other facts, --facts of demonstration; these also are transcendental, that is, transcend the senses, transcend the facts of observation.   For example, the three angles of a triangle are equal to two right angles, --that is universally true; it is a fact of demonstration, and is a deduction from a first truth which is self-evident, a fact of necessity.   But here the fact of demonstration transcends the fact of experience, philosophy is truer than sensation.   The whole matter of geometry is transcendental.

Transcendentalism does not take a few facts out of human history and say they are above nature; all that appears in nature it looks on as natural, not supernatural, not subternatural; so the distinction between natural and supernatural does not appear.   By this means philosophy is often in advance of observation; e. g., Newton's law of gravitation, Kepler's third law, the theory that a diamond might be burned, and Berkeley's theory of vision, --these are interpretations of nature, but also anticipations of nature, as all true philosophy must be.   Those men, however, did not philosophically know it to be so.   So by an actual law of nature, not only are known facts explained, but the unknown anticipated.

Evils have come from the transcendental method in physics; men have scorned observation, have taken but a few facts from which to learn universal laws, and so failed of getting what is universal, even general.   They have tried to divine the constitution of the world, to do without sensational experience in matters where knowledge depends on that and that is the sine qua non.   The generalizations of the transcendental naturalists have been often hasty; they attempt to determine what nature shall be, not to learn what nature is.

Thus a famous philosopher said there are only seven primary
planets in the solar systems, and from the nature of things,
a priori known, it is impossible there should be more.   He
had intelligence in advance of the mail; but the mail did not
confirm, for six months afterwards Dr. Piazzi discovered
one of the asteroids; and in a few years three more were
found, and now several more have been discovered, not to
mention the new planet Neptune.   Many of the statements of
Schelling in physics are of this same character.

II.   In politics, transcendentalism starts not from experience alone, but from consciousness; not merely from
human history, but also from human nature.   It does not so
much quote precedents, contingent facts of experience, as
ideas, necessary facts of consciousness.   It only quotes the
precedent to obtain or illustrate the idea.   It appeals to a
natural justice, natural right; absolute justice, absolute right.
Now the source and original of this justice and right it finds
in God--the conscience of God; the channel through which we
receive this justice and right is our own moral sense, our
conscience, which is our consciousness of the conscience of
God.   This conscience in politics and in ethics transcends
experience, and a priori tells us of the just, the right, the
good, the fair; not the relatively right alone, but absolute
right also.   As it transcends experience, so it anticipates
history; and the ideal justice of conscience is juster than the
empirical and contingent justice actually exercised at Washington or at Athens, as the ideal circle is rounder than one
the stone-cutter scratches on his rough seal.   In transcendental politics the question of expediency is always subordinate to the question of natural right; it asks not merely about
the cost of a war, but its natural justice.   It aims to organize the ideals of man's moral and social nature into political institutions; to have a government which shall completely represent the facts of man's social consciousness so
far as his nature is now developed.   But as this development
is progressive, so must government be; yet not progressive
by revolution, by violence; but by harmonious development,
progressive by growth.   The transcendental politician does
not merely interpret history, and look back to Magna Charta
and the Constitution; but into human nature, through to divine
nature; and so anticipates history, and in man and God finds
the origin and primary source of all just policy, all right
legislation.   So looking he transcends history.

For example, the great political idea of America, the
idea of the Declaration of Independence, is a composite idea

made up of three simple ones: 1. Each man is endowed with
certain unalienable rights.   2. In respect of these rights all
men are equal.   3. A government is to protect each man in
the entire and actual enjoyment of all the unalienable rights.
Now the first two ideas represent ontological facts, facts of
human consciousness; they are facts of necessity.   The third
is an idea derived from the two others, is a synthetic judgment a priori; it was not learned from sensational experience; there never was a government which did this, nor is
there now.   Each of the other ideas transcended history:
every unalienable right has been alienated, still is; no two
men have been actually equal in actual rights.   Yet the idea
is true, capable of proof by human nature, not of verification
by experience; as true as the proposition that three angles of
a triangle are equal to two right angles; but no more capable
of a sensational proof than that.   The American Revolution,
with American history since, is an attempt to prove by experience this transcendental proposition, to organize the
transcendental idea of politics.   The idea demands for its
organization, a democracy--a government of all, for all, and
by all; a government by natural justice, by legislation that is
divine as much as a true astronomy is divine, legislation
which enacts law representing a fact of the universe, a re-
solution of God.

All human history said, "That cannot be. "   Human
nature said, "It can, must, shall. "   The authors of the
American Revolution, as well as the fathers of New England,
were transcendentalists to that extent.   America had such
faith in the idea that she made the experiment in part.   She
will not quite give up yet.   But there is so much of the sensational philosophy in her politics that in half the land the
attempt is not made at all, the composite idea is denied,
each of the simple ideas is also denied; and in the other half
it is but poorly made.

In France men have an idea yet more transcendental;
to the intellectual idea of liberty, and the moral idea of
equality, they add the religious idea of fraternity, and so put
politics and all legislation on a basis divine and incontestable
as the truths of mathematics.   They say that rights and
duties are before all human laws and above all human laws.
America says, "The Constitution of the United States is above
the President, the Supreme Court above Congress. "   France
says, "The Constitution of the Universe is above the Constitution of France. "   Forty million people say that.   It transcends experience.   The grandest thing a nation ever said in
history.

The transcendental politician does not say that might
makes right, but that there is an immutable morality for nations as for men. Legislation must represent that, or the
law is not binding on any man. By birth man is a citizen of
the universe, subject to God; no oath of allegiance, no king,
no parliament, no congress, no people, can absolve him from
his natural fealty thereto, and alienate a man born to the
rights, born to the duties, of a citizen of God's universe.
Society, government, politics come not from a social compact
which men made and may unmake, but from a social nature
of God's making; a nation is to be self-ruled by justice. In
a monarchy, the king holds power as a trust, not a right: in
a democracy, the people have it as a right, the majority as
a trust; but the minority have lost no right, can alienate
none, delegate none beyond power of ultimate recall. A nation has a right to make just laws, binding because just.
Justice is the point common to one man and the world of
men, the balance-point. A nation is to seek the greatest
good of all, not of the greatest number; not to violate the
constitution of the universe, not sacrifice the minority to the
majority, nor one single man to the whole. But over all
human law God alone has eminent domain.

He too is a danger: the transcendental politician may
seek to ignore the past, and scorn its lessons; may take his
own personal whims for oracles of human nature; and so he
may take counsel from the selfishness of lazy men against
the selfishness of active men, counsel from the selfishness
of poor men against the selfishness of rich men, and think
he hears the voice of justice, or the reverse, as himself is
rich or poor, active or idle; there is danger that he be rash
and question as hastily in politics as in physics, and reckon
without his host, to find that the scot is not free when the
day of reckoning comes.

III. In ethics. Transcendentalism affirms that man
has moral faculties which lead him to justice and right, and
by his own nature can find out what is right and just, and
can know it and be certain of it. Right is to be done come
what will come. I am not answerable for the consequences
of doing right, only of not doing it, only of doing wrong.
The conscience of each man is to him the moral standard;
so to mankind is the conscience of the race. In morals conscience is complete and reliable as the eye for colors, the
ears for sounds, the touch and taste for their purposes.
While experience shows what has been or is, conscience
shows what should be and shall.

Transcendental ethics look not to the consequences of virtue, in this life or the next, as motive, therefore, to lead men to virtue. That is itself a good, an absolute good, to be loved not for what it brings, but is. It represents the even poise or balance-point between individual and social development. To know what is right, I need not ask what is the current practice, what say the Revised Statutes, what said holy men of old, but what says conscience? what, God? The common practice, the Revised Statutes, the holy men of old are helps, not masters. I am to be co-ordinate with justice.

Conscience transcends experience, and not only explains but anticipates that, and the transcendental system of morals is to be founded on human nature and absolute justice.

I am to respect my own nature and be an individual man, --your nature and be a social man. Truth is to be told and asked, justice done and demanded, right claimed and allowed, affection felt and received. The will of man is free; not absolutely free as God's, but partially free, and capable of progress to yet higher degrees of freedom.

Do you ask an example of a transcendental moralist? A scheme of morals was once taught to mankind wholly transcendental, the only such scheme that I know. In that was no alloy of expediency, no deference to experience, no crouching behind a fact of human history to hide from ideas of human nature; a scheme of morals which demands that you be you--I, I; balances individualism and socialism on the central point of justice; which puts natural right, natural duty, before all institutions, all laws, all traditions. You will pardon me for mentioning the name of Jesus of Nazareth in a lecture. But the whole of human history did not justify his ethics; only human nature did that. Hebrew ethics, faulty in detail, were worse in method and principle, referring all to an outward command, not an inward law. Heathen ethics less faulty in detail, not less in principles, referred all to experience and expediency, knew only what was, and what worked well here or there; not what ought to be, and worked well anywhere and forever. He transcended that, taught what should be, must, shall, and forever.

The danger is that the transcendental moralist shall too much abhor the actual rules of morality; where much is bad and ill-founded, shall deem all worthless. Danger, too, that he take a transient impulse, personal and fugitive, for a

universal law; follow a passion for a principle, and come to
naught; surrender his manhood, his free will to his unreflect-
ing instinct, become subordinate thereto.   Men that are
transcendental-mad we have all seen in morals; to be tran-
scendental-wise, sober, is another thing.   The notion that
every impulse is to be followed, every instinct totally obeyed,
will put man among the beasts, not angels.

      IV.   In religion.   Transcendentalism admits a religious
faculty, element, or nature in man, as it admits a moral, intellectual and sensational faculty, --that man by nature is a
religious being as well as moral, intellectual, sensational;
that this religious faculty is adequate to its purposes and
wants, as much so as the others, as the eye acquainting us
with light; and that this faculty is the source of religious
emotions, of the sentiments of adoration, worship.   Through
this we have consciousness of God as through the senses consciousness of matter.   In connection with reason it gives us
the primary ideas of religion, ideas which transcend experience.

      Now the transcendental philosophy legitimates the ideas
of religion by reference to human nature.   Some of them it
finds truths of necessity, which cannot be conceived of as
false or unreal without violence to reason; some it finds are
truths of consciousness, --of spontaneous consciousness, or
intuition; some, truths of voluntary consciousness, or demonstration, inductive or deductive.   Such ideas, capable of this
legitimation, transcend experience, require and admit no
further proof; as true before experience as after; true before
time, after time, eternally; absolutely true.   On that rock
transcendentalism founds religion, sees its foundation, and
doubts no more of religious truths than of the truths of mathematics.   All the truths of religion it finds can be verified in
consciousness to-day, what cannot is not religion.   But it does
not neglect experience.   In human history it finds confirma-
tions, illustrations, of the ideas of human nature, for history
represents the attempt of mankind to develop human nature.
So then as transcendentalism in philosophy legitimates religion
by a reference to truths of necessity, to truths of consciousness, it illustrates religion by facts of observation, facts of
testimony.

      By sensationalism religious faith is a belief, more or
less strange, in a probability, a credibility, a possibility. By
transcendentalism religious faith is the normal action of the
whole spiritual nature of man, which gives him certain knowl-

edge of a certainty not yet attainable by experience; where understanding ends, faith begins, and out-travels the understanding. Religion is natural to man, is justice, piety--free justice, free piety, free thought. The form thereof should fit the individual; hence there will be a unity of substance, diversity of form. So a transcendental religion demands a transcendental theology.

1. The transcendental philosophy appears in its doctrine of God. The idea of God is a fact given in the consciousness of man; consciousness of the infinite is the condition of a consciousness of the finite. I learn of a finite thing by sensation, I get an idea thereof; at the same time the idea of the infinite unfolds in me. I am not conscious of my own existence except as a finite existence, that is, as a dependent existence; and the idea of the infinite, of God on whom I depend, comes at the same time as the logical correlative of a knowledge of myself. So the existence of God is a certainty; I am as certain of that as of my own existence. Indeed without that knowledge I know nothing. Of this I am certain, --I am; but of this as certain, --God is; for if I am, and am finite and dependent, then this presupposes the infinite and independent. So the idea of God is a priori; rests on facts of necessity, on facts of consciousness.

Then transcendentalism uses the other mode, the a posteriori. Starting with the infinite, it finds signs and proofs of him everywhere, and gains evidence of God's existence in the limits of sensational observation; the thing refers to its maker, the thought to the mind, the effect to the cause, the created to the creator, the finite to the infinite; at the end of my arms are two major prophets, ten minor prophets, each of them pointing the transcendental philosopher to the infinite God, of which he has consciousness without the logical process of induction.

Then the character of God as given in the idea of him, given in consciousness, --that represents God as a being, not with the limitations of impersonality (that is to confound God with matter); not with the limitations of personality (that confounds him with man); but God with no limitations, infinite, absolute; looked at from sensation, infinite power; from thought, infinite intellect; from the moral sense, infinite conscience; from the emotional, infinite affection; from the religious, infinite soul; from all truth, the whole human nature names him Infinite Father!

God is immanent in matter, so it is; immanent in
spirit, so it is.   He acts also as God in matter and spirit,
acts perfectly; laws of matter or of spirit are modes of
God's acting, being; as God is perfect, so the mode of his
action is perfect and unchangeable.   Therefore, as God is
ever in matter and spirit, and where God is is wholly God
active, so no intervention is possible.   God cannot come
where he already is, so no miracle is possible.   A miracle
a parte humana is a violation of what is a law to man; a
miracle to God--a parte divina--is a violation of what is law
to God; the most extraordinary things that have been seem
miracles a parte humana, --laws, a parte divina.   But though
God is immanent in matter and in spirit, he yet transcends
both matter and spirit, has no limitations.   Indeed all perfection of immanence and transcendence belong to him, --the
perfection of existence, infinite being; the perfection of space,
immensity; the perfection of time, eternity; of power, all-
mightiness; of mind, all-knowingness; of affection, all-loving-
ness; of will, absolute freedom, absolute justice, absolute
right.   His providence is not merely general, but universal,
so special in each thing.   Hence the universe partakes of his
perfection, is a perfect universe for the end he made it for.

2.   The doctrine of the soul.   This teaches that man
by nature is immortal.   This doctrine it legitimates: 1. By
reference to facts of consciousness that men feel in general;
in the heart it finds the longing after immortality, in the
mind the idea of immortality, in religious consciousness the
faith in immortality, in human nature altogether the strong
confidence and continued trust therein.   2.   It refers also to
the nature of God, and reasons thus: God is all-powerful and
can do the best; all-wise, and can know it; all-good, and
must will it; immortality is the best, therefore it is.   All
this anticipates experience a priori.   3.   It refers to the
general arrangements of the world, where everything gets
ripe, matures, but man.   In the history of mankind it finds
confirmation of this doctrine, for every rude race and all
civilized tribes have been certain of immortality; but here and
there are men, sad and unfortunate, who have not by the
mind legitimated the facts of spontaneous consciousness,
whose nature the sensational philosophy has made blind, and
they doubt or deny what nature spontaneously affirms.

The nature of God being such, he immanent and active
in matter and spirit; the nature of man such, so provided
with faculties to love the true, the just, the fair, the good, --
it follows that man is capable of inspiration from God, com-

munion with God; not in raptures, not by miracle, but by the
sober use of all his faculties, moral, intellectual, affectional,
religious.   The condition thereof is this, the faithful use of
human nature, the coincidence of man's will with God's.   Inspiration is proportionate to the man's quantity of being,
made up of a constant and a variable, his quantity of gifts,
his quantity of faithful use.   In this way transcendentalism
can legitimate the highest inspiration, and explain the genius
of God's noblest son, not as monstrous, but natural.   In religion as in all things else there has been a progressive development of mankind.   The world is a school, prophets,
saints, saviours, men more eminently gifted and faithful, and
so most eminently inspired, --they are the school-masters to
lead men up to God.

There is danger in this matter also lest the transcendental religionist should despise the past and its sober teachings, should take a fancy personal and fugitive for a fact of
universal consciousness, embrace a cloud for an angel, and
miserably perish.   It is not for man to transcend his faculties, to be above himself, above reason, conscience, affection, religious trust.   It is easy to turn off from these and
be out of reason, conscience, affection, religion--beside
himself.   Madmen in religion are not rare, enthusiasts,
fanatics.

The sensational philosophy, with all its evils, has
done the world great service.   It has stood up for the body,
for common sense, protested against spiritual tyranny,
against the spiritualism of the middle ages which thought the
senses wicked and the material world profane.   To sensationalism we are indebted for the great advance of mankind
in physical science, in discovery, arts, mechanics, and for
many improvements in government.   Some of its men are
great names, --Bacon, Locke, Newton.   Let us do them no
dishonor; they saw what they could, told it; they saw not all
things that are, saw some which are not.   In our day no one
of them would be content with the philosophy they all agreed
in then.   Hobbes and Hume have done us service; the
Socinians, Priestley, Collins, Berkeley, Dodwell, Mandeville, Edwards.   To take the good and leave the ill is our
part; but the doubts which this philosophy raises, the doubt
of Hume, the doubt of Hobbes, of the English Deists in general, do not get answered by this philosophy.   For this we
have weapons forged by other hands, tempered in another
spring.

Transcendentalism has a work to do, to show that
physics, politics, ethics, religion rest on facts of necessity,
facts of intuition, facts of demonstration, and have their witness and confirmation in facts of observation.   It is the work
of transcendentalism to give us politics which represent God's
thought of a state, --the whole world, each man free; to give
us morals which leave the man a complete individual, no
chord rent from the human harp, --yet complete in his social
character, no string discordant in the social choir; to give
us religion worthy of God and man, --free goodness, free piety,
free thought.   That is not to be done by talking at random,
not by idleness, not by railing at authority, calumniating the
past or the present; not by idle brains with open mouth, who
outrage common sense; but by diligent toil, brave discipline,
patience to wait, patience to work.   Nothing comes of nothing, foolishness of fools; but something from something, wise
thought from thinking men; and of the wise thought comes a
lovely deed, life, laws, institutions for mankind.

The problem of transcendental philosophy is no less
than this, to revise the experience of mankind and try its
teachings by the nature of mankind; to test ethics by conscience, science by reason; to try the creeds of the churches,
the constitutions of the states by the constitution of the universe; to reverse what is wrong, supply what is wanting, and
command the just.   To do this in a nation like ours, blinded
still by the sensational philosophy, devoted chiefly to material
interests, its politics guided by the madness of party more
than sober reason; to do this in a race like the Anglo-Saxon,
which has an obstinate leaning to a sensational philosophy,
which loves facts of experience, not ideas of consciousness,
and believes not in the First-Fair, First-Perfect, First-Good,
is no light work; not to be taken in hand by such as cannot
bear the strife of tongues, the toil, the heat, the war of
thought; not to be accomplished by a single man, however
well-born and well-bred; not by a single age and race.   It
has little of history behind, for this philosophy is young.   It
looks to a future, a future to be made; a church whose creed
is truth, whose worship love; a society full of industry and
abundance, full of wisdom, virtue, and the poetry of life; a
state with unity among all, with freedom for each; a church
without tyranny, a society without ignorance, want, or crime,
a state without oppression; yes, a world with no war among
the nations to consume the work of their hands, and no re-
strictive policy to hinder the welfare of mankind.   That is
the human dream of the transcendental philosophy.   Shall it
ever become a fact? History says, No; human nature says, Yes.

LIFE AND CORRESPONDENCE

OF

THEODORE PARKER.

THE LIBRARY.

CHAPTER XVI.

The Library—Habits of Composition and Study—Articles—Greek Classics—Goethe—
Sentences—Verses—Translations from Heine and others—Some original lines.

WHEN Mr. Parker went to Boston, he fitted up the fourth story
of his house for a study, by lining the walls with shelves of

From John Weiss's biography of Parker

Engraved by H. Adlard, from a Photograph taken in 1846

Engraving of Parker in 1846

2. A DISCOURSE OF THE TRANSIENT AND PERMANENT IN CHRISTIANITY*

Heaven and earth shall pass away: but my words
shall not pass away. --Luke xxi. 33.

In this sentence we have a very clear indication that
Jesus of Nazareth believed the religion he taught would be
eternal, that the substance of it would last for ever. Yet
there are some who are affrighted by the faintest rustle which
a heretic makes among the dry leaves of theology; they
tremble lest Christianity itself should perish without hope.
Ever and anon the cry is raised, "The Philistines be upon
us, and Christianity is in danger. " The least doubt respecting the popular theology, or the existing machinery of the
church; the least sign of distrust in the religion of the pulpit
or the religion of the street, is by some good men supposed
to be at enmity with faith in Christ, and capable of shaking
Christianity itself. On the other hand, a few bad men, and
a few pious men, it is said, on both sides of the water, tell
us the day of Christianity is past. The latter--it is alleged--
would persuade us that, hereafter, Piety must take a new
form; the teachings of Jesus are to be passed by; that Religion is to wing her way sublime, above the flight of
Christianity, far away, toward heaven, as the fledged eaglet
leaves for ever the nest which sheltered his callow youth.
Let us, therefore, devote a few moments to this subject, and
consider what is <u>transient</u> in Christianity, and what is <u>perm-
anent</u> therein. The topic seems not inappropriate to the
times in which we live, or the occasion that calls us together.

Christ says, his Word shall never pass away. Yet,
at first sight, nothing seems more fleeting than a word. It
is an evanescent impulse of the most fickle element. It
leaves no track where it went through the air. Yet to this,
and this only, did Jesus intrust the truth wherewith he came
laden to the earth; truth for the salvation of the world. He
took no pains to perpetuate his thoughts: they were poured
forth where occasion found him an audience--by the side of
the lake, or a well; in a cottage, or the temple; in a fisher's

*Parker, Theodore. Collected Works, ed. F. Cobbe
(London: Trübner, 1863-79), VIII, 1-30.

boat, or the synagogue of the Jews.   He founds no institution
as a monument of his words.   He appoints no order of men
to preserve his bright and glad relations.   He only bids his
friends give freely the truth they had freely received.   He
did not even write his words in a book.   With a noble confidence, the result of his abiding faith, he scattered them
broadcast on the world, leaving the seed to its own vitality.
He knew that what is of God cannot fail, for God keeps his
own.   He sowed his seed in the heart, and left it there, to
be watered and warmed by the dew and the sun which heaven
sends.   He felt his words were for eternity.   So he trusted
them to the uncertain air; and for eighteen hundred years
that faithful element has held them good--distinct as when
first warm from his lips.   Now they are translated into
every human speech, and murmured in all earth's thousand
tongues, from the pine forests of the North to the palm
groves of eastern Ind.   They mingle as it were, with the
roar of a populous city, and join the chime of the desert
sea.   Of a Sabbath morn they are repeated from church to
church, from isle to isle, and land to land, till their music
goes round the world.   These words have become the breath
of the good, the hope of the wise, the joy of the pious, and
that for many millions of hearts.   They are the prayers of
our churches; our better devotion by fireside and fieldside;
the enchantment of our hearts.   It is these words that still
work wonders, to which the first recorded miracles were
nothing in grandeur and utility.   It is these which build our
temples and beautify our homes.   They raise our thoughts of
sublimity; they purify our ideal of purity; they hallow our
prayer for truth and love.   They make beauteous and divine
the life which plain men lead.   They give wings to our aspirations.   What charmers they are!   Sorrow is lulled at
their bidding.   They take the sting out of disease, and rob
Adversity of his power to disappoint.   They give health and
wings to the pious soul, broken-hearted and shipwrecked in
his voyage through life, and encourage him to tempt the
perilous way once more.   They make all things ours: Christ
our brother; time our servant; death our ally, and the witness of our triumph.   They reveal to us the presence of God,
which else we might not have seen so clearly, in the first
windflower of spring, in the falling of a sparrow, in the distress of a nation, in the sorrow or the rapture of the world.
Silence the voice of Christianity, and the world is well-nigh
dumb, for gone is that sweet music which kept in awe the
rulers and the people, which cheers the poor widow in her
lonely toil, and comes like light through the windows of
morning, to men who sit stooping and feeble with failing eyes

and a hungering heart.   It is gone--all gone! only the cold,
bleak world left before them.

Such is the life of these words; such the empire they
have won for themselves over men's minds since they were
spoken first.   In the meantime, the words of great men and
mighty, whose name shook whole continents, though graven
in metal, and stone, though stamped in institutions, and defended by whole tribes of priests and troops of followers--
their words have gone to the ground, and the world gives
back no echo of their voice.   Meanwhile, the great works,
also, of old times, castle, and tower, and town, their cities
and their empires, have perished, and left scarce a mark on
the bosom of the earth to show they once have been.   The
philosophy of the wise, the art of the accomplished, the song
of the poet, the ritual of the priest, though honoured as divine in their day, have gone down a prey to oblivion.   Silence
has closed over them; only their spectres now haunt the
earth.   A deluge of blood has swept over the nations; a night
of darkness, more deep than the fabled darkness of Egypt,
has lowered down upon that flood, to destroy or to hide what
the deluge had spared.   But through all this the words of
Christianity have come down to us from the lips of that Hebrew youth, gentle and beautiful as the light of a star, not
spent by their journey through time and through space.   They
have built up a new civilization, which the wisest gentile
never hoped for, which the most pious Hebrew never foretold.   Through centuries of wasting these words have flown
on, like a dove in the storm, and now wait to descend on
hearts pure and earnest, as the Father's spirit, we are told,
came down on his lowly Son.   The old heavens and the old
earth are indeed passed away, but the Word stands.   Nothing
shows clearer than this how fleeting is what man calls great,
how lasting what God pronounces true.

Looking at the Word of Jesus, at real Christianity,
the pure religion he taught, nothing appears more fixed and
certain.   Its influence widens as light extends; it deepens as
the nations grow more wise.   But looking at the history of
what men call Christianity, nothing seems more uncertain
and perishable.   While true religion is always the same
thing, in each century and every land, in each man that feels
it, the Christianity of the pulpit, which is the religion taught,
the Christianity of the people, which is the religion that is
accepted and lived out, has never been the same thing in any
two centuries or lands, except only in name.   The difference
between what is called Christianity by the Unitarians in our

times, and that of some ages past, is greater than the difference between Mahomet and the Messiah.   The difference
at this day between opposing classes of Christians, the difference between the Christianity of some sects, and that of
Christ himself, is deeper and more vital than that between
Jesus and Plato, pagan as we call him.   The Christianity of
the seventh century has passed away.   We recognize only the
ghost of superstition in its faded features, as it comes up at
our call.   It is one of the things which has been, and can be
no more, for neither God nor the world goes back.   Its
terrors do not frighten, nor its hopes allure us.   We rejoice
that it has gone.   But how do we know that our Christianity
shall not share the same fate?   Is there that difference between the nineteenth century, and some seventeen that have
gone before it, since Jesus, to warrant the belief that our
notion of Christianity shall last for ever?   The stream of
time has already beat down philosophies and theologies, temple
and church, though never so old and revered.   How do we
know there is not a perishing element in what we call
Christianity?   Jesus tells us, his Word is the word of God,
and so shall never pass away.   But who tells us that our
word shall never pass away?   that our notion of his Word
shall stand for ever?

Let us look at this matter a little more closely.   In
actual Christianity--that is, in that portion of Christianity
which is preached and believed--there seems to have been,
ever since the time of its earthly founder, two elements, the
one transient, the other permanent.   The one is the thought,
the folly, the uncertain wisdom, the theological notions, the
impiety of man; the other, the eternal truth of God.   These
two bear, perhaps, the same relation to each other that the
phenomena of outward nature, such as sunshine and cloud,
growth, decay, and reproduction, bear to the great law of
nature, which underlies and supports them all.   As in that
case more attention is commonly paid to the particular phenomena than to the general law, so in this case more is generally given to the transient in Christianity than to the permanent therein.

It must be confessed, though with sorrow, that transient things form a great part of what is commonly taught as
religion.   An undue place has often been assigned to forms
and doctrines, while too little stress has been laid on the
divine life of the soul, love to God, and love to man.   Religious forms may be useful and beautiful.   They are so,
whenever they speak to the soul, and answer a want thereof.

In our present state some forms are perhaps necessary.
But they are only the accident of Christianity, not its substance. They are the robe, not the angel, who may take
another robe quite as becoming and useful. One sect has
many forms; another, none. Yet both may be equally
Christian, in spite of the redundance or the deficiency. They
are a part of the language in which religion speaks, and
exist, with few exceptions, wherever man is found. In our
calculating nation, in our rationalizing sect, we have retained
but two of the rites so numerous in the early Christian
Church, and even these we have attenuated to the last degree, leaving them little more than a spectre of the ancient
form. Another age may continue or forsake both; may revive
old forms, or invent new ones to suit the altered circumstances of the times, and yet be Christians quite as good as
we, or our fathers of the dark ages. Whether the Apostles
designed these rites to be perpetual, seems a question which
belongs to scholars and antiquarians; not to us, as Christian
men and women. So long as they satisfy or help the pious
heart, so long they are good. Looking behind or around us,
we see that the forms and rites of the Christians are quite
as fluctuating as those of the heathens; from whom some of
them have been, not unwisely, adopted by the earlier Church.

Again, the doctrines that have been connected with
Christianity, and taught in its name, are quite as changeable
as the form. This also takes place unavoidably. If observations be made upon nature, which must take place so
long as man has senses and understanding, there will be a
philosophy of nature, and philosophical doctrines. These will
differ as the observations are just or inaccurate, and as the
deductions from observed facts are true or false. Hence
there will be different schools of natural philosophy, so long
as men have eyes and understandings of different clearness
and strength. And if men observe and reflect upon religion--
which will be done so long as man is a religious and reflective being--there must also be a philosophy of religion, a
theology and theological doctrines. These will differ, as men
have felt much or little of religion, as they analyze their
sentiments correctly or otherwise, and as they have reasoned
right or wrong. Now the true system of nature, which exists
in the outward facts, whether discovered or not, is always
the same thing, though the philosophy of nature, which men
invent, change every month, and be one thing at London and
the opposite at Berlin. Thus there is but one system of
nature as it exists in fact, though many theories of nature,
which exist in our imperfect notions of that system, and by

which we may approximate and at length reach it. Now there
can be but one religion which is absolutely true, existing in
the facts of human nature and the ideas of Infinite God. That,
whether acknowledged or not, is always the same thing, and
never changes.   So far as a man has any real religion--
either the principle or the sentiment thereof--so far he has
that, by whatever name he may call it.   For, strictly speaking, there is but one kind of religion, as there is but one
kind of love, though the manifestations of this religion, in
forms, doctrines, and life, be never so diverse.   It is
through these men approximate to the true expression of this
religion.   Now while this religion is one and always the same
thing, there may be numerous systems of theology or philosophies of religion.   These, with their creeds, confessions,
and collections of doctrines, deduced by reasoning upon the
facts observed, may be baseless and false, either because
the observation was too narrow in extent, or otherwise defective in point of accuracy, or because the reasoning was
illogical, and therefore the deduction spurious.   Each of these
three faults is conspicuous in the systems of theology.   Now
the solar system as it exists in fact is permanent, though
the notions of Thales and Ptolemy, of Copernicus and Descartes, about this system, prove transient, imperfect ap-
proximations to the true expression.   So the Christianity of
Jesus is permanent, though what passes for Christianity with
popes and catechisms, with sects and churches, in the first
century or in the nineteenth century, prove transient also.
Now it has sometimes happened that a man took his philosophy
of nature at second-hand, and then attempted to make his observations conform to his theory, and nature ride in his
panniers.   Thus some philosophers refused to look at the
moon through Galileo's telescope, for, according to their
theory of vision, such an instrument would not aid the sight.
Thus their preconceived notions stood up between them and
nature.   Now it has often happened that men took their theology thus at second-hand, and distorted the history of the
world and man's nature besides, to make religion conform to
their notions.   Their theology stood between them and God.
Those obstinate philosophers have disciples in no small
number.

What another has said of false systems of science will
apply equally to the popular theology: "It is barren in effects, fruitful in questions, slow and languid in its improvement, exhibiting in its generality the counterfeit of perfection,
but ill filled up in its details, popular in its choice, but suspected by its very promoters, and therefore bolstered up and

countenanced with artifices. Even those who have been determined to try for themselves, to add their support to
learning, and to enlarge its limits, have not dared entirely
to desert received opinions, nor to seek the spring-head of
things. But they think they have done a great thing if they
intersperse and contribute something of their own; prudently
considering, that by their assent they can save their modesty,
and by their contributions, their liberty. Neither is there,
nor ever will be, an end or limit to these things. One
snatches at one thing, another is pleased with another: there
is no dry nor clear sight of anything. Every one plays the
philosopher out of the small treasures of his own fancy; the
more sublime wits more acutely and with better success; the
duller with less success, --but equal obstinacy; and, by the
discipline of some learned men, sciences are bounded within
the limits of some certain authors which they have set down,
imposing them upon old men and instilling them into young.
So that now (as Tully cavilled upon Caesar's consulship) the
star Lyra riseth by an edict, and authority is taken for truth,
and not truth for authority; which kind of order and discipline
is very convenient for our present use, but banisheth those
which are better. "

    Any one who traces the history of what is called
Christianity, will see that nothing changes more from age to
age than the doctrines taught as Christian, and insisted on as
essential to Christianity and personal salvation. What is
falsehood in one province passes for truth in another. The
heresy of one age is the orthodox belief and "only infallible
rule" of the next. Now Arius, and now Athanasius, is lord
of the ascendant. Both were excommunicated in their turn,
each for affirming what the other denied. Men are burned
for professing what men are burned for denying. For centuries the doctrines of the Christians were no better, to say
the least, than those of their contemporary pagans. The
theological doctrines derived from our fathers seem to have
come from Judaism, Heathenism, and the caprice of philosophers, far more than they have come from the principle
and sentiment of Christianity. The doctrine of the Trinity,
the very Achilles of theological dogmas, belongs to philosophy
and not religion; its subtleties cannot even be expressed in
our tongue. As old religions became superannuated, and died
out, they left to the rising faith, as to a residuary legatee,
their forms and their doctrines; or rather, as the giant in
the fable left his poisoned garment to work the overthrow of
his conqueror. Many tenets that pass current in our theology
seem to be the refuse of idol temples, the off-scourings of

Jewish and heathen cities, rather than the sands of virgin
gold, which the stream of Christianity has worn off from the
rock of ages, and brought in its bosom for us.   It is wood,
hay, and stubble, wherewith men have built on the corner-
stone Christ laid.   What wonder the fabric is in peril when
tried by fire?   The stream of Christianity, as men receive
it, has caught a stain from every soil it has filtered through,
so that now it is not the pure water from the well of life
which is offered to our lips, but streams troubled and pol-
luted by man with mire and dirt.   If Paul and Jesus could
read our books of theological doctrines, would they accept as
their teaching what men have vented in their name?   Never
till the letters of Paul had faded out of his memory; never
till the words of Jesus had been torn out from the book of
life.   It is their notions about Christianity men have taught
as the only living word of God.   They have piled their own
rubbish against the temple of Truth where Piety comes up to
worship: what wonder the pile seems unshapely and like to
fall?   But these theological doctrines are fleeting as the leaves
on the trees.   They--

> Are found
> Now green in youth, now withered on the ground:
> Another race the following spring supplies;
> They fall successive, and successive rise.

Like the clouds of the sky, they are here to-day; tomorrow, all swept off and vanished; while Christianity itself,
like the heaven above, with its sun, and moon, and uncounted
stars, is always over our head, though the cloud sometimes
debars us of the needed light.   It must of necessity be the
case that our reasonings, and therefore our theological doctrines, are imperfect, and so perishing.   It is only gradually
that we approach to the true system of nature by observation
and reasoning, and work out our philosophy and theology by
the toil of the brain.   But meantime, if we are faithful, the
great truths of morality and religion, the deep sentiment of
love to man and love to God, are perceived intuitively, and
by instinct, as it were, though our theology be imperfect and
miserable.   The theological notions of Abraham, to take the
story as it stands, were exceedingly gross, yet a greater
than Abraham has told us Abraham desired to see my day,
saw it, and was glad.   Since these notions are so fleeting,
why need we accept the commandment of men as the doctrine
of God?

This transitoriness of doctrines appears in many in-

stances, of which two may be selected for a more attentive
consideration.   First, the doctrine respecting the origin and
authority of the Old and New Testament.   There has been a
time when men were burned for asserting doctrines of
natural philosophy which rested on evidence the most incontestable, because those doctrines conflicted with sentences in
the Old Testament.   Every word of that Jewish record was
regarded as miraculously inspired, and therefore as infallibly
true.   It was believed that the Christian religion itself rested
thereon, and must stand or fall with the immaculate Hebrew
text.   He was deemed no small sinner who found mistakes
in the manuscripts.   On the authority of the written word man
was taught to believe impossible legends, conflicting asser-
tions; to take fiction for fact, a dream for a miraculous
revelation of God, an Oriental poem for a grave history of
miraculous events, a collection of amatory idyls for a serious
discourse "touching the mutual love of Christ and the
Church"; they have been taught to accept a picture sketched
by some glowing Eastern imagination, never intended to be
taken for a reality, as a proof that the Infinite God spoke in
human words, appeared in the shape of a cloud, a flaming
bush, or a man who ate, and drank, and vanished into
smoke; that he gave counsels to-day, and the opposite tomorrow; that he violated his own laws, was angry, and was
only dissuaded by a mortal man from destroying at once a
whole nation--millions of men who rebelled against their
leader in a moment of anguish.   Questions in philosophy,
questions in the Christian religion, have been settled by an
appeal to that book.   The inspiration of its authors has been
assumed as infallible.   Every fact in the early Jewish history
has been taken as a type of some analogous fact in Christian
history.   The most distant events, even such as are still in
the arms of time, were supposed to be clearly foreseen and
foretold by pious Hebrews several centuries before Christ.
It has been assumed at the outset, with no shadow of evidence, that those writers held a miraculous communication
with God, such as he has granted to no other man.   What
was originally a presumption of bigoted Jews became an
article of faith, which Christians were burned for not believing.   This has been for centuries the general opinion of
the Christian church, both Catholic and Protestant, though the
former never accepted the Bible as the only source of religious truth.   It has been so.   Still worse, it is now the
general opinion of religious sects at this day.   Hence the
attempt, which always fails, to reconcile the philosophy of
our times with the poems in Genesis writ a thousand years
before Christ.   Hence the attempt to conceal the contradic-

tions in the record itself.   Matters have come to such a
pass, that even now he is deemed an infidel, if not by im-
plication an atheist, whose reverence for the Most High for-
bids him to believe that God commanded Abraham to sacrifice
his son, a thought at which the flesh creeps with horror; to
believe it solely on the authority of an Oriental story, written
down nobody knows when or by whom, or for what purpose;
which may be a poem, but cannot be the record of a fact,
unless God is the author of confusion and a lie.

Now, this idolatry of the Old Testament has not always existed.   Jesus says that none born of a woman is
greater than John the Baptist, yet the least in the kingdom
of heaven was greater than John.   Paul tells us the law--
the very crown of the old Hebrew revelation--is a shadow of
good things, which have now come; only a schoolmaster to
bring us to Christ; and when faith has come, that we are no
longer under the schoolmaster; that it was a law of sin and
death from which we are made free by the law of the spirit
of life.   Christian teachers themselves have differed so
widely in their notion of the doctrines and meaning of those
books, that it makes one weep to think of the follies deduced
therefrom.   But modern criticism is fast breaking to pieces
this idol which men have made out of the Scriptures.   It has
shown that here are the most different works thrown together; that their authors, wise as they sometimes were,
pious as we feel often their spirit to have been, had only
that inspiration which is common to other men equally pious
and wise; that they were by no means infallible, but were
mistaken in facts or in reasoning--uttered predictions which
time has not fulfilled; men who in some measure partook of
the darkness and limited notions of their age, and were not
always above its mistakes or its corruptions.

The history of opinions on the New Testament is quite
similar.   It has been assumed at the outset, it would seem
with no sufficient reason, without the smallest pretence on
its writers' part, that all of its authors were infallibly and
miraculously inspired, so that they could commit no error of
doctrine or fact.   Men have been bid to close their eyes at
the obvious difference between Luke and John--the serious
disagreement between Paul and Peter; to believe, on the
smallest evidence, accounts which shock the moral sense and
revolt the reason, and tend to place Jesus in the same series
with Hercules, and Apollonius of Tyana; accounts which Paul
in the Epistles never mentions, though he also had a vein of
the miraculous running quite through him.   Men have been

told that all these things must be taken as part of Christianity, and if they accepted the religion, they must take all these accessories along with it; that the living spirit could not be had without the killing letter. All the books which caprice or accident had brought together between the lids of the Bible were declared to be the infallible word of God, the only certain rule of religious faith and practice. Thus the Bible was made not a single channel, but the only certain rule of religious faith and practice. To disbelieve any of its statements, or even the common interpretation put upon those statements by the particular age or church in which the man belonged, was held to be infidelity, if not Atheism. In the name of him who forbid us to judge our brother, good men and pious men have applied these terms to others, good and pious as themselves. That state of things has by no means passed away. Men, who cry down the absurdities of Paganism in the worst spirit of the French "free-thinkers," call others infidels and Atheists, who point out, though reverently, other absurdities which men have piled upon Christianity. So the world goes. An idolatrous regard for the imperfect scripture of God's word is the apple of Atalanta, which defeats theologians running for the hand of Divine truth.

But the current notions respecting the infallible inspiration of the Bible have no foundation in the Bible itself. Which Evangelist, which Apostle of the New Testament, what Prophet or Psalmist of the Old Testament, ever claims infallible authority for himself or for others? Which of them does not in his own writings show that he was finite, and, with all his zeal and piety, possessed but a limited inspiration, the bound whereof we can sometimes discover? Did Christ ever demand that men should assent to the doctrines of the Old Testament, credit its stories, and take its poems for histories, and believe equally two accounts that contradict one another? Has he ever told you that all the truths of his religion, all the beauty of a Christian life, should be contained in the writings of those men who, even after his resurrection, expected him to be a Jewish king; of men who were sometimes at variance with one another, and misunderstood his Divine teachings? Would not those modest writers themselves be confounded at the idolatry we pay them? Opinions may change on these points, as they have often changed--changed greatly and for the worse since the days of Paul. They are changing now, and we may hope for the better; for God makes man's folly as well as his wrath to praise him, and continually brings good out of evil.

Another instance of the transitoriness of doctrines taught as Christian is found in those which relate to the nature and authority of Christ.   One ancient party has told us that he is the infinite God; another, that he is both God and man; a third, that he was a man, the son of Joseph and Mary--born as we are; tempted like ourselves; inspired, as we may be, if we will pay the price.   Each of the former parties believed its doctrine on this head was infallibly true, and formed the very substance of Christianity, and was one of the essential conditions of salvation, though scarce any two distinguished teachers, of ancient or modern times, agree in their expression of this truth.

Almost every sect that has ever been makes Christianity rest on the personal authority of Jesus, and not the immutable truth of the doctrines themselves, or the authority of God, who sent him into the world.   Yet it seems difficult to conceive any reason why moral and religious truths should rest for their support on the personal authority of their revealer, any more than the truths of science on that of him who makes them known first or most clearly.   It is hard to see why the great truths of Christianity rest on the personal authority of Jesus, more than the axioms of geometry rest on the personal authority of Euclid or Archimedes.   The authority of Jesus, as of all teachers, one would naturally think, must rest on the truth of his words, and not their truth on his authority.

Opinions respecting the nature of Christ seem to be constantly changing.   In the three first centuries after Christ, it appears, great latitude of speculation prevailed.   Some said he was God, with nothing of human nature, his body only an illusion; others, that he was man, with nothing of the Divine nature, his miraculous birth having no foundation in fact.   In a few centuries it was decreed by councils that he was God, thus honouring the Divine element; next, that he was man also, thus admitting the human side.   For some ages the Catholic Church seems to have dwelt chiefly on the Divine nature that was in him, leaving the human element to mystics and other heretical persons, whose bodies served to flesh the swords of orthodox believers.   The stream of Christianity has come to us in two channels--one within the Church, the other without the Church--and it is not hazarding too much to say, that since the fourth century the true Christian life has been out of the Established Church, and not in it, but rather in the ranks of Dissenters.   From the Reformation till the latter part of the last century, we are

told, the Protestant Church dwelt chiefly on the human side
of Christ, and since that time many works have been written
to show how the two--perfect Deity and perfect manhood--
were united in his character.   But, all this time, scarce any
two eminent teachers agree on these points, however orthodox
they may be called.   What a difference between the Christ of
John Gerson and John Calvin--yet were both accepted teachers
and pious men.   What a difference between the Christ of the
Unitarians and the Methodists--yet may men of both sects be
true Christians and acceptable with God.   What a difference
between the Christ of Matthew and John--yet both were disciples, and their influence is wide as Christendom and deep
as the heart of man.   But on this there is not time to enlarge.

Now it seems clear, that the notion men form about
the origin and nature of the Scriptures, respecting the nature
and authority of Christ, have nothing to do with Christianity
except as its aids or its adversaries; they are not the foundation of its truths.   These are theological questions, not religious questions.   Their connection with Christianity appears
accidental: for if Jesus had taught at Athens, and not at
Jerusalem; if he had wrought no miracle, and none but the
human nature had ever been ascribed to him; if the Old Testament had for ever perished at his birth--Christianity would
still have been the Word of God; it would have lost none of
its truths.   It would be just as true, just as beautiful, just
as lasting, as now it is; though we should have lost so many
a blessed word, and the work of Christianity itself would
have been, perhaps, a long time retarded.

To judge the future by the past, the former authority
of the Old Testament can never return.   Its present authority
cannot stand.   It must be taken for what it is worth.   The
occasional folly and impiety of its authors must pass for no
more than their value; while the religion, the wisdom, the
love, which make fragrant its leaves, will still speak to the
best hearts as hitherto, and in accents even more divine when
Reason is allowed her rights.   The ancient belief in the infallible inspiration of each sentence of the New Testament is
fast changing, very fast.   One writer, not a sceptic, but a
Christian of unquestioned piety, sweeps off the beginning of
Matthew; another, of a different church and equally religious,
the end of John.   Numerous critics strike off several epistles.
The Apocalypse itself is not spared, notwithstanding its con-
cluding curse.   Who shall tell us the work of retrenchment
is to stop here; that others will not demonstrate, what some

pious hearts have long felt, that errors of doctrine and errors
of fact may be found in many parts of the record, here and
there, from the beginning of Matthew to the end of Acts?
We see how opinions have changed ever since the Apostles'
time; and who shall assure us that they were not sometimes
mistaken in historical, as well as doctrinal matters; did not
sometimes confound the actual with the imaginary; and that
the fancy of these pious writers never stood in the place of
their recollection?

But what if this should take place? Is Christianity
then to perish out of the heart of the nations, and vanish from
the memory of the world, like the religions that were before
Abraham? It must be so, if it rest on a foundation which a
scoffer may shake, and a score of pious critics shake down.
But this is the foundation of a theology, not of Christianity.
That does not rest on the decision of Councils. It is not to
stand or fall with the infallible inspiration of a few Jewish
fishermen, who have writ their names in characters of light
all over the world. It does not continue to stand through the
forbearance of some critic, who can cut, when he will, the
thread on which its life depends. Christianity does not rest
on the infallible authority of the New Testament. It depends
on this collection of books for the historical statement of its
facts. In this we do not require infallible inspiration on the
part of the writers, more than in the record of other historical facts. To me it seems as presumptuous, on the one
hand, for the believer to claim this evidence for the truth of
Christianity, as it is absurd, on the other hand, for the
sceptic to demand such evidence to support these historical
statements. I cannot see that it depends on the personal
authority of Jesus. He was the organ through which the Infinite spoke. It is God that was manifested in the flesh by
him, on whom rests the truth which Jesus brought to light,
and made clear and beautiful in his life; and if Christianity be
true, it seems useless to look for any other authority to uphold it, as for some one to support Almighty God. So if it
could be proved--as it cannot--in opposition to the greatest
amount of historical evidence ever collected on any similar
point, that the Gospels were the fabrication of designing and
artful men, that Jesus of Nazareth had never lived, still
Christianity would stand firm, and fear no evil. None of the
doctrines of that religion would fall to the ground; for, if
true, they stand by themselves. But we should lose--oh,
irreparable loss!--the example of that character, so beautiful, so divine, that no human genius could have conceived it,
as none, after all the progress and refinement of eighteen

centuries, seems fully to have comprehended its lustrous
life.   If Christianity were true, we should still think it was
so, not because its record was written by infallible pens,
nor because it was lived out by an infallible teacher; but that
it is true, like the axioms of geometry, because it is true,
and is to be tried by the oracle God places in the breast.
If it rest on the personal authority of Jesus alone, then there
is no certainty of its truth if he were ever mistaken in the
smallest matter, as some Christians have thought he was in
predicting his second coming.

These doctrines respecting the Scriptures have often
changed, and are but fleeting.   Yet men lay much stress on
them.   Some cling to these notions as if they were Christianity itself.   It is about these and similar points that
theological battles are fought from age to age.   Men sometimes use worst the choicest treasure which God bestows.
This is especially true of the use men make of the Bible.
Some men have regarded it as the heathen their idol, or the
savage his fetish.   They have subordinated reason, conscience,
and religion to this.   Thus have they lost half the treasure it
bears in its bosom.   No doubt the time will come when its
true character shall be felt.   Then it will be seen, that,
amid all the contradictions of the Old Testament; its legends,
so beautiful as fictions, so appalling as facts; amid its predictions that have never been fulfilled; amid the puerile con-
ceptions of God, which sometimes occur, and the cruel denunciations that disfigure both Psalm and Prophecy, there is
a reverence for man's nature, a sublime trust in God, and
a depth of piety, rarely felt in these cold northern hearts of
ours.   Then the devotion of its authors, the loftiness of
their aim, and the majesty of their life, will appear doubly
fair, and Prophet and Psalmist will warm our hearts as
never before.   Their voice will cheer the young, and sanctify
the grey-headed; will charm us in the toil of life, and
sweeten the cup Death gives us when he comes to shake off
this mantle of flesh.   Then will it be seen, that the words
of Jesus are the music of heaven, sung in an earthly voice,
and the echo of these words in John and Paul owe their
efficacy to their truth and their depth, and to no accidental
matter connected therewith.   Then can the Word, which was
in the beginning and now is, find access to the innermost heart
of man, and speak there as now it seldom speaks.   Then
shall the Bible--which is a whole library of the deepest and
most earnest thoughts and feelings, and piety, and love, ever
recorded in human speech--be read oftener than ever before,
not with superstition, but with reason, conscience, and faith,

fully active.   Then shall it sustain men bowed down with
many sorrows; rebuke sin, encourage virtue, sow the world
broadcast and quick with the seed of love, that man may
reap a harvest for life everlasting.

With all the obstacles men have thrown in its path,
how much has the Bible done for mankind.   No abuse has de-
prived us of all its blessings!   You trace its path across the
world from the day of Pentecost to this day.   As a river
springs up in the heart of a sandy continent, having its father
in the skies, and its birth-place in distant, unknown mountains; as the stream rolls on, enlarging itself, making in that
arid waste a belt of verdure wherever it turns its way; creat-
ing palm groves and fertile plains, where the smoke of the
cottager curls up at eventide, and marble cities send the
gleam of their splendour far into the sky; such has been the
course of the Bible on the earth.   Despite of idolaters bowing
to the dust before it, it has made a deeper mark on the world
than the rich and beautiful literature of all the heathen.   The
first book of the Old Testament tells man he is made in the
image of God; the first of the New Testament gives us the
motto, Be perfect as your Father in heaven.   Higher words
were never spoken.   How the truths of the Bible have blessed
us!   There is not a boy on all the hills of New England; not
a girl born in the filthiest cellar which disgraces a capital in
Europe, and cries to God against the barbarism of modern
civilization; not a boy nor a girl all Christendom through--but
their lot is made better by that great book.

Doubtless the time will come when men shall see
Christ also as he is.   Well might he still say, "Have I been
so long with you, and yet hast thou not known me?"   No! we
have made him an idol, have bowed the knee before him,
saying, "Hail, king of the Jews!" called him "Lord, Lord!"
but done not the things which he said.   The history of the
Christian world might well be summed up in one word of the
evangelist--"and there they crucified him"; for there has
never been an age when men did not crucify the Son of God
afresh.   But if error prevail for a time and grow old in the
world, truth will triumph at the last, and then we shall see
the Son of God as he is.   Lifted up, he shall draw all nations
unto him.   Then will men understand the word of Jesus,
which shall not pass away.   Then shall we see and love the
divine life that he lived.   How vast has his influence been!
How his spirit wrought in the hearts of his disciples, rude,
selfish, bigoted, as at first they were!   How it has wrought
in the world!   His words judge the nations.   The wisest son

of man has not measured their height.   They speak to what
is deepest in profound men, what is holiest in good men,
what is divinest in religious men.   They kindle anew the
flame of devotion in hearts long cold.   They are spirit and
life.   His truth was not derived from Moses and Solomon;
but the light of God shone through him, not coloured, not
bent aside.   His life is the perpetual rebuke of all time since.
It condemns ancient civilization: it condemns modern civilization.   Wise men we have since had, and good men; but this
Galilean youth strode before the world whole thousands of
years, so much of Divinity was in him.   His words solve the
questions of this present age.   In him the Godlike and the
human met and embraced, and a divine life was born.   Measure him by the world's greatest sons--how poor they are!
Try him by the best of men--how little and low they appear!
Exalt him as much as we may, we shall yet, perhaps, come
short of the mark.   But still was he not our brother; the
son of man, as we are; the Son of God, like ourselves?   His
excellence--was it not human excellence?   His wisdom, love,
piety--sweet and celestial as they were--are they not what
we also may attain?   In him, as in a mirror, we may see
the image of God, and go on from glory to glory, till we are
changed into the same image, led by the spirit which en-
lightens the humble.   Viewed in this way, how beautiful is
the life of Jesus!   Heaven has come down to earth, or,
rather, earth has become heaven.   The Son of God, come of
age, has taken possession of his birthright.   The brightest
revelation is this--of what is possible for all men, if not
now, at least hereafter.   How pure is his spirit, and how
encouraging its words!   "Lowly sufferer, " he seems to say,
"see how I bore the cross.   Patient labourer, be strong; see
how I toiled for the unthankful and the merciless.   Mistaken
sinner, see of what thou art capable.   Rise up, and be
blessed. "

But if, as some early Christians began to do, you
take a heathen view, and make him a God, the Son of God in
a peculiar and exclusive sense, much of the significance of
his character is gone.   His virtue has no merit, his love no
feeling, his cross no burthen, his agony no pain.   His death
is an illusion, his resurrection but a show.   For if he were
not a man, but a god, what are all these things? what his
words, his life, his excellence of achievement?   It is all
nothing, weighed against the illimitable greatness of Him who
created the worlds and fills up all time and space!   Then
his resignation is no lesson, his life no model, his death no
triumph to you or me, who are not gods, but mortal men,

that know not what a day shall bring forth, and walk by faith
"dim sounding on our perilous way." Alas! we have despaired of man, and so cut off his brightest hope.

In respect of doctrines as well as forms, we see all
is transitory. "Everywhere is instability and insecurity."
Opinions have changed most on points deemed most vital.
Could we bring up a Christian teacher of any age--from the
sixth to the fourteenth century, for example, though a teacher
of undoubted soundness of faith, whose word filled the
churches of Christendom--clergymen would scarce allow him
to kneel at their altar, or sit down with them at the Lord's
table. His notions of Christianity could not be expressed in
our forms, nor could our notions be made intelligible to his
ears. The questions of his age, those on which Christianity
was thought to depend--questions which perplexed and divided
the subtle doctors--are no questions to us. The quarrels
which then drove wise men mad, now only excite a smile or
a tear, as we are disposed to laugh or weep at the frailty of
man. We have other straws of our own to quarrel for.
Their ancient books of devotion do not speak to us: their
theology is a vain word. To look back but a short period,
the theological speculations of our fathers during the last two
centuries; their "practical divinity"; even the sermons written
by genius and piety--are, with rare exceptions, found un-
readable: such a change is there in the doctrines.

Now who shall tell us that the change is to stop here;
that this sect or that, or even all sects united, have exhausted the river of life, and received it all in their canonized
urns, so that we need draw no more out of the eternal well,
but get refreshment nearer at hand? Who shall tell us that
another age will not smile at our doctrines, disputes, and
unchristian quarrels about Christianity, and make wide the
mouth at men who walked brave in orthodox raiment, de-
lighting to blacken the names of heretics, and repeat again
the old charge, "He hath blasphemed?" Who shall tell us
they will not weep at the folly of all such as fancied truth
shone only into the contracted nook of their school, or sect,
or coterie? Men of other times may look down equally on
the heresy-hunters, and men hunted for heresy, and wonder
at both. The men of all ages before us were quite as confident as we, that their opinion was truth, that their notion
was Christianity and the whole thereof. The men who lit the
fires of persecution, from the first martyr to Christian
bigotry down to the last murder of the innocents, had no
doubt their opinion was divine. The contest about transub-

stantiation, and the immaculate purity of the Hebrew and
Greek texts of the Scriptures, was waged with a bitterness
unequalled in these days.   The Protestant smiles at one, the
Catholic at the other, and men of sense wonder at both.   It
might teach us all a lesson, at least of forbearance.   No
doubt an age will come in which ours shall be reckoned a
period of darkness--like the sixth century--when men groped
for the wall, but stumbled and fell, because they trusted a
transient notion, not an eternal truth; an age when temples
were full of idols, set up by human folly; an age in which
Christian light had scarce begun to shine into men's hearts.
But while this change goes on, while one generation of
opinions passes away, and another rises up, Christianity itself, that pure religion, which exists eternal in the constitution of the soul and the mind of God, is always the same.
The word that was before Abraham, in the very beginning,
will not change, for that word is Truth.   From this Jesus
subtracted nothing; to this he added nothing.   But he came to
reveal it as the secret of God, that cunning men could not
understand, but which filled the souls of men meek and lowly
of heart.   This truth we owe to God; the revelation thereof
to Jesus, our elder brother, God's chosen son.

     To turn away from the disputes of the Catholics and
the Protestants, of the Unitarian and the Trinitarian of old
school and new school, and come to the plain words of Jesus
of Nazareth, Christianity is a simple thing, very simple.
It is absolute, pure morality; absolute, pure religion; the
love of man; the love of God acting without let or hindrance.
The only creed it lays down is the great truth which springs
up spontaneous in the holy heart--there is a God.   Its watch-
word is, Be perfect as your Father in heaven.   The only
form it demands is a divine life; doing the best thing in the
best way, from the highest motives; perfect obedience to the
great law of God.   Its sanction is the voice of God in your
heart; the perpetual presence of Him who made us and the
stars over our head; Christ and the Father abiding within us.
All this is very simple--a little child can understand it; very
beautiful--the loftiest mind can find nothing so lovely.   Try
it by reason, conscience, and faith--things highest in man's
nature--we see no redundance, we feel no deficiency.   Examine the particular duties it enjoins; humility, reverence,
sobriety, gentleness, charity, forgiveness, fortitude, resignation, faith, and active love; try the whole extent of
Christianity, so well summed up in the command, "Thou
shalt love the Lord thy God with all thy heart, and with all
thy soul, and with all thy mind--thou shalt love thy neighbour

as thyself"; and is there anything therein that can perish?
No, the very opponents of Christianity have rarely found fault
with the teachings of Jesus.   The end of Christianity seems
to be to make all men one with God as Christ was one with
Him; to bring them to such a state of obedience and goodness, that we shall think divine thoughts and feel divine
sentiments, and so keep the law of God by living a life of
truth and love.   Its means are purity and prayer; getting
strength from God, and using it for our fellow-men as well
as ourselves.   It allows perfect freedom.   It does not demand all men to think alike, but to think uprightly, and get
as near as possible at truth; not all men to live alike, but
to live holy, and get as near as possible to a life perfectly
divine.   Christ set up no pillars of Hercules, beyond which
men must not sail the sea in quest of truth.   He says, "I
have many things to say unto you, but ye cannot bear them
now....   Greater works than these shall ye do. "   Christianity
lays no rude hand on the sacred peculiarity of individual
genius and character.   But there is no Christian sect which
does not fetter a man.   It would make all men think alike,
or smother their conviction in silence.   Were all men
Quakers or Catholics, Unitarians or Baptists, there would be
much less diversity of thought, character, and life, less of
truth active in the world, than now.   But Christianity gives
us the largest liberty of the sons of God; and were all men
Christians after the fashion of Jesus, this variety would be
a thousand times greater than now: for Christianity is not a
system of doctrines, but rather a method of attaining oneness
with God.   It demands, therefore, a good life of piety within, of purity without, and gives the promise that whoso does
God's will shall know of God's doctrine.

         In an age of corruption, as all ages are, Jesus stood
and looked up to God.   There was nothing between him and
the Father of all; no old world, be it of Moses or Esaias, of
a living Rabbi or Sanhedrim of Rabbis; no sin or perverse-
ness of the finite will.   As the result of this virgin purity of
soul and perfect obedience, the light of God shone down into
the very deeps of his soul, bringing all of the Godhead which
flesh can receive.   He would have us do the same; worship
with nothing between us and God; act, think, feel, live, in
perfect obedience to Him; and we never are Christians as he
was the Christ, until we worship, as Jesus did, with no
mediator, with nothing between us and the Father of all.   He
felt that God's word was in him; that he was one with God.
He told what he saw--the truth: he lived what he felt--a life
of love.   The truth he brought to light must have been always

the same before the eyes of all-seeing God, nineteen centuries before Christ, or nineteen centuries after him.   A
life supported by the principle and quickened by the sentiment of religion, if true to both, is always the same thing
in Nazareth or New England.   Now that divine man received
these truths from God; was illumined more clearly by "the
light that lighteneth every man"; combined or involved all the
truths of religion and morality in his doctrine, and made
them manifest in his life.   Then his words and example
passed into the world, and can no more perish than the stars
be wiped out of the sky.   The truths he taught; his doctrines
respecting man and God; the relation between man and man,
and man and God, with the duties that grow out of that re-
lation--are always the same, and can never change till man
ceases to be man, and creation vanishes into nothing.   No;
forms and opinions change and perish; but the word of God
cannot fail.   The form religion takes, the doctrines wherewith she is girded, can never be the same in any two centuries or two men; for since the sum of religious doctrines
is both the result and the measure of a man's total growth in
wisdom, virtue, and piety, and since men will always differ
in these respects, so religious doctrines and forms will always differ, always be transient, as Christianity goes forth
and scatters the seed she bears in her hand.   But the
Christianity holy men feel in the heart, the Christ that is
born within us, is always the same thing to each soul that
feels it.   This differs only in degree, and not in kind, from
age to age, and man to man.   There is something in Christianity which no sect, from the "Ebionites" to the "Latter-
Day Saints, " ever entirely overlooked.   This is that common
Christianity which burns in the hearts of pious men.

        Real Christianity gives men new life.   It is the
growth and perfect action of the Holy Spirit God puts into the
sons of men.   It makes us outgrow any form or any system
of doctrines we have devised, and approach still closer to
the truth.   It would lead us to take what help we can find.
It would make the Bible our servant, not our master.   It
would teach us to profit by the wisdom and piety of David
and Solomon, but not to sin their sins, nor bow to their idols.
It would make us revere the holy words spoken by "godly men
of old, " but revere still more the word of God spoken
through conscience, reason, and faith, as the holiest of all.
It would not make Christ the despot of the soul, but the
brother of all men.   It would not tell us that even he had
exhausted the fulness of God, so that he could create none
greater; for with Him "all things are possible, " and neither

Old Testament nor New Testament ever hints that creation
exhausts the Creator.   Still less would it tell us, the wisdom, the piety, the love, the manly excellence of Jesus, was
the result of miraculous agency alone, but that it was won,
like the excellence of humbler men, by faithful obedience to
Him who gave his Son such ample heritage.   It would point
to him as our brother, who went before, like the good shepherd, to charm us with the music of his words, and with the
beauty of his life to tempt us up the steeps of mortal toil,
within the gate of heaven.   It would have us make the kingdom of God on earth, and enter more fittingly the kingdom
on high.   It would lead us to form Christ in the heart, on
which Paul laid such stress, and work out our salvation by
this.   For it is not so much by the Christ who lived so
blameless and beautiful eighteen centuries ago, that we are
saved directly, but by the Christ we form in our hearts and
live out in our daily life, that we save ourselves, God working with us both to will and to do.

        Compare the simpleness of Christianity, as Christ
sets it forth on the Mount, with what is sometimes taught
and accepted in that honoured name; and what a difference!
One is of God; one is of man.   There is something in
Christianity which sects have not reached; something that will
not be won, we fear, by theological battles, or the quarrels
of pious men; still we may rejoice that Christ is preached
in any way.   The Christianity of sects, of the pulpit, of society, is ephemeral--a transitory fly.   It will pass off and
be forgot.   Some new form will take its place, suited to the
aspect of the changing times.   Each will represent something
of truth, but no one the whole.   It seems the whole race of
man is needed to do justice to the whole of truth, as "the
whole Church, to preach the whole Gospel. "   Truth is intrusted for the time to a perishable ark of human contrivance.
Though often shipwrecked, she always comes safe to land,
and is not changed by her mishap.   That pure ideal religion
which Jesus saw on the mount of his vision, and lived out in
the lowly life of a Galilean peasant; which transforms his
cross into an emblem of all that is holiest on earth; which
makes sacred the ground he trod, and is dearest to the best
of men, most true to what is truest in them--cannot pass
away.   Let men improve never so far in civilization, or
soar never so high on the wings of religion and love, they
can never outgo the flight of truth and Christianity.   It will
always be above them.   It is as if we were to fly towards a
star, which becomes larger and more bright the nearer we
approach, till we enter and are absorbed in its glory.

If we look carelessly on the ages that have gone by,
or only on the surfaces of things as they come up before us,
there is reason to fear; for we confound the truth of God
with the word of man.   So at a distance the cloud and the
mountain seem the same.   When the drift changes with the
passing wind, an unpractised eye might fancy the mountain
itself was gone.   But the mountain stands to catch the clouds,
to win the blessing they bear, and send it down to moisten
the fainting violet, to form streams which gladden valley and
meadow, and sweep on at last to the sea in deep channels,
laden with fleets.   Thus the forms of the Church, the creeds
of the sects, the conflicting opinions of teachers, float round
the sides of the Christian mount, and swell and toss, and
rise and fall, and dart their lightning, and roll their thunder,
but they neither make nor mar the mount itself.   Its lofty
summit far transcends the tumult, knows nothing of the storm
which roars below, but burns with rosy light at evening and
at morn, gleams in the splendours of the mid-day sun, sees
his light when the long shadows creep over plain and moor-
land, and all night long has its head in the heavens, and is
visited by troops of stars which never set, nor veil their
face to aught so pure and high.

Let then the transient pass, fleet as it will; and may
God send us some new manifestation of the Christian faith,
that shall stir men's hearts as they were never stirred; some
new word, which shall teach us what we are, and renew us
all in the image of God; some better life, that shall fulfil the
Hebrew prophecy, and pour out the spirit of God on young
men and maidens, and old men and children; which shall
realize the word of Christ, and give us the Comforter, who
shall reveal all needed things!   There are Simeons enough in
the cottages and churches of New England, plain men and
pious women, who wait for the consolation, and would die in
gladness if their expiring breath could stir quicker the wings
that bear him on.   There are men enough, sick and "bowed
down, in no wise able to lift up themselves," who would be
healed could they kiss the hand of their Saviour, or touch but
the hem of his garment; men who look up and are not fed,
because they ask bread from heaven and water from the rock,
not traditions or fancies, Jewish or heathen, or new or old;
men enough who, with throbbing hearts, pray for the spirit
of healing to come upon the waters, which other than angels
have long kept in trouble; men enough who have lain long
time sick of theology, nothing bettered by many physicians,
and are now dead, too dead to bury their dead, who would
come out of their graves at the glad tidings.   God send us a

real religious life, which shall pluck blindness out of the
heart, and make us better fathers, mothers, and children!
a religious life, that shall go with us where we go, and make
every home the house of God, every act acceptable as a
prayer. We would work for this, and pray for it, though we
wept tears of blood while we prayed.

Such, then, is the Transient and such the Permanent
in Christianity. What is of absolute value never changes; we
may cling round it and grow to it for ever. No one can say
his notions shall stand. But we may all say, the truth, as
it is in Jesus, shall never pass-away. Yet there are always
some, even religious men, who do not see the permanent
element, so they rely on the fleeting, and, what is also an
evil, condemn others for not doing the same. They mistake
a defense of the truth for an attack upon the Holy of Holies,
the removal of a theological error for the destruction of all
religion. Already men of the same sect eye one another
with suspicion, and lowering brows that indicate a storm,
and, like children who have fallen out in their play, call
hard names. Now, as always, there is a collision between
these two elements. The question puts itself to each man,
"Will you cling to what is perishing, or embrace what is
eternal?" This question each must answer for himself.

My friends, if you receive the notions about Christianity which chance to be current in your sect or church,
solely because they are current, and thus accept the commandment of men instead of God's truth, there will always
be enough to commend you for soundness of judgment,
prudence, and good sense, enough to call you Christian for
that reason. But if this is all you rely upon, alas for you!
The ground will shake under your feet if you attempt to walk
uprightly and like men. You will be afraid of every new
opinion, lest it shake down your church: you will fear "lest,
if a fox go up, he will break down your stone wall. " The
smallest contradiction in the New Testament or Old Testament, the least disagreement between the law and the Gospel,
any mistake of the Apostles, will weaken your faith. It
shall be with you "as when a hungry man dreameth, and behold, he eateth; but he awaketh, and his soul is empty."

If, on the other hand, you take the true word of God,
and live out this, nothing shall harm you. Men may mock,
but their mouthfuls of wind shall be blown back upon their
own face. If the master of the house were called Beelzebub,
it matters little what name is given to the household. The

name Christian, given in mockery, will last till the world go
down.   He that loves God and man, and lives in accordance
with that love, needs not fear what man can do to him.   His
religion comes to him in his hour of sadness, it lays its
hand on him when he has fallen among thieves, and raises
him up, heals and comforts him.   If he is crucified, he
shall rise again.

My friends, you this day receive, with the usual
formalities, the man you have chosen to speak to you on
the highest of all themes--what concerns your life on earth,
your life in heaven.   It is a work for which no talents, no
prayerful diligence, no piety, is too great; an office that
would dignify angels, if worthily filled.   If the eyes of this
man be holden, that he <u>cannot</u> discern between the perishing
and the true, you will hold him guiltless of all sin in this;
but look for light where it can be had; for his office will
then be of no use to you.   But if he sees the truth, and is
sacred by worldly motives, and <u>will</u> not tell it, alas for him!
If the watchman see the foe coming, and blow not the
trumpet, the blood of the innocent is on him.

Your own conduct and character, the treatment you
offer this young man, will in some measure influence him.
The hearer affects the speaker.   There were some places
where even Jesus "did not many mighty works, because of
their unbelief. " Worldly motives--not seeming such--some-
times deter good men from their duty.   Gold and ease have,
before now, enervated noble minds.   Daily contact with men
of low aims takes down the ideal of life, which a bright spirit
casts out of itself.   Terror has sometimes palsied tongues
that, before, were eloquent as the voice of persuasion.   But
thereby Truth is not holden.   She speaks in a thousand
tongues, and with a pen of iron graves her sentence on the
rock for ever.   You may prevent the freedom of speech in
this pulpit if you will.   You may hire you servants to preach
as you bid; to spare your vices, and flatter your follies; to
prophesy smooth things, and say, It is peace, when there is
no peace.   Yet in so doing you weaken and enthral your-
selves.   And alas for that man who consents to think one
thing in his closet and preach another in his pulpit!   God
shall judge him in his mercy, not man in his wrath.   But
over his study and over his pulpit might be writ, <u>Emptiness;</u>
on his canonical robes, on his forehead and right hand,
<u>Deceit, Deceit.</u>

But, on the other hand, you may encourage your

brother to tell you the truth.   Your affection will then be
precious to him, your prayers of great price.   Every evidence of your sympathy will go to baptize him anew to holiness and truth.   You will then have his best words, his
brightest thoughts, and his most hearty prayers.   He may
grow old in your service, blessing and blest.   He will have--

> The sweetest, best of consolation,
>   The thought, that he has given,
>   To serve the cause of Heaven,
> The freshness of his early inspiration.

Choose as you will choose; but weal or woe depends
upon your choice.

3. THE POSITION AND DUTIES
OF THE AMERICAN SCHOLAR*

Men of a superior culture get it at the cost of the whole community, and therefore at first owe for their education. They must pay back an equivalent, or else remain debtors to mankind, debtors for ever; that is, beggars or thieves, such being the only class that are thus perpetually in debt, and a burden to the race.

It is true that every man, the rudest Prussian boor, as well as Von Humboldt, is indebted to mankind for his culture, to their past history and their existing institutions, to their daily toil. Taking the whole culture into the account, the debt bears about the same ratio to the receipt in all men. I speak not of genius, the inborn faculty which costs mankind nothing, only of the education thereof, which the man obtains. The Irishman who can only handle his spade, wear his garments, talk his wild brogue, and bid his beads, has four or five hundred generations of ancestors behind him, and is as long descended, and from as old a stock, as the accomplished patrician scholar at Oxford and Berlin. The Irishman depends on them all, and on the present generation, for his culture. But he has obtained his development with no special outlay and cost of the human race. In getting that rude culture, he has appropriated nothing to himself which is taken from another man's share. He has paid as he went along, so he owes nothing in particular for his education; and mankind has no claim on him as for value received. But the Oxford graduate has been a long time at school and college; not earning, but learning; living therefore at the cost of mankind, with an obligation and an implied promise to pay back when he comes of age and takes possession of his educated faculties. He therefore has not only the general debt which he shares with all men, but an obligation quite special and peculiar for his support while at study.

*Parker, Theodore. Collected Works, ed. F. Cobbe (London: Trübner, 1863-79), VII, 217-56.

This rule is general, and applies to the class of educated men, with some apparent exceptions, and a very few real ones.   Some men are born of poor but strong-bodied parents, and endowed with great abilities; they inherit nothing except their share of the general civilization of mankind, and the onward impulse which that has given.   These men devote themselves to study; and having behind them an ancestry of broad-shouldered, hard-handed, stalwart, temperate men and deep-bosomed, red-armed, and industrious mothers, they are able to do the work of two or three men at the time.   Such men work while they study; they teach while they learn; they hew their own way through the wood by superior strength and skill born in their bones, with an axe themselves have chipped out from the stone, or forged of metal, or paid for with the result of their first hewings.   They are specially indebted to nobody for their culture.   They pay as they go, owing the academic ferryman nothing for setting them over into the elysium of the scholar.

Only few men ever make this heroic and crucial experiment.   None but poor men's sons essay the trial.   Nothing but poverty has whips sharp enough to sting indolent men, even of genius, to such exertion of the manly part. But even this proud race often runs into another debt: they run up long scores with the body, which must one day be paid "with aching head and squeamish heart-burnings. " The credit on account of the hardy fathers is not without limit. It is soon exhausted; especially in a land where the atmosphere, the institutions, and the youth of the people all excite to premature and excessive prodigality of effort.   The body takes a mortgage on the spendthrift spirit, demands certain regular periodic payments, and will one day foreclose for breach of condition, impede the spirit's action in the premises, putting a very disagreeable keeper there, and finally expel the prodigal mortgagor.   So it oftens happens that a man, who in his youth scorned a pecuniary debt to mankind and would receive no favour, even to buy culture with, has yet unconsciously and against his will, contracted debts which trouble him in manhood, and impede his action all his life; with swollen feet and blear eyes famous Griesbach pays for the austere heroism of his penurious and needy youth.   The rosy bud of genius, on the poor man's tree, too often opens into a lean and ghastly flower.   Could not Burns tell us this?

With the rare exceptions just hinted at, any man of a superior culture owes for it when obtained.   Sometimes the debt is obvious: a farmer with small means and a large

family sends the most hopeful of his sons to college.   Look
at the cost of the boy's culture.   His hands are kept from
work that his mind may be free.   He fares on daintier food,
wears more and more costly garments.   Other members of
the family must feed and clothe him, earn his tuition-fees,
buy his books, pay for his fuel and room-rent.   For this the
father rises earlier than of old, yoking the oxen a great
while before day of a winter's morning, and toils till long
after dark of a winter's night, enduring cold and hardship.
For this the mother stints her frugal fare, her humble dress;
for this the brothers must forego sleep and pastime, must
toil harder, late and early both; for this the sisters must
seek new modes of profitable work, must wear their old
finery long after it is finery no more.   The spare wealth of
the family, stinted to spare it, is spent on this one youth.
From the father to the daughters, all lay their bones to extraordinary work for him; the whole family is pinched in
body, that this one youth may go brave and full.   Even the
family horse pays his tax to raise the education fee.

Men see the hopeful scholar, graceful and accomplished,
receiving his academic honours, but they see not the hard-
featured father standing unheeded in the aisle, nor the older
sister in an obscure corner of the gallery, who had toiled in
the factory for the favoured brother, tending his vineyard,
her own not kept; who had perhaps learned the letters of
Greek to hear him recite the grammar at home.   Father and
sister know not a word of the language in which his diploma
is writ and delivered.   At what cost of the family tree is
this one flower produced?   How many leaves, possible blossoms, --yea, possible branches--have been absorbed to create
this one flower, which shall perpetuate the kind, after being
beautiful and fragrant in its own season?   Yet, while these
leaves are growing for the blossom's sake, and the life of the tree
is directed thither with special and urgent emphasis, the
difference between branch and blossom, leaf and petal, is
getting more and more.   By and by the two cannot comprehend each other; the acorn has forgotten the leaf which reared
it, and thinks itself of another kin.   Grotius, who speaks a
host of languages, talking with the learned of all countries,
and of every age, has forgot his mother tongue, and speech
is at end with her that bore him.   The son, accomplished
with many a science, many an art, ceases to understand the
simple consciousness of his father and mother.   They are
proud of him--that he has outgrown them; he ashamed of them
when they visit him amid his scholarly company.   To them
he is a philosopher; they only clowns in his eyes.   He learns

to neglect, perhaps to despise them, and forgets his obligation and his debt.   Yet by their rudeness is it that he is refined.   His science and literary skill are purchased by their
ignorance and uncouthness of manner and speech.   Had the
educational cost been equally divided, all had still continued
on a level; he had known no Latin, but the whole family might
have spoken good English.   For all the difference which education has made betwixt him and his kinsfolk he is a debtor.

    In New England you sometimes see extremes of social
condition brought together.   The blue-frocked father, well advanced, but hale as an October morning, jostles into Boston
in a milk-cart, his red-checked grand-daughter beside him,
also coming for some useful daily work, while the youngest
son, cultured at the cost of that grand-daughter's sire and by
that father's toil, is already a famous man; perhaps also a
proud one, eloquent at the bar, or powerful in the pulpit, or
mighty in the senate.   The family was not rich enough to
educate all the children after this costly sort; one becomes
famous, the rest are neglected, obscure, and perhaps ignorant; the cultivated son has little sympathy with them.   So
the men that built up the cathedrals of Strasbourg and Milan
slept in mean hutches of mud and straw, dirty, cold, and
wet; the finished tower looks proudly down upon the lowly
thatch, all heedless of the cost at which itself arose.   It is
plain that this man owes for his education; it is plain whom
he owes.   But all men of a superior culture, though born to
wealth, get their education in the same way, only there is
this additional mischief to complicate the matter: the burden
of self-denial is not borne by the man's own family, but by
other fathers and mothers, other brothers and sisters.   They
also pay the cost of his culture, bear the burden for no
special end, and have no personal or family joy in the success; they do not even know the scholar they help to train.
They who hewed the topstone of society are far away when it
is hoisted up with shouting.   Most of the youths now-a-days
trained at Harvard College are the sons of rich men, yet they
also, not less, are educated at the public charge; beneficiaries
not of the "Hopkins' Fund, " but of the whole community.   Society is not yet rich enough to afford so generous a culture
to all who ask, who deserve, or who would pay for it a
hundred-fold.   The accomplished man who sits in his well-
endowed scholarship at Oxford, or rejoices to be "Master of
Trinity, " though he have the estate of the Westminsters and
Sutherlands behind him, is still the beneficiary of the public,
and owes for his schooling.

In the general way, among the industrious classes of
New England, a boy earns his living after he is twelve years
old. If he gets the superior education of the scholar solely
by the pecuniary aid of his father or others, when he is
twenty-five and enters on his profession, law, medicine, or
divinity, politics, school-keeping, or trade, he has not
earned his Latin grammar; has rendered no appreciable
service to mankind; others have worked that he might study,
and taught that he might learn. He has not paid the first
cent towards his own schooling; he is indebted for it to the
whole community. The ox-driver in the fields, the pavior in
the city streets, the labourer on the railroad, the lumberer
in the woods, the girl in the factory, each has a claim on
him. If he despises these persons, or cuts himself off from
sympathy with them; if he refuses to perform his function for
them after they have done their possible to fit him for it; he
is not only the perpetual and ungrateful debtor, but is more
guilty than the poor man's son who forgets the family that
sent him to college: for that family consciously and willingly
made the sacrifice, and got some satisfaction for it in the
visible success of their scheme, --nay, are sometimes proud
of the pride which scorns them, while with the mass of men
thus slighted there is no return for their sacrifice. They
did their part, faithfully did it; their beneficiary forgets his
function.

The democratic party in New England does not much
favour the higher seminaries of education. There has long
been a suspicion against them in the mass of the community,
and among the friends of the public education of the people a
serious distrust. This is the philosophy of that discontent:
public money spent on the higher seminaries is so much
taken from the humbler schools, so much taken from the
colleges of all for the college of the few; men educated at
such cost have not adequately repaid the public for the sacrifice made on their account; men of superior education have
not been eminently the friends of mankind, they do not eminently represent truth, justice, philanthropy, and piety; they
do not point men to lofty human life, and go thitherward in
advance of mankind; their superior education has narrowed
their sympathies, instead of widening; they use their opportunities against mankind, and not in its behalf; think, write,
legislate, and live not for the interest of mankind, but only
for a class; instead of eminent wisdom, justice, piety, they
have eminent cunning, selfishness, and want of faith. These
charges are matters of allegation; judge you if they be not
also matters of fact.

Now, there is a common feeling amongst men that the
scholar is their debtor, and, in virtue of this, that they have
a right to various services from him.   No honest man asks
the aid of a farmer or a blacksmith without intending to repay him in money; no assembly of mechanics would ask
another to come two hundred miles and give them a month's
work, or a day's work.   Yet they will ask a scholar to do
so.   What gratuitous services are demanded of the physician,
of the minister, of the man of science and letters in general!
No poor man in Boston but thinks he has a good claim on any
doctor; no culprit in danger of liberty or life but will ask the
services of a lawyer, wholly without recompense, to plead
his cause.   The poorest and most neglected class of men
look on every good clergyman as their missionary and
minister and friend; the better educated and more powerful
he is, the juster and greater do they feel their claim on him.
A pirate in gaol may command the services of any Christian
minister in the land.   Most of the high achievements in science, letters, and art, have had no apparent pay.   The pay
came beforehand: in general and from God, in the greater
ability, "the vision and the faculty divine," but in particular
also and from men, in the opportunity afforded them by
others for the use and culture thereof.   Divinely and humanly
they are well paid.   Men feel that they have this right to the
services of the scholar, in part because they dimly know that
his superior education is purchased at the general cost.
Hence, too, they are proud of the few able and accomplished
men, feeling that all have a certain property therein, as
having contributed their mite to the accumulation, by their
divine nature related to the men of genius, by their human
toil partners in the acquirements of the scholar.   This feeling is not confined to men who intellectually can appreciate
intellectual excellence.   The little parish in the mountains,
and the great parish in the city, are alike proud of the able-
headed and accomplished scholar who ministers to them;
though neither the poor clowns of the village nor the wealthy
clowns of the metropolis could enter into his consciousness
and understand his favourite pursuits or loftiest thought. Both
would think it insulting to pay such a man in full proportion
to his work or their receipt.   Nobody offers a salary to the
House of Lords: their lordship is their pay, and they must
give back, in the form of justice and sound government, an
equivalent for all they take in high social rank.   They must
pay for their nobility by being noble lords.

How shall the scholar pay for his education?   He is
to give a service for the service received.   Thus the miller

and the farmer pay one another, each paying with service in his own kind.   The scholar cannot pay back bread for bread, and cloth for cloth.   He must pay in the scholar's kind, not the woodman's or the weaver's.   He is to represent the higher modes of human consciousness; his culture and oppor- tunities of position fit him for that.   So he is not merely to go through the routine of his profession, as minister, doctor, lawyer, merchant, schoolmaster, politician, or maker of almanacks, and for his own advantage; he is also to repre- sent truth, justice, beauty, philanthropy, and religion--the highest facts of human experience; he must be common, but not vulgar, and, as a star, must dwell apart from the vul- garity of the selfish and the low.   He may win money with- out doing this, get fame and power, and thereby seem to pay mankind for their advance to him, while he rides upon their neck; but as he has not paid back the scholar's cost, and in the scholar's way, he is a debtor still, and owes for his past culture and present position.

Such is the position of the scholar everywhere, and such his consequent obligation.   But in America there are some circumstances which make the position and the duty still more important.   Beside the natural aristocracy of genius, talent, and educated skill, in most countries there is also a conventional and permanent nobility based on royal or patrician descent and immoveable aristocracy.   Its mem- bers monopolize the high places of society, and if not strong by nature are so by position.   Those men check the natural power of the class of scholars.   The descendant of some famous chief of old time takes rank before the Bacons, the Shakespeares, and the Miltons of new families, --born yes- terday, to-day gladdened and gladdening with the joy of their genius, --usurps their place, and for a time "shoves away the worthy bidden guest" from the honours of the public board.   Here there is no such class: a man born at all is well born; with a great nature, nobly born; the career opens to all that can run, to all men that wish to try; our aristoc- racy is moveable, and the scholar has scope and verge enough.

Germany has the largest class of scholars; men of talent, sometimes of genius, of great working power, ex- ceedingly well furnished for their work, with a knowledge of the past and the present.   On the whole, they seem to have a greater power of thought than the scholars of any other land.   They live in a country where intellectual worth is rated at its highest value.   As England is the paradise of

the patrician and the millionnaire, so is Germany for the
man of thought; Goethe and Schiller and the Humboldts took
precedence of the mere conventional aristocracy.   The empire of money is for England; that of mind is for Germany.
But there the scholar is positively hindered in his function
by the power of the government, which allows freedom of
thought, and by education tends to promote it, yet not its
correlative freedom of speech, and still less the consequent
of that--freedom of act.   Revelations of new thought are indeed looked for, and encouraged in certain forms, but the
corresponding revolution of old things is forbidden.   An idea
must remain an idea; the government will not allow it to become a deed, an institution, an idea organized in men.   The
children of the mind must be exposed to die, or, if left
alive, their feet are cramped, so that they cannot go alone;
useless, joyless, and unwed, they remain in their father's
house.   The government seeks to establish national unity of
action, by the sacrifice of individual variety of action, personal freedom: every man must be a soldier and a Christian,
wearing the livery of the government on the body and in the
soul, and going through the spiritual exercises of the church,
as through the manual exercise of the camp.   In a nation so
enlightened, personal freedom cannot be wholly sacrificed, so
thought is left free, but speech restricted by censorship--
speech with the human mouth or the iron lips of the press.
Now, as of old, is there a controversy between the temporal
and the spiritual powers, about the investiture of the children
of the soul.

Then, on the other side, the scholar is negatively impeded by the comparative ignorance of the people, by their
consequent lack of administrative power and self-help, and
their distrust of themselves.   There a great illumination has
gone on in the upper heavens of the learned, meteors corus-
cating into extraordinary glory; it has hardly dawned on the
low valleys of the common people.   If it shines there at all,
it is but as the Northern Aurora, with a little crackling
noise, lending a feeble and uncertain light, not enough to
walk with, and no warmth at all; a light which disturbs the
dip and alters the variation of the old historical compass,
bewilders the eye, hides the stars, and yet is not bright
enough to walk by without stumbling.   There is a learned
class, very learned and very large, with whom the scholar
thinks, and for whom he writes, most uncouthly, in the
language only of the schools; and, if not kept in awe by the
government, they are contented that a thought should remain
always a thought; while in their own heart they disdain all

authority but that of truth, justice, and love, they leave the
people subject to no rule but the priest, the magistrate, and
old custom, which usurp the place of reason, conscience,
and the affections.   There is a very enlightened pulpit, and
a very dull audience.   In America, it is said, for every
dough-faced representative there is a dough-faced constituency;
but in Germany there is not an intelligent people for each intelligent scholar.   So on condition a great thought be true
and revolutionary, it is hard to get it made a thing.   Ideas go
into a nunnery, not a family.   Phidias must keep his awful
Jove only in his head; there is no marble to carve it on.
Eichhorn and Strauss, and Kant, and Hegel, with all their
pother among the learned, have kept no boor from the com-
munion-table, nor made him discontented with the despotism
of the State.   They wrote for scholars, perhaps for gentlemen, for the enlightened, not for the great mass of the
people, in whom they had no confidence.   There is no class
of hucksters of thought, who retail philosophy to the million.
The million have as yet no appetite for it.   So the German
scholar is hindered from his function on either hand by the
power of the government, or the ignorance of the people.   He
talks to scholars and not men; his great ideas are often as
idle as shells in a lady's cabinet.

In America all is quite different.   There are no royal
or patrician patrons, no plebeian clients in literature, no immoveable aristocracy to withstand or even retard the new
genius, talent, or skill of the scholar.   There is no class
organized, accredited, and confided in, to resist a new idea;
only the unorganized inertia of mankind retards the circula-
tion of thought and the march of men.   Our historical men
do not found historical families; our famous names of to-day
are all new names in the State.   American aristocracy is
bottomed on money which no unnatural laws make steadfast
and immoveable.   To exclude a scholar from the company of
rich men, is not to exclude him from an audience that will
welcome and appreciate.

Then the government does not interfere to prohibit the
free exercise of thought.   Speaking is free, preaching free,
printing free.   No administration in America could put down
a newspaper or suppress the discussion of an unwelcome
theme.   The attempt would be folly and madness.   There is
no "tonnage and poundage" on thought.   It is seldom that lawless violence usurps the place of despotic government.   The
chief opponent of the new philosophy is the old philosophy.
The old has only the advantage of a few years; the advantage

of possession of the ground.   It has no weapons of defence
which the new has not for attack.   What hinders the growth
of the new democracy of to-day? --only the old democracy of
yesterday, once green, and then full-blown, but now going to
seed.   Everywhere else walled gardens have been built for
it to go quietly to seed in, and men appointed, in God's
name or the State's, to exterminate as a weed every new
plant of democratic thought which may spring up and suck
the soil or keep off the sun, so that the old may quietly
occupy the ground, and undisturbed continue to decay, and
contaminate the air.   Here it has nothing but its own stalk
to hold up its head, and is armed with only such spines as
it has grown out of its own substance.

Here the only power which continually impedes the
progress of mankind, and is conservative in the bad sense,
is wealth, which represents life lived, not now a living, and
labour accumulated, not now a doing.   Thus the obstacle to
free trade is not the notion that our meat must be home-
grown and our coat home-spun, but the money invested in
manufactures.   Slavery is sustained by no prestige of antiquity, no abstract fondness for a patriarchal institution, no
special zeal for "Christianity" which the churches often tell
us demands it, but solely because the Americans have invested some twelve hundred millions of dollars in the bodies
and souls of their countrymen, and fear they shall lose their
capital.   Witney's gin for separating the cotton from its blue
seed, making its culture and the labour of the slave profitable, did more to perpetuate slavery than all the "Compromises of the Constitution. "   The last argument in its favour
is always this: "It brings money, and we would not lose our
investment. "   Weapon a man with iron, he will stand and
fight; with gold, he will shrink and run.   The class of
capitalists are always cowardly; here they are the only
cowardly class that has much political or social influence.
Here gold is the imperial metal; nothing but wealth is consecrated for life: the tonsure gets covered up or grown over;
vows of celibacy are no more binding than dicers' oaths; allegiance to the State is as transferable as a cent, and may
be alienated by going over the border; church-communion
may be changed or neglected; as men will, they sign off from
Church and State; only the dollar holds its own continually,
and is the same under all administrations, "safe from the
bar, the pulpit, and the throne. "   Obstinate money continues
in office spite of the proscriptive policy of Polk and Taylor;
the laws may change, South Carolina move out of the nation,
the Constitution be broken, the Union dissolved, still money

holds its own.   That is the only peculiar weapon which the
old has wherewith to repel the new.

Here, too, the scholar has as much freedom as he
will take; himself alone stands in his own light, nothing else
between him and the infinite majesty of Truth.   He is free
to think, to speak, to print his word and organize his thought.
No class of men monopolize public attention or high place.
He comes up to the Genius of America, and she asks:
"What would you have, my little man?"   "More liberty, "
lisps he.   "Just as much as you can carry, " is the answer.
"Pay for it and take it, as much as you like, there it is. "
"But it is guarded!"   "Only by gilded flies in the day-time;
they look like hornets, but can only buzz, not bite with their
beak, nor sting with their tail.   At night it is defended by
daws and beetles, noisy, but harmless.   Here is marble,
my son, not classic and famous as yet, but good as the
Parian stone; quarry as much as you will, enough for a
nymph or a temple.   Say your wisest and do your best thing;
nobody will hurt you!"

Not much more is the scholar impeded by the ignorance of the people, not at all in respect to the substance of
his thought.   There is no danger that he will shoot over the
heads of the people by thinking too high for the multitude.
We have many authors below the market; scarce one above
it.   The people are continually looking for something better
than our authors give.   No American author has yet been too
high for the comprehension of the people, and compelled to
leave his writings "to posterity, after some centuries shall
have passed by. "   If he has thought with the thinkers, and
has something to say, and can speak it in plain speech, he
is sure to be widely understood.   There is no learned class
to whom he may talk Latin or Sanscrit, and who will understand him if he write as ill as Immanuel Kant; there is not
a large class to buy costly editions of ancient classics, however beautiful, or magnificent works on India, Egypt, Mex-
ico--the class of scholars is too poor for that, the rich men
have not the taste for such beauty; but there is an intelligent
class of men who will hear a man if he has what is worth
listening to, and says it plain.   It will be understood and
appreciated, and soon reduced to practice.   Let him think
as much in advance of men as he will, as far removed from
the popular opinion as he may, if he arrives at a great truth
he is sure of an audience, not an audience of fellow-scholars,
as in Germany, but of fellow-men; not of the children of distinguished or rich men--rather of the young parents of such,

an audience of earnest, practical people, who, if his thought
be a truth, will soon make it a thing.   They will appreciate
the substance of his thought, though not the artistic form
which clothes it.

      This peculiar relation of the man of genius to the
people comes from American institutions.   Here the greatest
man stands nearest to the people, and without a mediator
speaks to them face to face.   This is a new thing: in the
classic nations oratory was for the people, so was the
drama, and the ballad; that was all their literature.   But
this came to the people only in cities: the tongue travels
slow and addresses only the ear, while swiftly hurries on
the printed word and speaks at once to a million eyes.
Thucydides and Tacitus wrote for a few; Virgil sang the
labours of the shepherd in old Ascraean verse, but only to
the wealthy wits of Rome.   "I hate the impious crowd, and
stave them off, " was the scholar's maxim then.   All writing
was for the few.   The best English literature of the six-
teenth and seventeenth and eighteenth centuries is amenable
to the same criticism, except the dramatic and the religious.
It is so with all the permanent literature of Europe of that
time.   The same must be said even of much of the religious
literature of the scholars then.   The writings of Taylor, of
Barrow and South, of Bossuet, Massillon, and Bourdaloue,
clergymen though they were, speaking with a religious and
therefore a universal aim, always presuppose a narrow
audience of men of nice culture.   So they drew their figures
from the schoolmen, from the Greek anthology, from heathen
classics and the Christian Fathers.   Their illustrations were
embellishments to the scholar, but only palpable darkness to
the people.   This fact of writing for a few nice judges was
of great advantage to the form of the literature thus produced, but a disadvantage to the substance thereof; a misfortune to the scholar himself, for it belittled his sympathies
and kept him within a narrow range.   Even the religious
literature of the men just named betrays a lack of freedom,
a thinking for the learned and not for mankind; it has
breathed the air of the cloister, not the sky, and is tainted
with academic and monastic diseases.   So the best of it is
over-sentimental, timid, and does not point to hardy, manly
life.   Only Luther and Latimer preached to the million hearts
of their contemporaries.   The dramatic literature, on the
other hand, was for box, pit, and gallery; hence the width
of poetry in its great masters; hence many of its faults of
form; and hence the wild and wanton luxuriance of beauty
which flowers out all over the marvellous field of art where

Shakespeare walked and sung.   In the pulpit, excellence was
painted as a priest, or monk, or nun, loving nothing but
God; on the stage, as a soldier, magistrate, a gentleman or
simpleman, a wife and mother, loving also child and friend.
Only the literature of the player and the singer of ballads
was for the people.

Here all is changed, everything that is written is for
the hands of the million.   In three months Mr. Macaulay has
more readers in America than Thucydides and Tacitus in
twelve centuries.   Literature, which was once the sacrament
of the few, only a shew-bread to the people, is now the daily
meat of the multitude.   The best works get reprinted with
great speed; the highest poetry is soon in all the newspapers.
Authors know this, and write accordingly.   It is only scientific works which ask for a special public.   But even
science, the proudest of the day, must come down from the
clouds of the academy, lay off it scholastic garb, and appear
before the eyes of the multitude in common work-day clothes.
To large and mainly unlearned audiences Agassiz and Walker
set forth the highest teachings of physics and metaphysics,
not sparing difficult things, but putting them in plain speech.
Emerson takes his majestic intuitions of truth and justice,
which transcend the experience of the ages, and expounds
them to the mechanics' apprentices, to the factory girls at
Lowell and Chicopee, and to the merchants' clerks at Boston.
The more original the speaker, and the more profound, the
better is he relished; the beauty of the form is not appreciated, but the original substance welcomed into new life
over the bench, the loom, and even the desk of the counting-
house.   Of a deep man the people ask clearness also, thinking he does not see a thing wholly till he sees it plain.

From this new relation of the scholar to the people,
and the direct intimacy of his intercourse with men, there
comes a new modification of his duty; he is to represent the
higher facts of human consciousness to the people, and express them in the speech of the people; to think with the
sage and saint, but talk with common men.   It is easy to
discourse with scholars, and in the old academic carriage
drive through the broad gateway of the cultivated class; but
here the man of genius is to take the new thought on his
shoulders and climb up the stiff, steep hill, and find his way
where the wild asses quench their thirst, and the untamed
eagle builds his nest.   Hence our American scholar must
cultivate the dialectics of speech as well as thought. Power
of speech without thought, a long tongue in an empty head,

calls the people together once or twice, but soon its only
echo is from an audience of empty pews. Thought without
power of speech finds little welcome here; there are not
scholars enough to keep it in countenance. This popularity
of intelligence gives a great advantage to the man of letters,
who is also a man. He can occupy the whole space between
the extremes of mankind; can be at once philosopher in his
thought and people in his speech, deliver his word without
an interpreter to mediate, and, like King Mithridates in the
story, talk with the fourscore nations of his camp each in
his own tongue.

Further still, there are some peculiarities of the
American mind, in which we differ from our English brothers.
They are more inclined to the matter of fact, and appeal to
history; we, to the matter of ideas, and having no national
history but of a revolution, may appeal at once to human
nature. So while they are more historical, fond of names
and precedents, enamoured of limited facts and coy towards
abstract and universal ideas, with the maxim, "Stand by the
fixed," we are more metaphysical, ideal; do not think a
thing right because actual, nor impossible because it has
never been. The Americans are more metaphysical than the
English; have departed more from the old sensational philosophy, have welcomed more warmly the transcendental
philosophy of Germany and France. The Declaration of Independence, and all the State Constitutions of the North,
begin with a universal and abstract idea. Even preaching is
abstract and of ideas. Calvinism bears metaphysical fruit
in New England.

This fact modifies still more the function of the duty
of the scholar. It determines him to ideas, to facts for the
ideas they cover, not so much to the past as the future, to
the past only that he may guide the present and construct
the future. He is to take his run in the past to acquire the
momentum of history, his stand in the present, and leap into
the future.

In this manner the position and duty of the scholar in
America are modified and made peculiar; and thus is the
mode determined for him, in which to pay for his education
in the manner most profitable to the public that has been at
the cost of his training.

There is a test by which we measure the force of a
horse or a steam-engine; the raising of so many pounds

through so many feet in a given time.   The test of the
scholar's power is his ability to raise men in their development.

In America there are three chief modes of acting upon
the public, omitting others of small account.   The first is
the power which comes of National Wealth; the next, that of
Political Station; the third, power of Spiritual Wealth, so to
say, eminent wisdom, justice, love, piety, the power of
sentiments and ideas, and the faculty of communicating them
to other men, and organizing them therein.   For the sake of
shortness, let each mode of power be symbolized by its instrument, and we have the power of the purse, of the office,
and the pen.

The purse represents the favourite mode of power with
us.   This is natural in our present stage of national existence
and human development; it is likely to continue for a long
time.   In all civilized countries which have outgrown the
period when the sword was the favourite emblem, the purse
represents the favourite mode of power with the mass of men;
but here it is so with the men of superior education.   This
power is not wholly personal, but extra-personal, and the
man's centre of gravity lies out of himself, less or more;
somewhere between the man and his last cent, the distance
being greater or less as the man is less or greater than the
estate.   This is wielded chiefly by men of little education,
except the practical culture which they have gained in the
process of accumulation.   Their riches they get purposely,
their training by the way, and accidentally.   It is a singular
misfortune of the country, that while the majority of the
people are better cultivated and more enlightened than any
other population in the world, the greater part of the wealth
of the nation is owned by men of less education and conse-
quently of less enlightenment than the rich men of any leading
nation in Europe.   In England and France the wealth of this
generation is chiefly inherited, and has generally fallen to
men carefully trained, with minds disciplined by academic
culture.   Here wealth is new, and mainly in the hands of
men who have scrambled for it adroitly and with vigour.
They have energy, vigour, forecast, and a certain generosity,
but as a class, are narrow, vulgar, and conceited.   Nine-
tenths of the property of the people is owned by one-tenth of
the persons; and these capitalists are men of little culture,
little moral elevation.   This is an accident of our position
unavoidable, perhaps transient; but it is certainly a misfortune that the great estates of the country, and the social and

political power of such wealth, should be mainly in the hands
of such men.   The melancholy result appears in many a disastrous shape; in the tone of the pulpit, of the press, and
of the national politics; much of the vulgarity of the nation is
to be ascribed to this fact, that wealth belongs to men who
know nothing better.

      The office represents the next most popular mode of
power.   This also is extra-personal, the man's centre of
gravity is out of himself, somewhere between him and the
lowest man in the State; the distance depending on the proportion of manhood in him and the multitude, if the office is
much greater than the man, then the officer's centre of
gravity is further removed from his person.   This is sought
for by the ablest and best educated men in the land.   But
there is a large class of educated persons who do not aspire
to it from lack of ability, for in our form of government it
commonly takes some saliency of character to win the high
places of office and use respectably this mode of power,
while it demands no great or lofty talents to accumulate the
largest fortune in America.   It is true the whirlwind of an
election, by the pressure of votes, may now and then take a
very heavy body up to a great height.   Yet it does not keep
him from growing giddy and ridiculous while there, and after
a few years lets him fall again into complete insignificance,
whence no Hercules can ever lift him up.   A corrupt administration may do the same, but with the same result.
This consideration keeps many educated men from the political arena; others are unwilling to endure the unsavoury
atmosphere of politics, and take part in a scramble so vulgar; but still a large portion of the educated and scholarly
talent of the nation goes to that work.

      The power of the pen is wholly personal.   It is the
appropriate instrument of the scholar, but it is least of all
desired and sought for.   The rich man sends his sons to
trade, to make too much of inheritance yet more by fresh
acquisitions of superfluity.   He does not send them to literature, art, or science.   You find the scholar slipping in to
other modes of action, not the merchants and politicians mi-
grating into this.   He longs to act by the gravity of his
money or station, not draw merely by his head.   The office
carries the day before the pen; the purse takes precedence
of both.   Educated men do not so much seek places that demand great powers, as those which bring much gold.   Self-
denial for money or office is common, for scholarship rare
and unpopular.   To act by money, not mind, is the ill-

concealed ambition of many a well-bred man; the desire of
this colours his day-dream, which is less of wisdom and
more of wealth, or of political station; so a first-rate clergyman desires to be razeed to a second-rate politician, and
some "tall admiral" of a politician consents to be cut down
and turned into a mere sloop of trade.   The representative
in Congress becomes a president of an insurance office or a
bank, or the agent of a cotton-mill; the judge deserts his
station on the bench, and presides over a railroad; the governor or senator wants a place in the post-office; the historian longs for a "chance in the custom-house. "   The pen
stoops to the office, that to the purse.   The scholar would
rather make a fortune by a balsam of wild cherry than write
Hamlet or Paradise Lost for nothing; rather than help mankind by making a Paradise Regained.   The well-endowed
minister thinks how much more money he might have made
had he speculated in stocks and not theology, and mourns
that the kingdom of heaven does not pay in this present life
fourfold.   The professor of Greek is sorry he was not a
surveyor and superintendent of a railroad, he should have
so much more money; that is what he has learned from
Plato and Diogenes.   We estimate the skill of an artist like
that of a pedler, not by the pictures he has made, but by
the money.   There is a mercantile way of determining literary merit, not by the author's books, but by his balance
with the publisher.   No church is yet called after a man who
is merely rich, something in the New Testament might hinder
that; but the ministers estimate their brother minister by the
greatness of his position, not of his character; not by his
piety and goodness, not even by his reason and understanding,
the culture he has attained thereby, and the use he makes
thereof, but by the wealth of his church and the largeness of
his salary; so that he is not thought the fortunate and great
minister who has a large outgo of spiritual riches, rebukes
the sins of the nation and turns many to righteousness, but
he who has a large material income, ministers, though
poorly, to rich men, and is richly paid for that function.
The well-paid clergymen of a city tell the professor of theology that he must teach "such doctrines as the merchants
approve, " or they will not give money to the college, and he,
it, and the "cause of the Lord, " will all come to the ground
at the same time and in kindred confusion.   So blind money
would put out the heavenly eyes of science, and lead her also
to his own ditch.   It must not be forgotten that there are
men in the midst of us, rich, respectable, and highly
honoured with social rank and political power, who practically
and in strict conformity with their theory, honour Judas, who

made money by his treachery, far more than Jesus who laid
down his life for men whose money is deemed better than
manhood. It must indeed be so. Any outrage that is profitable to the controlling portion of society is sure to be welcome to the leaders of the State, and is soon pronounced
divine by the leaders of the church.

It would seem as if the pen ought to represent the
favourite mode of power at a college; but even there the
waters of Pactolus are thought fairer than the Castalian,
Heliconian spring, or "Siloa's brook that flowed fast by the
oracle of God." The college is named after the men of
wealth, not genius. How few professorships in America bear
the names of men of science or letters, and not of mere rich
men! Which is thought the greatest benefactor of a college,
he who endows it with money or with mind? Even there it
is the purse, not the pen that is the symbol of honour, and
the University is "up for California," not Parnassus.

Even in politics the purse turns the scale. Let a
party wrestle never so hard, it cannot throw the dollar.
Money controls and commands talent, not talent money. The
successful shopkeeper frowns on and browbeats the accomplished politician, who has too much justice for the wharf and
the board of brokers; he notices that the rich men avert their
eye, or keep their beaver down, trembles and is sad, fearing
that his daughter will never find a fitting spouse. The purse
buys up able men of superior education, corrupts and keeps
them as its retained attorneys, in congress or the church,
not as counsel but advocate, bribed to make the worse appear
the better reason, and so help money to control the State and
wield its power against the interest of mankind. This is
perfectly well known; but no politician or minister, bribed to
silence or to speech, ever loses his respectability because
he is bought by respectable men, --if he get his pay. In all
countries but this the office is before the purse; here the
State is chiefly an accessory of the Exchange, and our politics
only mercantile. This appears sometimes against our will,
in symbols not meant to tell the tale. Thus in the House of
Representatives in Massachusetts, a cod-fish stares the
speaker in the face--not a very intellectual looking fish.
When it was put there it was a symbol of the riches of the
State, and so of the Commonwealth. With singular and unconscious satire it tells the legislature to have an eye "to
the main chance," and, but for its fidelity to its highest instincts and its obstinate silence, might be a symbol good
enough for the place.

Now, after the office and the purse have taken their
votaries from the educated class, the ablest men are certainly not left behind. Three roads open before our young
Hercules as he leaves college, having respectively as finger-
post, the pen, the office, and the purse. Few follow the
road of letters. This need not be much complained of;--nay,
it might be rejoiced in, if the purse and the office in their
modes of power did represent the higher consciousness of
mankind. But no one contends it is so.

Still there are men who devote themselves to some
literary callings, which have no connection with political
office, and which are not pursued for the sake of great
wealth. Such men produce the greater part of the permanent literature of the country. They are eminently scholars;
permanent scholars who act by their scholar-craft, not by the
state-craft of the politician, or the purse-craft of the capitalist. How are these men paying their debt and performing
their function? The answer must be found in the science and
the literature of the land.

American science is something of which we may well
be proud. Mr. Liebig, in Germany, has found it necessary
to defend himself from the charge of following science for the
loaves and fishes thereof; and he declares that he espoused
chemistry not for her wealthy dower, not even for the
services her possible children might render to mankind, but
solely for her own sweet sake. Amongst the English race,
on both sides of the ocean, science is loved rather for the
fruit than the blossom; its service to the body is thought of
more value than its service to the mind. A man's respectability would be in danger, in America, if he loved any
science better than the money or fame it might bring. It is
characteristic of us that a scholar should write for reputation
and gold. Here, as elsewhere, the unprofitable parts of
science fall to the lot of poor men. When the rich man's
son has the natural calling that way, public opinion would
dissuade him from the study of nature. The greatest scientific attainments do not give a man so high social consideration as a political office or a successful speculation--
unless it be the science which makes money. Scientific
schools we call after merely rich men, not men of wealthy
minds. It is true we name streets and squares, towns and
counties, after Franklin, but it is because he keeps the lightning from factories, churches, and barns; tells us not "to
give too much for the whistle, " and teaches "the way to make
money plenty in every man's pocket. " We should not name

them after Cuvier and La Place.

Notwithstanding this, the scientific scholars of
America, both the home-born and the adopted sons, have
manfully paid for their culture, and done honour to the land.
This is true of men in all departments of science, --from
that which searches the deeps of the sky to that which ex-
plores the shallows of the sea.   Individuals, States, and the
nation, have all done themselves honour by the scientific re-
searches and discoveries that have been made.   The outlay
of money and of genius for things which only pay the head
and not the mouth of man, is beautiful and a little surprising
in such a utilitarian land as this.   Time would fail me to
attend to particular cases.

Look at the literature of America.   Reserving the exceptional portion thereof to be examined in a moment, let us
study the instantial portion of it, American literature as a
whole.   This may be distributed into two main divisions:
First comes the permanent literature, consisting of works
not designed merely for a single and transient occasion, but
elaborately wrought for a general purpose.   This is literature proper.   Next follows the transient literature, which is
brought out for a particular occasion, and designed to serve
a special purpose.   Let us look at each.

The permanent literature of America is poor and
meagre; it does not bear the mark of manly hands of original, creative minds.   Most of it is rather milk for babes
than meat for men, though much of it is neither fresh meat
nor new milk, but the old dish often served up before.   In
respect to its form, this portion of our literature is an
imitation.   That is natural enough, considering the youth of
the country.   Every nation, like every man, even one born
to genius, begins by imitation.   Raphael, with servile pencil, followed his masters in his youth; but at length his
artistic eye attracted new-born angels from the calm still-
ness of their upper heaven, and with liberal, free hand, with
masterly and original touch, the painter of the newness
amazed the world.

The early Christian literature is an imitation of the
Hebrew or the classic type; even after centuries had passed
by, Sidonius, though a bishop of the church, and destined to
become a saint, uses the old heathen imagery, referring to
Triptolemus as a model for Christian work, and talks about
Triton and Galatea to the Christian Queen of the Goths.

Saint Ambrose is a notorious imitator of pagan Cicero. The
Christians were all anointed with Jewish nard; and the sour
grapes they ate in sacrament have set on edge their children's teeth till now.   The modern nations of Europe began
their literature by the driest copies of Livy and Virgil. The
Germans have the most original literature of the last hundred years.   But till the middle of the past century their
permanent literature was chiefly in Latin and French, with
as little originality as our own.   The real poetic life of the
nation found vent in other forms.   It is natural, therefore,
and according to the course of history, that we should begin
in this way.   The best political institutions of England are
cherished here, so her best literature; and it is not surprising that we are content with this rich inheritance of artistic
toil.   In many things we are independent, but in much that
relates to the higher works of man, we are still colonies of
England.   This appears not only in the vulgar fondness for
English fashions, manners, and the like, which is chiefly an
affectation, but in the servile style with which we copy the
great or little models of English literature.   Sometimes this
is done consciously, oftener without knowing it.

But the substance of our permanent literature is as
faulty as its form.   It does not bear marks of a new, free,
vigorous mind at work, looking at things from the American
point of view, and, though it put its thought in antique forms,
yet thinking originally and for itself.   It represents the
average thought of respectable men, directed to some particular subject, and their average morality.   It represents
nothing more; how could it, while the ablest men have gone
off to politics or trade?   It is such literature as almost
anybody might get up if you would give him a little time to
make the preliminary studies.   There is little in it that is
national; little individual and of the writer's own mind; it is
ground out in the public literary mill.   It has no noble sentiments, no great ideas; nothing which makes you burn; nothing
which makes you much worse or much better.   You may feed
on this literature all your days, and whatsoever you may
gain in girth, you shall not take in thought enough to add
half an inch to your stature.

Out of every hundred American literary works printed
since the century began, about eight will be of this character.
Compare the four most conspicuous periodicals of America
with the four great Quarterlies of England, and you see how
inferior our literature is to theirs--in all things, in form
and in substance too.   The European has the freedom of a

well-bred man--it appears in the movement of his thought,
his use of words, in the easy grace of his sentences, and
the general manner of his work; the American has the stiff-
ness and limitations of a big, raw boy, in the presence of
his schoolmaster.   They are proud of being English, and so
have a certain lofty nationality which appears in their thought
and the form thereof, even in the freedom to use and invent
new words.   Our authors of this class seem ashamed that
they are Americans, and accordingly are timid, ungraceful,
and weak.   They dare not be original when they could.
Hence this sort of literature is dull.   A man of the average
mind and conscience, heart, and soul, studies a particular
subject a short time--for this is the land of brief processes
--and writes a book thereof, or thereon; a critic of the same
average makes his special study of the book, not its theme,
"reviews" the work; is as ready and able to pass judgment
on Bowditch's translation of La Place in ten days after its
appearance as ten years, and distributes praise and blame,
not according to the author's knowledge, but the critic's ignorant caprice; and then average men read the book and the
critique with no immoderate joy or unmeasured grief.   They
learn some new facts, no new ideas, and get no lofty impulse.   The book was written without inspiration, without
philosophy, and is read with small profit.   Yet it is curious
to observe the praise which such men receive, how soon
they are raised to the House of Lords in English literature.
I have known three American Sir Walter Scotts, half a dozen
Addisons, one or two Macaulays--a historian that was Hume
and Gibbon both in one, several Burnses, and Miltons by the
quantity, not "mute," the more is the pity, but "inglorious"
enough; nay, even vain-glorious at the praise which some
penny-a-liner or dollar-a-pager foolishly gave their cheap
extemporary stuff.   In sacred literature it is the same: in
a single winter at Boston we had two American Saint Johns,
in full blast for several months.   Though no Felix trembles,
there are now extant in the United States not less than six
American Saint Pauls, in no manner of peril except the most
dangerous--of idle praise.

          A living, natural, and full-grown literature contains
two elements.   One is of mankind in general; that is human
and universal.   The other is of the tribe in special, and of
the writer in particular.   This is national and even personal:
you see the idiosyncracy of the nation and the individual
author in the work.   The universal human substance accepts
the author's form, and the public wine of mankind runs into
the private bottle of the author.   Thus the Hebrew literature

of the Old Testament is fresh and original in substance and
in form; the two elements are plain enough, the universal
and the particular.   The staple of the Psalms of David is
human, of mankind, it is trust of God; but the twist, the
die, the texture, the pattern, all that is Hebrew--of the
tribe, and personal--of David, shepherd, warrior, poet,
king.   You see the pastoral hill-sides of Judaea in his holy
hymns; nay, "Uriah's beauteous wife" now and then sidles
into his sweetest psalm.   The Old Testament books smell of
Palestine, of its air and its soil.   The Rose of Sharon has
Hebrew earth about its roots.   The geography of the Holy
Land, its fauna and its flora both, even its wind and sky, its
early and its latter rain, all appear in the literature of historian and bard.   It is so in the Iliad.   You see how the
sea looked from Homer's point of view, and know how he
felt the west wind, cold and raw.   The human element has
an Ionian form and a Homeric hue.   The ballads of the
people in Scotland and England are national in the same way;
the staple of human life is wrought into the Scottish form.
Before the Germans had any permanent national literature of
this character, their fertile mind found vent in legends,
popular stories, now the admiration of the learned.   These
had at home the German dress, but as the stories travelled
into other lands, they kept their human flesh and blood, but
took a different garb, and acquired a different complexion
from every country which they visited; and, like the streams
of their native Swabia, took the colour of the soil they
travelled through.

        The permanent and instantial literature of America is
not national in this sense.   It has little that is American;
it might as well be written by some bookwright in Leipsic
or London, and then imported.   The individuality of the
nation is not there, except in the cheap, gaudy binding of
the work.   The nationality of America is only stamped on
the lids, and vulgarly blazoned on the back.

        Is the book a history?--it is written with no such
freedom as you should expect of a writer, looking at the
breadth of the world from the lofty stand-point of America.
There is no new philosophy of history in it.   You would not
think it was written in a democracy that keeps the peace
without armies or a national gaol.   Mr. Macaulay writes the
history of England as none but a North Briton could do.
Astonishingly well-read, equipped with literary skill at least
equal to the masterly art of Voltaire, mapping out his subject like an engineer, and adorning it like a painter, you yet

see, all along, that the author is a Scotchman and a Whig.
Nobody else could have written so.   It is of Mr. Macaulay.
But our American writer thinks about matters just as everybody else does; that is, he does not think at all, but only
writes what he reads, and then, like the good-natured bear
in the nursery story, "thinks he has been thinking." It is
no such thing, he has been writing the common opinion of
common men, to get the applause of men as common as
himself.

Is the book of poetry?--the substance is chiefly old,
the form old, the allusions are old.   It is poetry of society,
not of nature.   You meet in it the same everlasting mythology, the same geography, botany, zoology, the same symbols; a new figure of speech suggested by the sight of nature,
not the reading of books, you could no more find than a
fresh shad in the Dead Sea.   You take at random eight or
ten "American poets" of this stamp, you see at once what
was the favourite author with each new bard; you often see
what particular work of Shelley, or Tennyson, or Milton, or
George Herbert, or, if the man has culture enough, of
Goethe, or Uhland, Jean Paul, or Schiller, suggested the
"American original." His inspiration comes from literature,
not from the great universe of nature or of human life.   You
see that this writer has read Percy's Reliques, and the
German Wunderhorn; but you would not know that he wrote
in a republic--in a land full of new life, with great rivers
and tall mountains, with maple and oak trees that turn red
in the autumn; amongst a people who hold town-meetings,
have free schools for everybody, read newspapers voraciously,
who have lightning rods on their steeples, ride in railroads,
are daguerreotyped by the sun, and who talk by lightning
from Halifax to New Orleans; who listen to the whippoorwill
and the bobolink, who believe in Slavery and the Declaration
of Independence, in the devil and the five points of Calvinism.   You would not know where our poet lived, or that he
lived anywhere.   Reading the Iliad, you doubt that Homer
was born blind; but our bard seems to have been deaf also,
and for expressing what was national in his time, might
likewise have been dumb.

Is it a volume of sermons?--they might have been
written at Edinburgh, Madrid, or Constantinople, as well as
in New England; as well preached to the "Homo Sapiens" of
Linnaeus, or the man in the moon, as to the special audience that heard, or heard them not, but only paid for having
the things preached.   There is nothing individual about them;

the author seems as impersonal as Spinoza's conception of
God. The sermons are like an almanack calculated for the
meridian of no place in particular, for no time in special.
There is no allusion to anything American. The author
never mentions a river this side of the Jordan; knows no
mountain but Lebanon, Zion, and Carmel, and would think it
profane to talk of the Alleghanies and the Mississippi, of
Monadnock and the Androscoggin. He mentions Babylon and
Jerusalem, not New York and Baltimore; you would never
dream that he lived in a church without a bishop, and a
State without a king, in a democratic nation that held three
million slaves, with ministers chosen by the people. He is
surrounded, clouded over, and hid by the traditions of the
"ages of faith" behind him. He never thanks God for the
dew and snow, only for "the early and the latter rain" of a
classic sacred land; a temperance man, he blesses God for
the wine because the great Psalmist did so thousands of
years ago. He speaks of the olive and the fig-tree which he
never saw, not of the apple-tree and the peach before his
eyes all day long, their fruit the joy of his children's heart.
If you guessed at his time and place, you would think he
lived, not under General Taylor, but under King Ahab, or
Jeroboam; that his audience rode on camels or in chariots,
not in steam-cars; that they fought with bows and arrows
against the children of Moab; that their favourite sin was the
worship of some graven image, and that they made their
children pass through the fire unto Moloch, not through the
counting-house unto Mammon. You would not know whether
the preacher was married or a bachelor, rich or poor,
saint or sinner; you would probably conclude he was not
much of a saint, nor even much of a sinner.

　　The authors of this portion of our literature seem
ashamed of America. One day she will take her revenge.
They are the parasites of letters, and live on what other
men have made classic. They would study the Holy Land,
Greece, Etruria, Egypt, Nineveh, spots made famous by
great and holy men, and let the native races of America
fade out, taking no pains to study the monuments which so
swiftly pass away from our own continent. It is curious
that most of the accounts of the Indians of North America
come from men not natives here, from French and Germans; and characteristic that we should send an expedition
to the Dead Sea, while wide tracts of this continent lie all
untouched by the white man's foot; and, also, that while we
make such generous and noble efforts to christianize and
bless the red, yellow, and black heathens at the world's end,

we should leave the American Indian and Negro to die in savage darkness, the South making it penal to teach a black man to write or read.

Yet, there is one portion of our permanent literature, if literature it may be called, which is wholly indigenous and original. The lives of the early martyrs and confessors are purely Christian, so are the legends of saints and other pious men: there was nothing like this in the Hebrew or heathen literature; cause and occasion were alike wanting for it. So we have one series of literary productions that could be written by none but Americans, and only here: I mean the Lives of Fugitive Slaves. But as these are not work of the men of superior culture, they hardly help to pay the scholar's debt. Yet all the original romance of America is in them, not in the white man's novel.

Next is the transient literature, composed chiefly of speeches, orations, state papers, political and other occasional pamphlets, business reports, articles in the journals, and other productions designed to serve some present purpose. These are commonly the work of educated men, though not of such as make literature a profession. Taking this department as a whole, it differs much from the permanent literature; here is freshness of thought and newness of form. If American books are mainly an imitation of old models, it would be difficult to find the prototype of some American speeches. They "would have made Quintilian stare and gasp." Take the State papers of the American government during the administration of Mr. Polk, the speeches made in Congress at the same time, the State papers of the several States--you have a much better and more favourable idea of the vigour and originality of the American mind, than you would get from all the bound books printed in that period. The diplomatic writings of American politicians compare favourably with those of any nation in the world. In eloquence no modern nation is before us, perhaps none is our equal. Here you see the inborn strength and manly vigour of the American mind. You meet the same spirit which fells the forest, girdles the land with railroads, annexes Texas, and covets Cuba, Nicaragua, all the world. You see that the authors of this literature are workers also. Others have read of wild beasts; here are the men that have seen the wolf.

A portion of this literature represents the past, and has the vices already named. It comes from human history

and not human nature; as you read it, you think of the inertia and the cowardliness of mankind; nothing is progressive, nothing noble, generous, or just, only respectable.
The past is preferred before the present; money is put before men, a vested right before a natural right.   Such literature appears in all countries.   The ally of despotism,
and the foe of mankind, it is yet a legitimate exponent of a
large class of men.   The leading journals of America, political and commercial, or literary, are poor and feeble;
our reviews of books afford matter for grave consideration.
You would often suppose them written by the same hand
which manufactures the advertisements of the grand caravan,
or some patent medicine; or, when unfavourable, by some of
the men who write defamatory articles on the eve of an
election.

     But a large part of this transient literature is very
different in its character.   Its authors have broken with the
traditions of the past; they have new ideas, and plans for
putting them in execution; they are full of hope; are national
to the extreme, bragging and defiant.   They put the majority
before institutions; the rights of the majority before the
privilege of a few; they represent the onward tendency and
material prophecy of the nation.   The new activity of the
American mind here expresses its purpose and its prayer.
Here is strength, hope, confidence, even audacity; all is
American.   But the great idea of the absolute right does not
appear, all is more national than human; and in what concerns the nation, it is not justice, the point where all interests are balanced, and the welfare of each harmonizes
with that of all, which is sought; but the "greatest good of
the greatest number;" that is, only a privilege had at the
cost of the smaller number.   Here is little respect for universal humanity; little for the eternal laws of God, which
override all the traditions and contrivances of men; more
reverence for a statute, or constitution, which is indeed the
fundamental law of the political State, but is often only an
attempt to compromise between the fleeting passions of the
day and the immutable morality of God.

     Amid all the public documents of the nation and the
several States, in the speeches and writings of favourite men,
who represent and so control the public mind, for fifty
years, there is little that "stirs the feelings infinite" within
you; much to make us more American, not more manly.
There is more head than heart; native intellect enough; culture that is competent, but little conscience, or real religion.

How many newspapers, how many politicians in the land go
at all beyond the Whig idea of protecting the property now
accumulated, or the democratic idea of insuring the greatest
material good of the greatest number?   Where are we to
look for the representative of justice, of the unalienable
rights of all the people and all the nations?   In the triple
host of article-makers, speech-makers, lay and clerical,
and makers of laws, you find but few who can be trusted to
stand up for the unalienable rights of men; who will never
write, speak, nor vote in the interests of a party, but always in the interest of mankind, and will represent the justice of God in the forum of the world.

This literature, like the other, fails of the high end
of writing and of speech; with more vigour, more freedom,
more breadth of vision, and an intense nationality, the
authors thereof are just as far from representing the higher
consciousness of mankind, just as vulgar as the tame and
well-licked writers of the permanent literature.   Here are
the men who have cut their own way through the woods, men
with more than the average intelligence, daring, and strength;
but with less than the average justice which is honesty in the
abstract, less than the average honesty which is justice concentrated upon small particulars.

Examine both these portions of American literature,
the permanent and the fleeting--you see their educated
authors are no higher than the rest of men.   They are the
slaves of public opinion, as much as the gossip in her little
village.   It may not be the public opinion of a coterie of
crones, but of a great party; that makes little odds, they are
worshippers of the same rank, idolaters of the same wealth;
the gossipping granny shows her littleness the size of life,
while their deformity is magnified by the solar microscope
of high office.   Many a popular man exhibits his pigmy soul
to the multitude of a whole continent, idly mistaking it for
greatness.   They are swayed by vulgar passions, seek vulgar ends, address vulgar motives, use vulgar means; they
may command by their strength, they cannot refine by their
beauty or instruct by their guidance, and still less inspire
by any eminence of manhood which they were born to or have
won.   They build on the surface-sand for to-day, not on the
rock of ages for ever.   With so little conscience, they heed
not the solemn voice of history, and respect no more the
prophetic instincts of mankind.

To most men, the approbation of their fellows is one
of the most desirable things.   This approbation appears in

the various forms of admiration, respect, esteem, confidence, veneration, and love. The great man obtains this after a time, and in its highest forms, without seeking it, simply by faithfulness to his nature. He gets it by rising and doing his work, in the course of nature, as easily and as irresistibly as the sun gathers to the clouds the evaporation of land and sea, and, like the sun, to shed it down in blessings on mankind. Little men seek this, consciously or not knowing it, by stooping, cringeing, flattering the pride, the passion, or the prejudice of others. So they get the approbation of men, but never of man. Sometimes this is sought for by the attainment of some accidental quality, which low-minded men hold in more honour than the genius of sage or poet, or the brave manhood of some great hero of the soul. In England, though money is power, it is patrician birth which is nobility, and valued most; and there, accordingly, birth takes precedence of all--of genius, and even of gold. Men seek the companionship or the patronage of titled lords, and social rank depends upon nobility of blood. The few bishops in the upper house do more to give conventional respectability to the clerical profession there, than all the solid intellect of Hooker, Barrow, and of South, the varied and exact learning of philosophic Cudworth, the eloquence and affluent piety of Taylor, and Butler's vast and manly mind. In America, social rank depends substantially on wealth, an accident as much as noble birth, but moveable. Here gold takes precedence of all, --of genius, and even of noble birth.

> Though your sire
> Had royal blood within him, and though you
> Possess the intellect of angels too,
> 'Tis all in vain; the world will ne'er inquire
> On such a score:--Why should it take the pains?
> "tis easier to weigh purses, sure, than brains.

Wealth is sought, not merely as a means of power, but of nobility. When obtained, it has the power of nobility; so poor men of superior intellect and education, powerful by nature, not by position, fear to disturb the opinion of wealthy men, to instruct their ignorance or rebuke their sin. Hence the aristocracy of wealth, illiterate and vulgar, goes unrebuked, and debases the natural aristocracy of mind and culture which bows down to it. The artist prostitutes his pencil and his skill, and takes his law of beauty from the fat clown, whose barns and pigs, and wife, he paints for daily bread. The preacher does the same; and though the stench

of the rum-shop infests the pulpit, and death hews down the
leaders of his flock, the preacher must cry, "Peace, peace,"
or else be still, for rum is power! But this power of
wealth has its antagonistic force--the power of numbers.
Much depends on the dollar. Nine-tenths of the property is
owned by one-tenth of all these men--but much also on the
votes of the million. The few are strong by money, the
many by their votes. Each is worshipped by its votaries,
and its approbation sought. He that can get the men controls the money too. So while one portion of educated men
bows to the rich, and consecrates their passion and their
prejudice, another portion bows, equally prostrate, to the
passions of the multitude of men. The many and the rich
have each a public opinion of their own, and both are tyrants.
Here the tyranny of public opinion is not absolutely greater
than in England, Germany, or France, but is far greater in
comparison with other modes of oppression. It seems inherent in a republic; it is not in a republic of noble men.
But here this sirocco blows flat to the ground full many an
aspiring blade. Wealth can establish banks or factories;
votes can lift the meanest man into the highest political
place, can dignify any passion with the name and force of
human law; so it is thought by the worshippers of both, seeking the approbation of the two, that public opinion can make
truth of lies, and right even out of foulest wrong. Politicians begin to say, there is no law of God above the ephemeral laws of men.

There are few American works of literature which
appeal to what is best in men; few that one could wish should
go abroad and live. America has grown beyond hope in population, the free and bond, in riches, in land, in public material prosperity, but in a literature that represents the
higher elements of manliness far less than wise men thought.
They looked for the fresh new child; it is born with wrinkles,
and dreadfully like his grandmother, only looking older and
more effete. Our muse does not come down from an
American Parnassus, with a new heaven in her eye, men
not daring to look on the face of anointed beauty, coming to
tell of noble thought, to kindle godlike feelings with her celestial spark, and stir mankind to noble deeds. She finds
Parnassus steep and high, and hard to climb; the air austere
and cold, the light severe, too stern for her effeminate
nerves. So she has a little dwelling in the flat and close-
pent town, hard by the public street; breathes its Boeotian
breath; walks with the money-lenders at high change; has her
account at the bank, her pew in the most fashionable church

and least austere; she gets approving nods in the street,
flattery in the penny prints, sweetmeats and sparkling wine
in the proper places.   What were the inspirations of all
God's truth to her?   He "taunts the lofty land with little
men. "

There still remains the exceptional literature; some
of it is only fugitive, some meant for permanent duration.
Here is a new and different spirit; a respect for human nature above human history, for man above all the accidents of
man, for God above all the alleged accidents of God; a veneration for the eternal laws which He only makes and man
but finds; a law before all statutes, above all constitutions,
and holier than all the writings of human hands.   Here you
find most fully the sentiments and ideas of America, not
such as rule the nation now, but which, unconsciously to the
people, have caused the noble deeds of our history, and now
prophesy a splendid future for this young giant here.   These
sentiments and ideas are brought to consciousness in this
literature.   Here a precedent is not a limitation; a fact of
history does not eclipse an idea of nature; an investment is
not thought more sacred than a right.   Here is more hope
than memory; little deference to wealth and rank, but a constant aspiration for truth, justice, love, and piety; little fear
of the public opinion of the many or the few, rather a scorn
thereof, almost a defiance of it.   It appears in books, in
pamphlets, in journals, and in sermons, sorely scant in
quantity as yet.   New and fresh, it is often greatly deficient
in form; rough, rude, and uncouth, it yet has in it a soul
that will live.   Its authors are often men of a wide and fine
culture, though mainly tending to underrate the past achievements of mankind.   They have little reverence for great
names.   They value the Greek and Hebrew mind for no more
than it is worth.   With them a wrong is no more respected
because well descended, and supported by all the riches, all
the votes; a right, not less a right because unjustly kept out
of its own.   These men are American all through; so intensely national, that they do not fear to tell the nation of
the wrong it does.

The form of this literature is American.   It is indigenous to our soil, and could come up in no other land.   It
is unlike the classic literature of any other nation.   It is
American as the Bible is Hebrew, and the Odyssey is Greek.
It is wild and fantastic, like all fresh original literature at
first.   You see in it the image of republican institutions--the
free school, free state, free church; it reflects the counte-

nance of free men. So the letters of old France, of modern
England, of Italy and Spain, reflect the monarchic, oligarchic,
and ecclesiastic institutions of those lands. Here appears
the civilization of the nineteenth century, the treasures of
human toil for many a thousand years. More than that, you
see the result of a fresh contact with nature, and original
intuitions of divine things. Acknowledging inspiration of old,
these writers of the newness believe in it now not less, not
miraculous, but normal. Here is humanity that overleaps
the bounds of class and of nation, and sees a brother in the
beggar, pirate, slave, one family of men variously dressed
in cuticles of white or yellow, black or red. Here, too, is
a new loveliness, somewhat akin to the savage beauty of our
own wild woods, seen in their glorious splendour an hour before autumnal suns go down and leave a trail of glory lingering in the sky. Here, too, is a piety somewhat heedless of
scriptures, liturgies, and forms and creeds; it finds its law
written in nature, its glorious everlasting gospel in the soul
of man; careless of circumcision and baptismal rites, it
finds the world a temple, and rejoices everywhere to hold
communion with the Infinite Father of us all, and keep a
sacrament in daily life, conscious of immortality, and feed-
ing continually on angels' bread.

    The writers of this new literature are full of faults;
yet they are often strong, though more by their direction
than by native force of mind; more by their intuitions of the
first good, first perfect, and first fair, than through their
historical knowledge or dialectic power. Their ship sails
swift, not because it is sharper built, or carries broader
sails than other craft, but because it steers where the current of the ocean coincides with the current of the sky, and
so is borne along by nature's wind and nature's wave. Un-
invited, its ideas steal into parlour and pulpit, its kingdom
coming within men and without observation. The shoemaker
feels it as he toils in his narrow shop; it cheers the maiden
weaving in the mill, whose wheels the Merrimac is made to
turn; the young man at college bids it welcome to his ingenuous soul. So at the breath of spring new life starts up
in every plant; the sloping hills are green with corn, and
sunny banks are blue and fragrant with the wealth of violets,
which only slept till the enchanter came. The sentiments of
this literature burn in the bosom of holy-hearted girls, of
matrons, and of men. Ever and anon its great ideas are
heard even in Congress, and in the speech of old and young,
which comes tingling into most unwilling ears.

This literature has a work to do, and is about its
work.   Let the old man crow loud as he may, the young one
will crow another strain; for it is written of God, that our
march is continually onward, and age shall advance over age
for ever and for ever.

Already America has a few fair specimens from this
new field to show.   Is the work history?   The author writes
from the stand-point of American democracy, --I mean philanthropy, the celestial democracy, not the satanic; writes
with a sense of justice and in the interest of men; writes to
tell a nation's purpose in its deeds, and so reveal the universal law of God, which overrules the affairs of States as
of a single man.   You wonder that history was not before so
writ that its facts told the nation's ideas, and its labours
were lessons, and so its hard-won life became philosophy.

Is it poetry the man writes?   It is not poetry like the
old.   The poet has seen nature with his own eyes, heard her
with his own mortal, bodily ears, and felt her presence, not
vicariously through Milton, Uhland, Ariosto, but personally,
her heart against his heart.   He sings of what he knows,
sees, feels, not merely of what he reads in others' song.
Common things are not therefore unclean.   In plain New
England life he finds his poetry, as magnets iron in the
blacksmith's dust, and as the bee finds dew-bright cups of
honey in the common woods and common weeds.   It is not
for him to rave of Parnassus, while he knows it not, for
the soul of song has a seat upon Monadnock, Wachusett, or
Katahdin, quite as high.   So Scottish Burns was overtaken by
the muse of poetry, who met him on his own bleak hills,
and showed him beauty in the daisy and the thistle, and the
tiny mouse, till to his eye the hills ran o'er with loveliness,
and Caledonia became a classic land.

Is it religion the author treats of?   It is not worship
by fear, but through absolute faith, a never-ending love; for
it is not worship of a howling and imperfect God, grim,
jealous, and revengeful, loving but a few, and them not well,
--but of the Infinite Father of all mankind, whose universal
providence will sure achieve the highest good of all that are.

These men are few; in no land are they numerous, or
were or will be.   There were few Hebrew prophets, but a
tribe of priests; there are but few mighty bards that hover
o'er the world; but here and there a sage, looking deep and
living high, who feels the heart of things, and utters oracles

which pass for proverbs, psalms and prayers, and stimulate
a world of men.   They draw the nations, as conjoining
moon and sun draw waters shore-ward from the ocean
springs; and as electrifying heat they elevate the life of men.
Under their influence you cannot be as before.   They stimulate the sound, and intoxicate the silly; but in the heart of
noble youths their idea becomes a fact, and their prayer a
daily life.

Scholars of such a stamp are few and rare, not without great faults.   For every one of them there will be many
imitators, as for each lion a hundred lion-flies, thinking
their buzz as valiant as his roar, and wondering the forest
does not quake thereat, and while they feed on him fancy
they suck the breasts of heaven.

Such is the scholars' position in America; such their
duty, and such the way in which they pay the debt they owe.
Will men of superior culture not all act by scholar-craft and
by the pen?   It were a pity if they did.   If a man work
nobly, the office is as worthy, and the purse as blessed in
its work.   The pen is power; the office is power; the purse
is power; and if the purse and office be nobly held, then in
a high mode the cultivated man pays for his bringing up, and
honours with wide sympathies the mass of men who give him
chance to ride and rule.   If not; if these be meanly held,
for self and not for man, then the scholar is a debtor and
a traitor too.

The scholar never had so fair a chance before; here
is the noblest opportunity for one that wields the pen; it is
mightier than the sword, the office, or the purse.   All
things concede at last to beauty, justice, truth and love, and
these he is to represent.   He has what freedom he will pay
for and take.   Let him talk never so heroic, he will find fit
audience, nor will it long be few.   Men will rise up and
welcome his quickening words as vernal grass at the first
rains of spring.   A great nation which cannot live by bread
alone, asks for the bread of life; while the State is young,
a single great and noble man can deeply influence the nation's mind.   There are great wrongs which demand redress;
the present men who represent the office and the purse will
not end these wrongs.   They linger for the pen, with magic
touch, to abolish and destroy this ancient serpent-brood.
Shall it be only rude men and unlettered who confront the
dragons of our time which prowl about the folds by day and
night, while the scholar, the appointed guardian of mankind,

but "sports with Amaryllis in the shade, or with the tangles
of Neaera's hair?" The nation asks of her scholar better
things than ancient letters ever brought; asks his wonders
for the million, not the few alone. Great sentiments burn
now in half-unconscious hearts, and great ideas kindle their
glories round the heads of men. Unconscious electricity,
truth and right, flashes out of the earth, out of the air. It
is for the scholar to attract this ground-lightning and this
lightning of the sky, condense it into useful thunder to destroy the wrong, then spread it forth a beauteous and a
cheering light, shedding sweet influence and kindling life
anew. A few great men of other times tell us what may be
now.

Nothing will be done without toil--talent is only power
of work, and genius greater power for higher forms of work
--nothing without self-denial; nothing great and good save by
putting your idea before yourself, and counting it dearer
than your flesh and blood. Let it hide you, not your obesity
conceal the truth God gave you to reveal. The quality of intellectual work is more than the quantity. Out of the cloudy
world Homer has drawn a spark that lasts three thousand
years. "One, but a lion, " should be the scholar's maxim;
let him do many things for daily need; one great thing for
the eternal beauty of his art. A single poem of Dante, a
book for the bosom, lives through the ages, surrounding its
author with the glory of genius in the night of time. One
sermon on the mount, compact of truths brought down from
God, all molten by such pious trust in Him, will stir men's
hearts by myriads, while words, dilute with other words are
a shame to the speaker, and a dishonour to men who have
ears to hear.

It is a great charity to give beauty to mankind; part
of the scholar's function. How we honour such as create
mere sensuous loveliness! Mozart carves it on the unseen
air; Phidias sculptures it out from the marble stone; Raphael
fixes ideal angels, maidens, matrons, men and his triple
God upon the canvas; and the lofty Angelo, with more than
Amphionic skill, bids the hills rise into a temple which constrains the crowd to pray. Look, see how grateful man re-
pays these architects of beauty with never-ending fame!
Such as create a more than sensuous loveliness, for Homers,
Miltons, Shakespeares, who sing of man in never-dying and
creative song--see what honours we have in store for such;
what honour given for what service paid! But there is a
beauty higher than that of art, above philosophy and merely

intellectual grace; I mean the loveliness of noble life; that
is a beauty in the sight of man and God. This is a new
country, the great ideas of a noble man are easily spread
abroad; soon they will appear in the life of the people, and
be a blessing in our future history to ages yet unborn.   A
few great souls can correct the licentiousness of the American press, which is now but the type of covetousness and
low ambition; correct the mean economy of the State, and
amend the vulgarity of the American church, now the poor
prostitute of every wealthy sin.

Oh, ingenuous young maid or man, if such you are,
--if not, then let me dream you such, --seek you this beauty,
complete perfection of a man, and having this, go hold the
purse, the office, or the pen, as suits you best; but out of
that life, writing, voting, acting, living in all forms, you
shall pay men back for your culture, and in the scholar's
noble kind, and represent the higher facts of human thought.
Will men still say, "This wrong is consecrated; it has
stood for ages, and shall stand for ever!" Tell them, "No.
A wrong, though old as sin, is not now sacred, nor shall
it stand!" Will they say, "This right can never be; that
excellence is lovely, but impossible!" Show them the fact,
who will not hear the speech; the deed goes where the word
fails, and life enchants where rhetoric cannot persuade.

Past ages offer their instruction, much warning, and
a little guidance, many a wreck along the shore of time, a
beacon here and there. Far off in the dim distance, present as possibilities, not actual as yet, future generations,
with broad and wishful eyes, look at the son of genius,
talent, educated skill, and seem to say, "A word for us; it
will not be forgot!" Truth and Beauty, God's twin daughters,
eternal both, yet ever young, wait there to offer each faithful man a budding branch, --in their hands budding, in his
to blossom and mature its fruit, --wherewith he sows the
field of time, gladdening the millions yet to come.

4. THE POLITICAL DESTINATION OF AMERICA AND THE SIGNS OF THE TIMES*

Every nation has a peculiar character, in which it differs from all others that have been, that are, and possibly from all that are to come; for it does not yet appear that the Divine Father of the nations ever repeats himself and creates either two nations or two men exactly alike. However, as nations, like men, agree in more things than they differ, and in obvious things too, the special peculiarity of any one tribe does not always appear at first sight. But if we look through the history of some nation which has passed off from the stage of action, we find certain prevailing traits which continually reappear in the language and laws thereof; in its arts, literature, manners, modes of religion--in short, in the whole life of the people. The most prominent thing in the history of the Hebrews is their continual trust in God, and this marks them from their first appearance to the present day. They have accordingly done little for art, science, philosophy, little for commerce and the useful arts of life, but much for religion; and the psalms they sung two or three thousand years ago are at this day the hymns and prayers of the whole Christian world. Three great historical forms of religion, Judaism, Christianity, and Mahometanism, all have proceeded from them.

He that looks at the Ionian Greeks, finds in their story always the same prominent characteristic, a devotion to what is beautiful. This appears often to the neglect of what is true, right, and therefore holy. Hence, while they have done little for religion, their literature, architecture, sculpture, furnish us with models never surpassed, and perhaps not equalled. Yet they lack the ideal aspiration after religion that appears in the literature and art, and even language of some other people, quite inferior to the Greeks in elegance and refinement. Science, also, is most largely indebted to these beauty-loving Greeks, for truth is one form of loveliness.

*Parker, Theodore. Collected Works, ed. F. Cobbe (London: Trübner, 1863-79), IV, 77-110.

If we take the Romans, from Romulus their first king, to Augustulus, the last of the Caesars, the same traits of national character appear, only the complexion and dress thereof changed by circumstances.   There is always the same hardness and materialism the same skill in organizing men, the same turn for affairs and genius for legislation. Rome borrowed her theology and liturgical forms; her art, science, literature, philosophy, and eloquence; even her art of war was an imitation.   But law sprung up indigenous in her soil; her laws are the best gift she offers to the human race, --the "monument more lasting than brass, " which she has left behind her.

We may take another nation, which has by no means completed its history, the Saxon race, from Hengist and Horsa to Sir Robert Peel; there also is a permanent peculiarity in the tribe.   They are yet the same bold, handy, practical people as when their bark first touched the savage shores of Britain; not over religious; less pious than moral; not so much upright before God, as downright before men; servants of the understanding more than children of reason; not following the guidance of an intuition, and the light of an idea, but rather trusting to experiment, facts, precedents, and usages; not philosophical, but commercial; warlike through strength and courage, not from love of war or its glory; material, obstinate, and grasping, with the same admiration of horses, dogs, oxen, and strong drink; the same willingness to tread down any obstacle, material, human, or divine, which stands in their way; the same impatient lust of wealth and power; the same disposition to colonize and re-annex other lands; the same love of liberty and love of law; the same readiness in forming political confederations.

In each of these four instances, the Hebrews, the Ionians, the Romans, and the Anglo-Saxon race, have had a nationality so strong, that while they have mingled with other nations in commerce and in war, as victors and vanquished, they have stoutly held their character through all; they have thus modified feebler nations joined with them.   To take the last, neither the Britons nor the Danes affected very much the character of the Anglo-Saxons; they never turned it out of its course.   The Normans gave the Saxon manners, refinement, letters, elegance.   The Anglo-Saxon bishop of the eleventh century, dressed in untanned sheep-skins, "the wooly side out and the fleshy side in;" he ate cheese and flesh, drank milk and mead.   The Norman taught him to wear cloth, to eat also bread and roots, to drink wine.   But in

other respects the Norman left him as he found him.   England has received her kings and her nobles from Normandy,
Anjou, the Provence, Scotland, Holland, Hanover, often
seeing a foreigner ascend her throne; yet the sturdy Anglo-
Saxon character held its own,   spite of the new element in-
fused into its blood: change the ministries, change the dyn-
asties often as they will, John Bull is obstinate as ever,
and himself changes not; no philosophy or religion makes
him less material.   No nation but the English could have
produced a Hobbes, a Hume, a Paley, or a Bentham; they
are all instantial and not exceptional men in that race.

    Now this idiosyncrasy of a nation is a sacred gift;
like the genius of a Burns, a Thorwaldsen, a Franklin, or
a Bowditch, it is given for some divine purpose, to be
sacredly cherished and patiently unfolded.   The cause of the
peculiarities of a nation or an individual man we cannot fully
determine as yet, and so we refer it to the chain of causes
which we call Providence.   But the national persistency in a
common type is easily explained.   The qualities of father and
mother are commonly transmitted to their children, but not
always, for peculiarities may lie latent in a family for generations, and reappear in the genius or the folly of a child--
often in the complexion and features: and, besides, father
and mother are often no match.   But such exceptions are
rare, and the qualities of a race are always thus reproduced,
the deficiency of one man getting counterbalanced by the re-
dundancy of the next: the marriages of a whole tribe are not
far from normal.

    Some nations, it seems, perish through defect of this
national character, as individuals fail of success through excess or deficiency in their character.   Thus the Celts--that
great flood of a nation which once swept over Germany,
France, England, and, casting its spray far over the Alps,
at one time threatened destruction to Rome itself--seem to
have been so filled with love of individual independence, that
they could never accept a minute organization of human
rights and duties; and so their children would not group
themselves into a city, as other races, and submit to a
strong central power, which should curb individual will
enough to insure national unity of action.   Perhaps this was
once the excellence of the Celts, and thereby they broke the
trammels and escaped from the theocratic or despotic traditions of earlier and more savage times, developing the
power of the individual for a time, and the energy of a nation
loosely bound; but when they came in contact with the Romans,

Franks, and Saxons, they melted away as snow in April--
only, like that, remnants thereof yet lingering in the mountains and islands of Europe.   No external pressure of famine
or political oppression now holds the Celts in Ireland together, or gives them national unity of action enough to resist the Saxon foe.   Doubtless in other days this very peculiarity of the Irish has done the world some service.   Nations
succeed each other as races of animals in the geological
epochs, and, like them also, perish when their work is done.

The peculiar character of a nation does not appear
nakedly, without relief and shadow.   As the waters of the
Rhone, in coming from the mountains, have caught a stain
from the soils they have traversed which mars the cerulean
tinge of the mountain snow that gave them birth, so the peculiarities of each nation become modified by the circumstances to which it is exposed, though the fundamental character of a nation, it seems, has never been changed.   Only
when the blood of the nation is changed by additions from
another stock is the idiosyncrasy altered.

Now, while each nation has its peculiar genius or
character which does not change, it has also and accordingly
a particular work to perform in the economy of the world,
a certain fundamental idea to unfold and develop.   This is
its national task, for in God's world, as in a shop, there is
a regular division of labour.   Sometimes it is a limited
work, and when it is done the nation may be dismissed, and
go to its repose.   Non omnia possumus omnes is as true of
nations as of men; one has a genius for one thing, another
for something different, and the idea of each nation and its
special work will depend on the genius of the nation.   Men
do not gather grapes of thorns.

In addition to this specific genius of the nation and
its corresponding work, there are also various accidental or
subordinate qualities, which change with circumstances, and
so vary the nation's aspect that its peculiar genius and peculiar duty are often hid from its own consciousness, and
even obscured to that of the philosophic looker-on.   These
subordinate peculiarities will depend first on the peculiar
genius, idea and work of the nation, and next on the transient circumstances, geographical, climatic, historical and
secular, to which the nation has been exposed.   The past
helped form the circumstances of the present age, and they
the character of the men now living.   Thus new modifications
of the national type continually take place; new variations are

played, but on the same old strings and of the same old tune. Once circumstances made the Hebrews entirely pastoral, now as completely commercial; but the same trust in God, the same national exclusiveness, appear as of old. As one looks at the history of the Ionians, Romans, Saxons, he sees unity of national character, a continuity of idea and of work; but it appears in the midst of variety, for while these remained ever the same to complete the economy of the world, subordinate qualities--sentiments, ideas, actions-- changed to suit the passing hour. The nation's course was laid towards a certain point, but they stood to the right hand or the left, they sailed with much canvas or little, and swift or slow, as the winds and waves compelled: nay, sometimes the national ship "heaves to," and lies with her "head to the wind," regardless of her destination; but when the storm is overblown resumes her course. Men will carelessly think the ship has no certain aim, but only drifts.

The most marked characteristic of the American nation is Love of Freedom; of man's natural rights. This is so plain to a student of American history, or of American politics, that the point requires no arguing. We have a genius for liberty: the American idea is freedom, natural rights. Accordingly, the work providentially laid out for us to do seems this, --to organize the rights of man. This is a problem hitherto unattempted on a national scale, in human history. Often enough attempts have been made to organize the powers of priests, kings, nobles, in a theocracy, monarchy, oligarchy, powers which had no foundation in human duties or human rights, but solely in the selfishness of strong men. Often enough have the mights of men been organized, but not the rights of man. Surely there has never been an attempt made on a national scale to organize the rights of man as man; rights resting on the nature of things; rights derived from no conventional compact of men with men; not inherited from past generations, nor received from parliaments and kings, nor secured by their parchments; but rights that are derived straightway from God, the Author of Duty and the Source of Right, and which are secured in the great charter of our being.

At first view it will be said, the peculiar genius of America is not such, nor such her fundamental idea, nor that her destined work. It is true that much of the national conduct seems exceptional when measured by that standard, and the nation's course as crooked as the Rio Grande; it is true that America sometimes seems to spurn liberty, and

sells the freedom of three million men for less than three
million annual bales of cotton; true, she often tramples,
knowingly, consciously, tramples on the most unquestionable
and sacred rights.   Yet, when one looks through the whole
character and history of America, spite of the exceptions,
nothing comes out with such relief as this love of freedom,
this idea of liberty, this attempt to organize right.   There
are numerous subordinate qualities which conflict with the
nation's idea and work, coming from our circumstances, not
our soul, as well as many others which help the nation perform her providential work.   They are signs of the times,
and it is important to look carefully among the most prominent of them, where, indeed, one finds striking contradictions.

        The first is an impatience of authority.   Every thing
must render its reason, and show cause for its being.   We
will not be commanded, at least only by such as we choose
to obey.   Does some one say, "Thou shalt," or "Thou shalt
not," we ask, "Who are you?"   Hence comes a seeming irreverence.   The shovel hat, the symbol of authority, which
awed our fathers, is not respected unless it covers a man,
and then it is the man we honour, and no longer the shovel
hat.   "I will complain of you to the government!" said a
Prussian nobleman to a Yankee stage-driver, who uncivilly
threw the nobleman's trunk to the top of the coach.   "Tell
the government to go to the devil!" was the symbolical reply.

        Old precedents will not suffice us, for we want some-
thing anterior to all precedents; we go beyond what is written, asking the cause of the precedent and the reason of the
writing.   "Our fathers did so," says some one.   "What of
that?" say we.   "Our fathers--they were giants, were they?
Not at all, only great boys, and we are not only taller than
they, but mounted on their shoulders to boot, and see twice
as far.   My dear wise man, or wiseacre, it is we that are
the ancients, and have forgotten more than all our fathers
knew.   We will take their wisdom joyfully, and thank God for
it, but not their authority, we know better; and of their nonsense not a word.   It was very well that they lived, and it
is very well that they are dead.   Let them keep decently
buried, for respectable dead men never walk."

        Tradition does not satisfy us.   The American scholar
has no folios in his library.   The antiquary unrolls his codex,
hid for eighteen hundred years in the ashes of Herculaneum,
deciphers its fossil wisdom, telling us what great men thought

in the bay of Naples, and two thousand years ago. "What do you tell of that for?" is the answer to his learning. "What has Pythagoras to do with the price of cotton? You may be a very learned man; you can read the hieroglyphics of Egypt, I dare say, and know so much about the Pharaohs, it is a pity you had not lived in their time, when you might have been good for something; but you are too old-fashioned for our business, and may return to your dust." An eminent American, a student of Egyptian history, with a scholarly indignation declared, "There is not a man who cares to know whether Shoophoo lived one thousand years before Christ, or three."

The example of other and ancient States does not terrify or instruct us. If slavery were a curse to Athens, the corruption of Corinth, the undoing of Rome, and all history shows it was so, we will learn no lesson from that experience, for we say, "We are not Athenians, men of Corinth, nor pagan Romans, thank God, but free republicans, Christians of America. We live in the nineteenth century, and though slavery worked all that mischief then and there, we know how to make money out of it, twelve hundred millions of dollars, as Mr. Clay counts the cash."

The example of contemporary nations furnishes us little warning or guidance. We will set our own precedents, and do not like to be told that the Prussians or the Dutch have learned some things in the education of the people before us, which we shall do well to learn after them. So when a good man tells us of their schools and their colleges, "patriotic" schoolmasters exclaim, "It is not true; our schools are the best in the world! But if it were true, it is unpatriotic to say so; it aids and comforts the enemy." Jonathan knows little of war; he has heard his grandfather talk of Lexington and Saratoga; he thinks he should like to have a little touch of battle on his own account: so when there is difficulty in setting up the fence betwixt his estate and his neighbours, he blusters for awhile, talks big, and threatens to strike his father; but, not having quite the stomach for that experiment, falls to beating his other neighbour, who happens to be poor, weak, and of a sickly constitution; and when he beats her at every step, --

> For 'tis no war, as each one knows,
> When only one side deals the blows,
> And t'other bears 'em, --

Jonathan thinks he has covered himself with "imperishable
honours," and sets up his general for a great king.   Poor
Jonathan--he does not know the misery, the tears, the blood,
the shame, the wickedness, and the sin he has set a-going,
and which one day he is to account for with God, who forgets nothing!

Yet while we are so unwilling to accept the good principles, to be warned by the fate, or guided by the success,
of other nations, we gladly and servilely copy their faults,
their follies, their vice and sin.   Like all upstarts, we pique
ourselves on our imitation of aristocratic ways.   How many
a blusterer in Congress, --for there are two denominations
of blusterers, differing only in degree, your great blusterer
in Congress and your little blusterer in a bar-room, --has
roared away hours long against aristocratic influence, in
favour of the "pure democracy," while he played the oligarch
in his native village, the tyrant over his hired help, and
though no man knows who his grandfather was, spite of the
herald's office, conjures up some trumpery coat of arms!
Like a clown, who, by pinching his appetite, has bought a
gaudy cloak for Sabbath wearing, we chuckle inwardly at our
brave apery of foreign absurdities, hoping that strangers will
be astonished at us--which, sure enough, comes to pass.
Jonathan is as vain as he is conceited, and expects that the
Fiddlers, and the Trollopes, and others, who visit us peri-
odically as the swallows, and likewise for what they can
catch, shall only extol, or at least stand aghast at the brave
spectacle we offer, of "the freest and most enlightened nation
in the world"; and if they tell us that we are an ill-mannered
set, raw and clownish, that we pick our teeth with a fork,
loll back in our chairs, and make our countenance hateful
with tobacco, and that with all our excellences we are a nation of "rowdies,"--why, we are offended, and our feelings
are hurt.   There was an African chief, long ago, who ruled
over a few miserable cabins, and one day received a French
traveller from Paris, under a tree.   With the exception of a
pair of shoes, our chief was as naked as a pestle, but with
great complacency he asked the traveller, "What do they say
of me at Paris?"

Such is our dread of authority, that we like not old
things; hence we are always a-changing.   Our house must be
new, and our book, and even our church.   So we choose a
material that soon wears out, though it often outlasts our
patience.   The wooden house is an apt emblem of this sign
of the times.   But this love of change appears not less in

important matters.   We think "Of old things all are over old,
of new things none are new enough. " So the age asks of all
institutions their right to be: What right has the government
to existence?   Who gave the majority a right to control the
minority, to restrict trade, levy taxes, make laws, and all
that?   If the nation goes into a committee of the whole and
makes laws, some little man goes into a committee of one
and passes his counter resolves.   The State of South Carolina is a nice example of this self-reliance, and this ques-
tioning of all authority.   That little brazen State, which contains only about half so many free white inhabitants as the
single city of New York, but which none the less claims to
have monopolized most of the chivalry of the nation, and its
patriotism, as well as political wisdom--that chivalrous little
State says, "If the nation does not make laws to suit us; if
it does not allow us to imprison all black seamen from the
North; if it prevents the extension of Slavery wherever we
wish to carry it--then the State of South Carolina will nullify,
and leave the other nine-and-twenty States to go to ruin!"

Men ask what right have the churches to the shadow
of authority which clings to them--to make creeds, and to
bind and to loose! So it is a thing which has happened, that
when a church excommunicates a young stripling for heresy,
he turns round, fulminates his edict, and excommunicates
the church.   Said a sly Jesuit to an American Protestant at
Rome, "But the rites and customs and doctrines of the Catholic church go back to the second century, the age after the
apostles!"   "No doubt of it, " said the American, who had
also read the Fathers, "they go back to the times of the
apostles themselves; but that proves nothing, for there were
as great fools in the first century as the last.   A fool or a
folly is no better because it is an old folly or an old fool.
There are fools enough now, in all conscience.   Pray don't
go back to prove their apostolical succession. "

There are always some men who are born out of due
season, men of past ages, stragglers of former generations,
who ought to have been born before Dr. Faustus invented printing,
but who are unfortunately born now, or, if born long ago,
have been fraudulently and illegally concealed by their
mothers, and are now, for the first time, brought to light.
The age lifts such aged juveniles from the ground, and bids
them live, but they are sadly to seek in this day; they are
old-fashioned boys; their authority is called in question; their
traditions and old-wives' fables are laughed at, at any rate
disbelieved; they get profanely elbowed in the crowd--men

not knowing their great age and consequent venerableness;
the shovel hat, though apparently born on their head, is
treated with disrespect.   The very boys laugh pertly in their
face when they speak, and even old men can scarce forbear
a smile, though it may be a smile of pity.   The age affords
such men a place, for it is a catholic age, large-minded,
and tolerant, --such a place as it gives to ancient armour,
Indian Bibles, and fossil bones of the mastodon; it puts them
by in some room seldom used, with other old furniture, and
allows them to mumble their anilities by themselves; now and
then takes off its hat; looks in, charitably, to keep the medi-
aeval relics in good heart, and pretends to listen, as they
discourse of what comes of nothing and goes to it; but in
matters which the age cares about, commerce, manufactures,
politics, which it cares much for, even in education, which
it cares far too little about, it trusts no such counsellors,
nor tolerates nor ever affects to listen.

        Then there is a philosophical tendency, distinctly vis-
ible; a groping after ultimate facts, first principles, and
universal ideas.   We wish to know first the fact, next the
law of that fact, and then the reason of the law.   A sign of
this tendency is noticeable in the titles of books; we have no
longer "treatises" on the eye, the ear, sleep, and so forth,
but in their place we find works professing to treat of the
"philosophy" of vision, of sound, of sleep.   Even in the pulpits, men speak about the "philosophy" of religion; we have
philosophical lectures, delivered to men of little culture,
which would have amazed our grandfathers, who thought a
shoemaker should never go beyond his last, even to seek for
the philosophy of shoes.   "What a pity, " said a grave Scotchman, in the beginning of this century, "to teach the beautiful
science of geometry to weavers and cobblers. "   Here nothing
is too good or high for any one tall and good enough to get
hold of it.   What audiences attend the Lowell lectures in
Boston--two or three thousand men, listening to twelve lectures on the philosophy of fish!   It would not bring a dollar
or a vote, only thought to their minds!   Young ladies are
well versed in the philosophy of the affections, and understand
the theory of attraction, while their grandmothers, good easy
souls, were satisfied with the possession of the fact.   The
circumstance, that philosophical lectures get delivered by
men like Walker, Agassiz, Emerson, and their coadjutors,
men who do not spare abstruseness, get listened to, and even
understood, in town and village, by large crowds of men, of
only the most common culture; this indicates a philosophical
tendency, unknown in any other land or age.   Our circle of

professed scholars, men of culture and learning, is a very
small one, while our circle of thinking men is dispropor-
tionately large. The best thought of France and Germany
finds a readier welcome here than in our parent land: nay,
the newest and the best thought of England finds its earliest
and warmest welcome in America. It was a little remarkable, that Bacon and Newton should be reprinted here, and
La Place should have found his translator and expositor coming out of an insurance office in Salem! Men of no great
pretensions object to an accomplished and eloquent politician:
"That is all very well; he made us cry and laugh, but the
discourse was not philosophical; he never tells us the reason
of the thing; he seems not only not to know it, but not to
know that there is a reason for the thing, and if not, what
is the use of this bobbing on the surface?" Young maidens
complain of the minister, that he has no philosophy in his
sermons, nothing but precepts, which they could read in the
Bible as well as he; perhaps in heathen Seneca. He does
not feed their souls.

One finds this tendency where it is least expected:
there is a philosophical party in politics, a very small party
it may be, but an actual one. They aim to get at everlasting ideas and universal laws, not made by man, but by God,
and for man, who only finds them; and from them they aim
to deduce all particular enactments, so that each statute in
the code shall represent a fact in the universe; a point of
thought in God; so, indeed, that legislation shall be divine in
the same sense that a true system of astronomy is divine--
or the Christian religion--the law corresponding to a fact.
Men of this party, in New England, have more ideas than
precedents, are spontaneous more than logical; have intuitions, rather than intellectual convictions, arrived at by the
process of reasoning. They think it is not philosophical to
take a young scoundrel and shut him up with a party of old
ones, for his amendment; not philosophical to leave children
with no culture, intellectual, moral, or religious, exposed
to the temptations of a high and corrupt civilization, and
then, when they go astray--as such barbarians needs must,
in such temptations--to hang them by the neck for the example's sake. They doubt if war is a more philosophical
mode of getting justice between two nations, than blows to
settle a quarrel between two men. In either case they do
not see how it follows that he who can strike the hardest
blow is always in the right. In short, they think that judicial
murder, which is hanging, and national murder, which is
war, are not more philosophical than homicide, which one

man commits on his own private account.

Theological sects are always the last to feel any
popular movement. Yet all of them, from the Episcopalians
to the Quakers, have each a philosophical party, which bids
fair to outgrow the party which rests on precedent and
usage, to overshadow and destroy it. The Catholic church
itself, though far astern of all the sects, in regard to the
great movements of the age, shares this spirit, and abroad,
if not here, is well nigh rent asunder by the potent medicine
which this new Daniel of philosophy has put into its mouth.
Everywhere in the American churches there are signs of a
tendency to drop all that rests merely on tradition and hear-
say, to cling only to such facts as bide the test of critical
search, and such doctrines as can be verified in human consciousness here and to-day. Doctors of divinity destroy the
faith they once preached.

True, there are antagonistic tendencies; for, soon as
one pole is developed, the other appears; objections are
made to philosophy, the old cry is raised--"Infidelity, "
"Denial, " "Free-thinking. " It is said that philosophy will
corrupt the young men, will spoil the old ones, and deceive
the very elect. "Authority and tradition, " say some, "are
all we need consult; reason must be put down, or she will
soon ask terrible questions. " There is good cause for these
men warring against reason and philosophy; it is purely in
self-defence. But this counsel and that cry come from those
quarters before mentioned, where the men of past ages have
their place, where the forgotten is re-collected, the obsolete
preserved, and the useless held in esteem. The counsel is
not dangerous; the bird of night, who overstays his hour, is
only troublesome to himself, and was never known to hurt a
dovelet or a mouseling after sunrise. In the night only is
the owl destructive. Some of those who thus cry out against
this tendency, are excellent men in their way, and highly
useful, valuable as conveyancers of opinions. So long as
there are men who take opinions as real estate, "to have
and to hold for themselves and their heirs for ever, " why
should there not be such conveyancers of opinions, as well
as of land? And as it is not the duty of the latter func-
tionary to ascertain the quality or the value of the land, but
only its metes and bounds, its appurtenances, and the title
thereto; to see if the grantor is regularly seized and possessed thereof, and has good right to convey and devise the
same, and to make sure that the whole conveyance is regularly made out--so is it with these conveyancers of opinion;

so should it be, and they are valuable men. It is a good
thing to know that we hold, under Scotus, and Ramus, and
Albertus Magnus, who were regularly seized of this or that
opinion. It gives an absurdity the dignity of a relic. Sometimes these worthies, who thus oppose reason and her kin,
seem to have a good deal in them, and, when one examines,
he finds more than he looked for. They are like a nest of
boxes from Hingham and Nuremburg, you open one, and behold another; that, and lo! a third. So you go on, opening
and opening, and finding and finding, till at last you come
to the heart of the matter, and then you find a box that is
very little, and entirely empty.

Yet, with all this tendency--and it is now so strong
that it cannot be put down, nor even howled down, much as
it may be howled over--there is a lamentable want of first
principles, well known and established; we have rejected the
authority of tradition, but not yet accepted the authority of
truth and justice. We will not be treated as striplings, and
are not old enough to go alone as men. Accordingly, nothing seems fixed. There is a perpetual see-sawing of opposite principles. Somebody said ministers ought to be ordained on horseback, because they are to remain so short a
time in one place. It would be as emblematic to inaugurate
American politicians, by swearing them on a weathercock.
The great men of the land have as many turns in their
course as the Euripus or the Missouri. Even the facts
given in the spiritual nature of man are called in question.
An eminent Unitarian divine regards the existence of God as
a matter of opinion, thinks it cannot be demonstrated, and
publicly declares that it is "not a certainty." Some American Protestants no longer take the Bible as the standard of
ultimate appeal, yet venture not to set up in that place reason, conscience, the soul getting help of God; others, who
affect to accept the Scripture as the last authority, yet,
when questioned as to their belief in the miraculous and divine birth of Jesus of Nazareth, are found unable to say yes
or no, not having made up their minds.

In politics, it is not yet decided whether it is best to
leave men to buy where they can buy cheapest, and sell
where they can sell dearest, or to restrict that matter.

It was a clear case to our fathers, in '76, that all
men were "created equal," each with "Unalienable Rights."
That seemed so clear, that reasoning would not make it
appear more reasonable; it was taken for granted, as a self-

evident proposition. The whole nation said so. Now, it is
no strange thing to find it said that negroes are not "created
equal" in unalienable rights with white men. Nay, in the
Senate of the United States, a famous man declares all this
talk a dangerous mistake. The practical decision of the nation looks the same way. So, to make our theory accord
with our practice, we ought to recommit the Declaration to
the hands which drafted that great State paper, and instruct
Mr. Jefferson to amend the document, and declare that "All
men are created equal, and endowed by their Creator with
certain unalienable rights, if born of white mothers; but if
not, not."

In this lack of first principles, it is not settled in
the popular consciousness, that there is such a thing as an
absolute right, a great law of God, which we are to keep,
come what will come. So the nation is not upright, but goes
stooping. Hence, in private affairs, law takes the place of
conscience, and, in public, might of right. So the bankrupt
pays his shilling in the pound, and gets his discharge, but
afterwards, becoming rich, does not think of paying the other
nineteen shillings. He will tell you the law is his conscience; if that be satisfied, so is he. But you will yet find
him letting money at one or two per cent a month, contrary
to law; and then he will tell you that paying a debt is a
matter of law, while letting money is only a matter of conscience. So he rides either indifferently--now the public
hack, and now his own private nag, according as it serves
his turn.

So a rich State borrows money and "repudiates" the
debt, satisfying its political conscience, as the bankrupt his
commercial conscience, with the notion that there is no
absolute right; that expediency is the only justice, and that
King People can do no wrong. No calm voice of indignation
cries out from the pulpit and the press, and the heart of the
people, to shame the repudiators into decent morals; because
it is not settled in the popular mind that there is any absolute right. Then, because we are strong and the Mexicans
weak, because we want their land for a slave-pasture, and
they cannot keep us out of it, we think that is reason enough
for waging an infamous war of plunder. Grave men do not
ask about "the natural justice" of such an undertaking, only
about its cost. Have we not seen an American Congress
vote a plain lie, with only sixteen dissenting voices in the
whole body; has not the head of the nation continually repeated that lie; and do not both parties, even at this day,
sustain the vote?

Now and then there rises up an honest man, with a great Christian heart in his bosom, and sets free a score or two of slaves inherited from his father; watches over and tends them in their new-found freedom; or another, who, when legally released from payment of his debts, restores the uttermost farthing.   We talk of this and praise it, as an extraordinary thing.   Indeed it is so; justice is an unusual thing, and such men deserve the honour they thus win.   But such praise shows that such honesty is a rare honesty.   The northern man, born on the battle-ground of freedom, goes to the South and becomes the most tyrannical of slave-drivers. The son of the Puritan, bred up in austere ways, is sent to Congress to stand up for truth and right, but he turns out a "dough-face," and betrays the duty he went to serve.   Yet he does not lose his place, for every dough-faced representative has a dough-faced constituency to back him.

It is a great mischief that comes from lacking first principles, and the worst part of it comes from lacking first principles in morals.   Thereby our eyes are holden so that we see not the great social evils all about us.   We attempt to justify slavery, even to do it in the name of Jesus Christ. The whig party of the North loves slavery; the democratic party does not even seek to conceal its affection therefor.   A great politician declares the Mexican war wicked, and then urges men to go and fight it; he thinks a famous general not fit to be nominated for President, but then invites men to elect him.   Politics are national morals, the morals of Thomas and Jeremiah, multiplied by millions.   But it is not decided yet that honesty is the best policy for a politician; it is thought that the best policy is honesty, at least as near it as the times will allow.   Many politicians seem undecided how to turn, and so sit on the fence between honesty and dishonesty.   Mr. Facing-bothways is a popular politican in America just now, sitting on the fence between honesty and dishonesty, and like the blank leaf between the Old and New Testaments, belonging to neither dispensation.   It is a little amusing to a trifler to hear a man's fitness for the Presidency defended on the ground that he has no definite convictions or ideas!

There was once a man who said he always told a lie when it would serve his special turn.   It is a pity he went to his own place long ago.   He seemed born for a party politician in America.   He would have had a large party, for he made a great many converts before he died, and left a numerous kindred busy in the editing of newspapers, writing addresses for the people, and passing "resolutions. "

It must strike a stranger as a little odd that a republic should have a slaveholder for President five-sixths of
the time, and most of the important offices be monopolized
by other slaveholders; a little surprising that all the pulpits
and most of the presses should be in favour of slavery, at
least not against it.   But such is the fact.   Everybody knows
the character of the American government for some years
past, and of the American parties in politics.   "Like master,
like man, " used to be a true proverb in old England, and
"Like people, like ruler, " is a true proverb in America;
true now.   Did a decided people ever choose dough-faces?--
a people that loved God and man, choose representatives that
cared for neither truth nor justice?   Now and then, for dust
gets into the brightest eyes; but did they ever choose such
men continually?   The people are always fairly represented;
our representatives do actually represent us, and in more
senses than they are paid for.   Congress and the Cabinet are
only two thermometers hung up in the capital, to show the
temperature of the national morals.

But amid this general uncertainty there are two capital
maxims which prevail amongst our hucksters of politics: to
love your party better than your country, and yourself better
than your party.   There are, it is true, real statesmen
amongst us, men who love justice and do the right; but they
seem lost in the mob of vulgar politicians and the dust of
party editors.

Since the nation loves freedom above all things, the
name democracy is a favourite name.   No party could live
a twelvemonth that should declare itself anti-democratic.
Saint and sinner, statesman and politician, alike love the
name.   So it comes to pass that there are two things which
bear that name; each has its type and its motto.   The motto
of one is, "You are as good as I, and let us help one
another. "   That represents the democracy of the Declaration
of Independence, and of the New Testament; its type is a
free school, where children of all ranks meet under the guidance of intelligent and Christian men, to be educated in mind,
and heart, and soul.   The other has for its motto, "I am as
good as you, so get out of my way. "   Its type is the bar-
room of a tavern--dirty, offensive, stained with tobacco, and
full of drunken, noisy, quarrelsome "rowdies, " just returned
from the Mexican war, and ready for a "buffalo hunt, " for
privateering, or to go and plunder any one who is better off

than themselves, especially if also better.   That is not exactly the democracy of the Declaration, or of the New
Testament; but of--no matter whom.

Then, again, there is a great intensity of life and
purpose.   This displays itself in our actions and speeches;
in our speculations; in the "revivals" of the more serious
sects; in the excitements of trade; in the general character
of the people.   All that we do we overdo.   It appears in our
hopefulness; we are the most aspiring of nations.   Not content with half the continent, we wish the other half.   We have
this characteristic of genius: we are dissatisfied with all that
we have done.   Somebody once said we were too vain to be
proud.   It is not wholly so; the national idea is so far above
us that any achievement seems little and low.   The American
soul passes away from its work soon as it is finished.   So
the soul of each great artist refuses to dwell in his finished
work, for that seems little to his dream.   Our fathers
deemed the Revolution a great work; it was once thought a
surprising thing to found that little colony on the shores of
New England; but young America looks to other revolutions,
and thinks she has many a Plymouth colony in her bosom.   If
other nations wonder at our achievements, we are a dis-
appointment to ourselves, and wonder we have not done more.
Our national idea out-travels our experience, and all experience.   We began our national career by setting all history at
defiance--for that said, "A republic on a large scale cannot
exist. "   Our progress since has shown that we were right in
refusing to be limited by the past.   The political ideas of the
nation are transcendant, not empirical.   Human history could
not justify the Declaration of Independence and its large
statements of the new idea: the nation went behind human
history and appealed to human nature.

We are more spontaneous than logical; we have ideas,
rather than facts or precedents.   We dream more than we
remember, and so have many orators and poets, or poetas-
ters, with but few antiquaries and general scholars.   We are
not so reflective as forecasting.   We are the most intuitive
of modern nations.   The very party in politics which has the
least culture, is richest in ideas which will one day become
facts.   Great truths--political, philosophical, religious--lie
a-burning in many a young heart which cannot legitimate nor
prove them true, but none the less feels, and feels them
true.   A man full of new truths finds a ready audience with
us.   Many things which come disguised as truths under such
circumstances pass current for a time, but by and by their

bray discovers them.   The hope which comes from this intensity of life and intuition of truths is a national characteristic.   It gives courage, enterprise, and strength.   They can
who think they can.   We are confident in our star; other nations may see it or not, we know it is there above the clouds.
We do not hesitate at rash experiments--sending fifty thousand
soldiers to conquer a nation with eight or nine millions of
people.   We are up to everything, and think ourselves a
match for anything.   The young man is rash, for he only
hopes, having little to remember; he is excitable, and loves
excitement; change of work is his repose; he is hot and noisy,
sanguine and fearless, with the courage that comes from
warm blood and ignorance of dangers; he does not know what
a hard, tough, sour old world he is born into.   We are a
nation of young men.   We talked of annexing Texas and
northern Mexico, and did both; now we grasp at Cuba, Central America, --all the continent, --and speak of a railroad to
the Pacific as a trifle for us to accomplish.   Our national
deeds are certainly great, but our hope and promise far out-
brags them all.

     If this intensity of life and hope has its good side, it
has also its evil; with much of the excellence of youth we
have its faults--rashness, haste, and superficiality.   Our
work is seldom well done.   In English manufactures there is
a certain solid honesty of performance; in the French a certain air of elegance and refinement: one misses both these in
American works.   It is said America invents the most
machines, but England builds them best.   We lack the phleg-
matic patience of older nations.   We are always in a hurry,
morning, noon, and night.   We are impatient of the process,
but greedy of the result; so that we make short experiments
but long reports, and talk much though we say little.   We
forget that a sober method is a short way of coming to the
end, and that he who, before he sets out, ascertains where
he is going and the way thither, ends his journey more pros-
perously than one who settles these matters by the way.
Quickness is a great desideratum with us.   It is said an
American ship is known far off at sea by the quantity of canvas she carries.   Rough and ready is a popular attribute.
Quick and off would be a symbolic motto for the nation at
this day, representing one phase of our character.   We are
sudden in deliberation; the "one-hour rule" works well in
Congress.   A committee of the British Parliament spends
twice or thrice our time in collecting facts, understanding and
making them intelligible, but less than our time in speech-
making after the report; speeches there commonly being for

the purpose of facilitating the business, while here one sometimes is half ready to think, notwithstanding our earnestness,
that the business is to facilitate the speaking.   A State re-
vises her statutes with a rapidity that astonishes a European.
Yet each revision brings some amendment, and what is found
good in the constitution or laws of one State gets speedily
imitated by the rest; each new State of the North becoming
more democratic than its predecessor.

We are so intent on our purpose that we have no time
for amusement.   We have but one or two festivals in the
year, and even then we are serious and reformatory.   Jonathan thinks it a very solemn thing to be merry.   A French-
man said we have but two amusements in America--theology
for the women and politics for the men; preaching and voting.
If this be true, it may help to explain the fact that most men
take their theology from their wives, and women politics
from their husbands.   No nation ever tried the experiment of
such abstinence from amusement.   We have no time for
sport, and so lose much of the poetry of life.   All work and
no play does not always make a dull boy, but it commonly
makes a hard man.

We rush from school into business early; we hurry
while in business; we aim to be rich quickly, making a fortune at a stroke, making or losing it twice or thrice in a
lifetime.   "Soft and fair, goes safe and far, " is no proverb
to our taste.   We are the most restless of people.   How we
crowd into cars and steamboats; a locomotive would well
typify our fuming, fizzing spirit.   In our large towns life
seems to be only a scamper.   Not satisfied with bustling
about all day, when night comes we cannot sit still, but alone
of all nations have added rockers to our chairs.

All is haste, from the tanning of leather to the education of a boy, and the old saw holds its edge good as ever
--"the more haste the worse speed. "   The young stripling,
innocent of all manner of lore, whom a judicious father has
barrelled down in a college, or law-school, or theological
seminary, till his beard be grown, mourns over the few
years he must spend there awaiting that operation.   His rule
is, "to make a spoon or spoil a horn"; he longs to be out in
the world "making a fortune, " or "doing good, " as he calls
what his father better names "making noisy work for re-
pentance, and doing mischief. "   So he rushes into life not
fitted, and would fly towards heaven, this young Icarus, his
wings not half fledged.   There seems little taste for thorough-

ness. In our schools as our farms, we pass over much
ground, but pass over it poorly.

In education the aim is not to get the most we can,
but the least we can get along with. A ship with over-much
canvas and over-little ballast were no bad emblem of many
amongst us. In no country is it so easy to get a reputation
for learning--accumulated thought, because so few devote
themselves to that accumulation. In this respect our standard is low. So a man of one attainment is sure to be
honoured, but a man of many and varied abilites is in danger
of being undervalued. A Spurzheim would be warmly welcomed, while a Humboldt would be suspected of superficiality,
as we have not the standard to judge him by. Yet in no
country in the world is it so difficult to get a reputation for
eloquence, as many speak, and that well. It is surprising
with what natural strength and beauty the young American
addresses himself to speak. Some hatter's apprentice, or
shoemaker's journeyman, at a temperance or anti-slavery
meeting, will speak words like the blows of an axe, that cut
clean and deep. The country swarms with orators, more
abundantly where education is least esteemed--in the West
or South.

We have secured national unity of action for the white
citizens, without much curtailing individual variety of action,
so we have at the North pretty well solved that problem
which other nations have so often boggled over; we have
balanced the centripetal power, the government and laws,
with the centrifugal power, the mass of individuals, into
harmonious proportions. If one were to leave out of sight
the three million slaves, one-sixth part of the population, the
problem might be regarded as very happily solved. As the
consequences of this, in no country is there more talent, or
so much awake and active. In the South this unity is attained
by sacrificing all the rights of three million slaves, and almost all the rights of the other coloured population. In
despotic countries this unity is brought about by the sacrifice
of freedom, individual variety of action, in all except the
despot and his favourites; so, much of the nation's energy is
stifled in the chains of the State, while here it is friendly to
institutions which are friendly to it, goes to its work, and
approves itself in the vast increase of wealth and comfort
throughout the North, where there is no class of men which
is so oppressed that it cannot rise. One is amazed at the
amount of ready skill and general ability which he finds in
all the North, where each man has a little culture, takes his

newspaper, manages his own business, and talks with some
intelligence of many things--especially of politics and theology.   In respect to this general intellectual ability and
power of self-help, the mass of people seem far in advance
of any other nation.   But at the same time our scholars,
who always represent the nation's higher modes of consciousness, will not bear comparison with the scholars of England,
France, and Germany, men thoroughly furnished for their
work.   This is a great reproach and mischief to us, for we
need most accomplished leaders, who by their thought can
direct this national intensity of life.   Our literature does not
furnish them; we have no great men there; Irving, Channing,
Cooper, are not names to conjure with in literature.   One
reads thick volumes devoted to the poets of America, or her
prose writers, and finds many names which he wonders he
never heard of before; but when he turns over their works,
he finds consolation and recovers his composure.

     American literature may be divided into two depart-
ments: the permanent literature, which gets printed in books,
that sometimes reach more than one edition; and the evanescent literature, which appears only in the form of speeches,
pamphlets, reviews, newspaper articles, and the like ex-
tempore productions.   Now our permanent literature, as a
general thing, is superficial, tame, and weak; it is not
American; it has not our ideas, our contempt of authority,
our philosophical turn, nor even our uncertainty as to first
principles, still less our national intensity, our hope, and
fresh intuitive perceptions of truth.   It is a miserable imitation.   Love of freedom is not there.   The real national
literature is found almost wholly in speeches, pamphlets,
and newspapers.   The latter are pretty thoroughly American:
mirrors in which we see no very flattering likeness of our
morals or our manners.   Yet the picture is true: that vulgarity, that rant, that bragging violence, that recklessness
of truth and justice, that disregard of right and duty, are a
part of the nation's everyday life.   Our newspapers are low
and "wicked to a fault;" only in this weakness are they un-
American.   Yet they exhibit, and abundantly, the four qualities we have mentioned as belonging to the signs of our
times.   As a general rule, our orators are also American,
with our good and ill.   Now and then one rises who has
studied Demosthenes in Leland or Francis, and got a second-
hand acquaintance with old models: a man who uses literary
common-places, and thinks himself original and classic because he can quote a line or so of Horace, in a Western
House of Representatives, without getting so many words

wrong as his reporter; but such men are rare, and after
making due abatement for them, our orators all over the
land are pretty thoroughly American, a little turgid, hot,
sometimes brilliant, hopeful, intuitive, abounding in half
truths, full of great ideas; often inconsequent; sometimes
coarse; patriotic, vain, self-confident, rash, strong, and
young-mannish. Of course the most of our speeches are
vulgar, ranting, and worthless; but we have produced some
magnificent specimens of oratory, which are fresh, original,
American, and brand new.

The more studied, polished, and elegant literature is
not so; that is mainly an imitation. It seems not a thing of
native growth. Sometimes, as in Channing, the thought and
the hope are American, but the form and the colouring old
and foreign. We dare not be original; our American pine
must be cut to the trim pattern of the English yew, though
the pine bleed at every clip. This poet tunes his lyre at the
harp of Goethe, Milton, Pope, or Tennyson. His songs
might be better sung on the Rhine than the Kennebec. They
are not American in form or feeling; they have not the
breath of our air; the smell of our ground is not in them.
Hence our poet seems cold and poor. He loves the old
mythology; talks about Pluto--the Greek devil, the fates and
furies--witches of old time in Greece, but would blush to use
our mythology, or breathe the name in verse of our devil,
or our own witches, lest he should be thought to believe what
he wrote. The mother and sisters, who with many a pinch
and pain sent the hopeful boy to college, must turn over the
classical dictionary before they can find out what the youth
would be at in his rhymes. Our poet is not deep enough to
see that Aphrodite came from the ordinary waters, that
Homer only hitched into rhythm and furnished the accomplishment of verse to street-talk, nursery tales, and old men's
gossip in the Ionian towns; he thinks what is common is unclean. So he sings of Corinth and Athens, which he never
saw, but has not a word to say of Boston, and Fall River,
and Baltimore, and New York, which are just as meet for
song. He raves of Thermopylae and Marathon, with never a
word for Lexington and Bunker Hill, for Cowpens, and
Lundy's Lane, and Bemis's Heights. He loves to tell of the
Ilyssus, of "smooth-sliding Mincius, crowned with vocal
reeds," yet sings not of the Petapsco, the Susquehanna, the
Aroostook, and the Willimantick. He prates of the narcissus
and the daisy, never of American dandelions and blue-eyed
grass; he dwells on the lark and the nightingale, but has not a
thought for the brown thrasher and the bobolink, who every

morning in June rain down such showers of melody on his
affected head.   What a lesson Burns teaches us, addressing
his "rough bur-thistle, " his daisy, "wee crimson tippit thing,"
and finding marvellous poetry in the mouse whose nest his
plough turned over!   Nay, how beautifully has even our sweet
poet sung of our own Green river, our waterfowl, of the
blue and fringed gentian, the glory of autumnal days.

    Hitherto, spite of the great reading public, we have no
permanent literature which corresponds to the American idea.
Perhaps it is not time for that; it must be organized in deeds
before it becomes classic in words; but as yet we have no
such literature which reflects even the surface of American
life, certainly nothing which portrays our intensity of life,
our hope, or even our daily doings and drivings, as the
Odyssey paints old Greek life, or Don Quixote and Gil Blas
portray Spanish life.   Literary men are commonly timid; ours
know they are but poorly fledged as yet, so dare not fly
away from the parent tree, but hop timidly from branch to
branch.   Our writers love to creep about in the shadow of
some old renown, not venturing to soar away into the un-
winged air, to sing of things here and now, making our life
classic.   So, without the grace of high culture, and the
energy of American thought, they become weak, cold, and
poor; are "curious, not knowing, not exact, but nice. "   Too
fastidious to be wise, too unlettered to be elegant, too critical
to create, they prefer a dull saying that is old to a novel
form of speech, or a natural expression of a new truth.   In
a single American work, --and a famous one too, --there are
over sixty similes, not one original, and all poor.   A few
men, conscious of this defect, this sin against the Holy Spirit
of Literature, go to the opposite extreme, and are American-
mad; they wilfully talk rude, write innumerous verse, and
play their harps all jangling, out of tune.   A yet fewer few
are American without madness.   One such must not here be
passed by, alike philosopher and bard, in whose writings
"ancient wisdom shines with new-born beauty, " and who has
enriched a genius thoroughly American in the best sense,
with a cosmopolitan culture and literary skill, which were
wonderful in any land.   But of American literature in general, and of him in special, more shall be said at another
time.

    Another remarkable feature is our excessive love of
material things.   This is more than a Utilitarianism, a
preference of the useful over the beautiful.   The Puritan at
Plymouth had a corn-field, a cabbage-garden, and a patch for

potatoes, a school-house, and a church, before he sat down
to play the fiddle. He would have been a fool to reverse
this process. It were poor economy and worse taste to have
painters, sculptors, and musicians, while the rude wants of
the body are uncared for. But our fault in this respect is,
that we place too much the charm of life in mere material
things, --houses, lands, well-spread tables, and elegant furniture, --not enough in man, in virture, wisdom, genius, religion, greatness of soul, and nobleness of life. We mistake
a perfection of the means of manliness for the end--manhood
itself. Yet the housekeeping of a Shakespeare, Milton,
Franklin, had only one thing worth boasting of. Strange to
say, that was the master of the house. A rich and vulgar
man once sported a coach and four, and at its first turn out
rode into the great commercial street of a large town in New
England. "How fine you must feel with your new coach and
four, " said one of his old friends, though not quite so rich.
"Yes, " was the reply, "as fine as a beetle in a gold snuff-
box. " All of his kindred are not so nice and discriminating
in their self-consciousness.

   This practical materialism is a great affliction to us.
We think a man cannot be poor and great also. So we see a
great man sell himself for a little money, and it is thought
"a good operation. " A conspicuous man, in praise of a certain painter, summed up his judgment with this: "Why, sir,
he has made twenty thousand dollars by his pictures. " "A
good deal more than Michael Angelo, Leonardo, and Raphael
together, " might have been the reply. But it is easier to
weigh purses than artistic skill. It was a characteristic
praise bestowed in Boston on a distinguished American writer,
that his book brought him more money than any man had ever
realized for an original work in this country. "Commerce, "
said Mr. Pitt, "having got into both houses of Parliament,
privilege must be done away, " --the privilege of wit and
genius, not less than rank. Clergymen estimate their own
and their brothers' importance, not by their apostolical gifts,
or even apostolic succession, but by the value of the living.

   All other nations have this same fault, it may be said.
But there is this difference: in other nations the things of a
man are put before the man himself; so a materialism which
exalts the accidents of the man--rank, wealth, birth, and the
like--above the man, is not inconsistent with the general idea
of England or Austria. In America it is a contradiction.
Besides, in most civilized countries, there is a class of men
living on inherited wealth, who devote their lives to politics,

art, science, letters, and so are above the mere material
elegance which surrounds them.   That class has often in-
flicted a deep wound on society, which festers long and leads
to serious trouble in the system, but at the same time it
redeems a nation from the reproach of mere material vulgarity; it has been the source of refinement, and has warmed
into life much of the wisdom and beauty which have thence
spread over all the world.   In America there is no such
class.   Young men inheriting wealth very rarely turn to anything noble; they either convert their talents into gold, or
their gold into furniture, wines, and confectionary.   A young
man of wealth does not know what to do with himself or it;
a rich young woman seems to have no resource but marriage!   Yet it must be confessed, that at least in one part
of the United States wealth flows freely for the support of
public institutions of education.

Here it is difficult for a man of science to live by his
thought.   Was Bowditch one of the first mathematicians of
his age?   He must be at the head of an annuity office.   If
Socrates should be set up as a dealer in money, and outwit
the brokers as formerly the Sophists, and shave notes as
skilfully as of old, we should think him a great man.   But
if he adopted his old plan, what should we say of him?

Manliness is postponed and wealth preferred.   "What
a fine house is this, " one often says: "what furniture; what
feasting.   But the master of the house!--why, every stone
out of the wall laughs at him.   He spent all of himself in
getting this pretty show together, and now it is empty, and
mocks its owner.   He is the emblematic coffin at the Egyptian feast. "   "Oh, man!" says the looker-on, "why not furnish
thyself with a mind, and conscience, a heart and a soul, before getting all this brass and mahogany together; this beef
and these wines?"   The poor wight would answer, --"Why,
sir, there were none such in the market!"   The young man
does say, "I will first of all things be a man, and so being,
will have this thing and the other, " putting the agreeable
after the essential.   But he says, "First of all, by hook or
by crook, I will have money, the manhood may take care of
itself. "   He has it, --for tough and hard as the old world is,
it is somewhat fluid before a strong man who resolutely
grapples with difficulty and will swim through; it can be
made to serve his turn.   He has money, but the man has
evaporated in the process; when you look he is not there.
True, other nations have done the same thing, and we only
repeat their experiment.   The old devil of conformity says

to our American Adam and Eve, "Do this and you shall be
as gods," a promise as likely to hold good as the devil's
did in the beginning. A man was meant for something more
than a tassel to a large estate, and a woman to be more
than a rich housekeeper.

With this offensive materialism we copy the vices of
feudal aristocracy abroad, making our vulgarity still more
ridiculous. We are ambitious or proud of wealth, which is
but labour stored up, and at the same time are ashamed of
labour, which is wealth in process. With all our talk about
democracy, labour is thought less honourable in Boston than
in Berlin and Leipsic. Thriving men are afraid their
children will be shoemakers, or ply some such honourable
and useful craft. Yet little pains are taken to elevate the
condition or improve the manners and morals of those who
do all the manual work of society. The strong man takes
care that his children and himself escape that condition. We
do not believe that all stations are alike honourable if
honourably filled; we have little desire to equalize the burdens of life, so that there shall be no degraded class; none
cursed with work, none with idleness. It is popular to en-
dow a college; vulgar to take an interest in common schools.
Liberty is a fact, equality a word, and fraternity, we do not
think of yet.

In this struggle for material wealth and the social
rank which is based thereon, it is amusing to see the shifting of the scenes; the social aspirations of one, and the contempt with which another rebuts the aspirant. An old man
can remember when the most exclusive of men, and the most
golden, had scarce a penny in their purse, and grumbled at
not finding a place where they would. Now the successful
man is ashamed of the steps he rose by. The gentleman
who came to Boston half a century ago, with all his worldly
goods tied up in a cotton handkerchief, and that not of so
large a pattern as are made now-a-days, is ashamed to
recollect that his father was a currier, or a blacksmith, or
a skipper at Barnstable or Beverly; ashamed, also, of his
forty or fifty country cousins, remarkable for nothing but
their large hands and their excellent memory. Nay, he is
ashamed of his own humble beginnings, and sneers at men
starting as he once started. The generation of English
"Snobs" came in with the Conqueror, and migrated to America
at an early day, where they continue to thrive marvellously
--the chief "conservative party" in the land.

Through this contempt for labour, a certain affectation runs through a good deal of American society, and
makes our aristocracy vulgar and contemptible.   What if
Burns had been ashamed of his plough, and Franklin had
lost his recollection of the candle-moulds and the composing
stick?   Mr. Chubbs, who got rich to-day, imitates Mr.
Swipes, who got rich yesterday, buys the same furniture,
gives similar entertainments, and counts himself "as good a
man as Swipes, any day. "   Nay, he goes a little beyond
him, puts his servants in livery, with the "Chubbs arms"
on the button; but the new-found family arms are not descriptive of the character of the Chubbses, or of their origin
and history--only of their vanity.   Then Mr. Swipes looks
down on poor Chubbs, and curls his lip with scorn; calls
him a "parvenu, " "an upstart, " "a plebeian"; speaks of him
as one of "that sort of people, " "one of your ordinary men";
"thrifty and well off in the world, but a little vulgar. "   At
the same time Mr. Swipes looks up to Mr. Bung, who got
rich the day before yesterday, as a gentleman of old family
and quite distinguished, and receives from that quarter the
same treatment he bestows on his left-hand neighbour.   The
real gentleman is the same all the world over.   Such are by
no means lacking here, while the pretended gentlemen swarm in
America.   Chaucer said a good word long ago:

> --This is not mine intendément
> To clepen no wight in no age
> Only gentle for his lineáge;
> But whoso that is virtuous,
> And in his port not outragéous:
> When such one thou see'st thee beforn,
> Though he be not gentle born,
> Thou mayest well see this is soth,
> That he is gentle, because he doth
> As 'longeth to a gentleman;
> Of them none other deem I can;
> For certainly withouten drede,
> A churl is deeméd by his deed,
> Of high or low, as ye may see,
> Or of what kindred that he be.

It is no wonder vulgar men, who travel here and eat
our dinners, laugh at this form of vulgarity.   Wiser men see
its cause, and prophesy its speedy decay.   Every nation has
its aristocracy, or controlling class: in some lands it is
permanent, an aristocracy of blood; men that are descended
from distinguished warriors, from the pirates and freebooters

of a rude age.   The nobility of England are proud of their
fathers' deeds, and emblazon the symbols thereof in their
family arms, emblems of barbarism.   Ours is an aristocracy
of wealth, not got by plunder, but by toil, thrift, enterprise;
of course it is a moveable aristocracy: the first families of
the last century are now forgot, and their successors will
give place to new names.   Now earning is nobler than rob-
bing, and work is before war; but we are ashamed of both,
and seek to conceal the noble source of our wealth.   An
aristocracy of gold is far preferable to the old and immoveable nobility of blood, but it has also its peculiar vices: it
has the effrontery of an upstart, despises its own ladder, is
heartless and lacks noble principle, vulgar and cursing.   This
lust of wealth, however, does us a service, and gives the
whole nation a stimulus which it needs, and, low as the motive is, drives us to continual advancement.   It is a great
merit for a nation to secure the largest amount of useful and
comfortable and beautiful things which can be honestly earned,
and used with profit to the body and soul of man.   Only when
wealth becomes an idol, and material abundance is made the
end, not the means, does the love of it become an evil.   No
nation was ever too rich, or over-thrifty, though many a
nation has lost its soul by living wholly for the senses.

Now and then we see noble men living apart from this
vulgarity and scramble; some rich, some poor, but both content to live for noble aims, to pinch and spare for virtue,
religion, for truth and right.   Such men never fail from any
age or land, but everywhere they are the exceptional men.
Still they serve to keep alive the sacred fire in the hearts of
young men, rising amid the common mob as oaks surpass
the brambles or the fern.

In these secondary qualities of the people which mark
the special signs of the times, there are many contradictions,
quality contending with quality; all by no means balanced into
harmonious relations.   Here are great faults not less than
great virtues.   Can the national faults be corrected?   Most
certainly; they are but accidental, coming from our circumstances, our history, our position as a people--heterogeneous,
new, and placed on a new and untamed continent.   They come
not from the nation's soul; they do not belong to our fundamental idea, but are hostile to it.   One day our impatience
of authority, our philosophical tendency, will lead us to a
right method, that of fixed principles, and then we shall have
a continuity of national action.   Considering the pains taken
by the fathers of the better portion of America to promote

religion here, remembering how dear is Christianity to the
heart of all, conservative and radical--though men often
name as Christian what is not--and seeing how truth and
right are sure to win at last, --it becomes pretty plain that
we shall arrive at true principles, laws of the universe,
ideas of God; then we shall be in unison also with it and
Him.   When that great defect--lack of first principles--is
corrected, our intensity of life, with the hope and confidence
it inspires, will do a great work for us.   We have already
secured an abundance of material comforts hitherto unknown;
no land was ever so full of corn and cattle, clothing, comfortable houses, and all things needed for the flesh.   The
desire of those things, even the excessive desire thereof,
performs an important part in the divine economy of the
human race; nowhere is its good effect more conspicuous
than in America, where in two generations the wild Irishman
becomes a decent citizen, orderly, temperate, and intelligent.   This done or even a-doing, as it is now, we shall go
forth to realize our great national idea, and accomplish the
great work of organizing into institutions the unalienable
rights of man.   The great obstacle in the way of that is
African slavery--the great exception in the nation's history;
the national sin.   When that is removed, as soon it must be,
lesser but kindred evils will easily be done away; the truth
which the land-reformers, which the associationists, the
free-traders, and others, have seen, dimly or clearly, can
readily be carried out.   But while this monster vice continues, there is little hope of any great and permanent national reform.   The positive things which we chiefly need
for this work, are first, education, next, education, and
then education, a vigorous development of the mind, conscience, affections, religious power of the whole nation.   The
method and the means for that I shall not now discuss.

The organization of human rights, the performance of
human duties, is an unlimited work.   If there shall ever be
a time when it is all done, then the race will have finished
its course.   Shall the American nation go on in this work,
or pause, turn off, fall, and perish?   To me it seems almost treason to doubt that a glorious future awaits us.
Young as we are, and wicked, we have yet done something
which the world will not let perish.   One day we shall attend
more emphatically to the rights of the hand, and organize
labour and skill; then to the rights of the head, looking after
education, science, literature, and art; and again to the
rights of the heart, building up the State with its laws, society with its families, the church with its goodness and piety.

One day we shall see that it is a shame, and a loss, and a
wrong, to have a criminal, or an ignorant man, or a pauper,
or an idler, in the land; that the gaol, and the gallows, and
the almshouse are a reproach which need not be.   Out of
new sentiments and ideas, not seen as yet, new forms of
society will come, free from the antagonism of races,
classes, men--representing the American idea in its length,
breadth, depth, and height, its beauty, and its truth, and
then the old civilization of our time shall seem barbarous
and even savage.   There will be an American art commensurate with our idea and akin to this great continent; not an
imitation, but a fresh, new growth.   An American literature
also must come with democratic freedom, democratic thought,
democratic power--for we are not always to be pensioners
of other lands, doing nothing but import and quote; a literature with all of German philosophic depth, with English solid
sense, with French vivacity and wit, Italian fire of sentiment and soul, with all of Grecian elegance of form, and
more than Hebrew piety and faith in God.   We must not look
for the maiden's ringlets on the baby's brow; we are yet but
a girl; the nameless grace of maturity, and womanhood's
majestic charm, are still to come.   At length we must have
a system of education, which shall uplift the humblest,
rudest, worst born child in all the land; which shall bring
forth and bring up noble men.

An American State is a thing that must also be; a
State of free men who give over brawling, resting on industry, justice, love, not on war, cunning, and violence--
a State where liberty, equality, and fraternity are deeds as
well as words.   In its time the American Church must also
appear, with liberty, holiness, and love for its watchwords,
cultivating reason, conscience, affection, faith, and leading
the world's way in justice, peace, and love.   The Roman
Church has been all men know what and how; the American
Church, with freedom for the mind, freedom for the heart,
freedom for the soul, is yet to be, sundering no chord of the
human harp, but tuning all to harmony.   This also must
come; but hitherto no one has risen with genius fit to plan
its holy walls, conceive its columns, project its towers, or
lay its corner-stone.   Is it too much to hope all this?   Look
at the arena before us--look at our past history.   Hark!
there is the sound of many million men, the trampling of
their freeborn feet, the murmuring of their voice; a nation
born of this land that God reserved so long a virgin earth,
in a high day married to the human race, --rising and
swelling, and rolling on, strong and certain as the Atlantic

tide; they come numerous as ocean waves when east winds blow, their destination commensurate with the continent, with ideas vast as the Mississippi, strong as the Alleghenies, and awful as Niagara; they come murmuring little of the past, but, moving in the brightness of their great idea, and casting its light far on to other lands and distant days--come to the world's great work, to organize the rights of man.

5. THE WRITINGS OF
RALPH WALDO EMERSON*

1. <u>Nature, &c.</u> Boston: 1836. 1 vol. 12mo.
2. <u>Essays.</u> By R. W. Emerson. Boston: 1841. 1 vol. 12 mo.
3. <u>Essays: Second Series.</u> By R. W. Emerson. <u>Ibid.</u>: 1844. 1 vol. 12mo.
4. <u>Poems.</u> by R. W. Emerson. <u>Ibid.</u>: 1847. 1 vol. 12mo.
5. <u>Nature, Addresses and Orations.</u> By R. W. Emerson. <u>Ibid.</u>: 1849. 1 vol. 12mo.
6. <u>Representative Men: Seven Lectures.</u> By R. W. Emerson. <u>Ibid.</u>: 1850. 1 vol. 12mo.

When a hen lays an egg in the farmer's mow, she cackles quite loud and long. "See, " says the complacent bird, "see what an egg I have laid!" all the other hens cackle in sympathy, and seem to say, "what a nice egg has got laid! was there ever such a family of hens as our family?" But the cackling is heard only a short distance, in the neighbouring barnyards; a few yards above, the blue sky is silent. By and by the rest will drop their daily burden, and she will cackle with them in sympathy--but ere long the cackling is still; the egg has done its service, been addled, or eaten, or perhaps proved fertile of a chick, and it is forgotten, as well as the cackler who laid the ephemeral thing. But when an acorn in June first uncloses its shell, and the young oak puts out its earliest shoot, there is no noise; none attending its growth, yet it is destined to last some half a thousand years as a living tree, and serve as long after that for sound timber. Slowly and in silence, unseen in the dim recesses of the earth, the diamond gets formed by small accretions, age after age. There is no cackling in the caverns of the deep, as atom journeys to its fellow atom and the crystal is slowly getting made, to shine on the bosom of loveliness, or

---

*Parker, Theodore. <u>Collected Works</u>, ed. F. Cobbe (London: Trübner, 1863-79), X, 196-253. This appraisal of Emerson first appeared in the March, 1850 issue of the <u>Massachusetts Quarterly Review</u>.

glitter in the diadem of an emperor, a thing of beauty and a joy for ever.

As with eggs, so is it with little books; when one of them is laid in some bookseller's mow, the parent and the literary barnyard are often full of the foolishest cackle, and seem as happy as the ambiguous offspring of frogs, in some shallow pool, in early summer. But by and by it is again with the books as with the eggs; the old noise is all hushed, and the little books all gone, while new authors are at the same work again.

Gentle reader, we will not find fault with such books, they are as useful as eggs; yea, they are indispensable; the cackle of authors, and that of hens--why should they not be allowed? Is it not written that all things shall work after their kind, and so produce; and does not this rule extend from the hen-roost to the American Academy and all the Royal Societies of literature in the world? Most certainly. But when a great book gets written, it is published with no fine flourish of trumpets; the world does not speedily congratulate itself on the accession made to its riches; the book must wait awhile for its readers. Literary gentlemen of the tribe of Bavius and Maevius are popular in their time, and get more praise than bards afterwards famous. What audience did Athens and Florence give to their Socrates and their Dante? What price did Milton get for the Paradise Lost? How soon did men appreciate Shakespeare? Not many years ago, George Steevens, who "edited" the works of that bard, thought an "Act of Parliament was not strong enough" to make men read his sonnets, though they bore the author up to a great height of fame, and he sat where Steevens "durst not soar." In 1686, there had been four editions of Flatman's Poems; five of Waller's; eight of Cowley's; but in eleven years, of the Paradise Lost only three thousand copies were sold; yet the edition was cheap, and Norris of Bemerton went through eight or nine editions in a quite short time. For forty-one years, from 1623 to 1664, England was satisfied with two editions of Shakespeare, making, perhaps one thousand copies in all. Says Mr. Wordsworth of these facts: "There were readers in multitudes; but their money went for other purposes, as their admiration was fixed elsewhere." Mr. Wordsworth himself furnishes another example. Which found the readiest welcome, the Excursion and the Lyrical Poems of that writer, or Mr. Macaulay's Lays of Ancient Rome? How many a little philosophist in Germany went up in his rocket-like ascension, while the bookseller at Königsberg despaired over the unsaleable sheets of Immanuel Kant!

Says an Eastern proverb, "the sage is the instructor
of a hundred ages," so he can afford to wait till one or two
be past away, abiding with the few, waiting for the fit and
the many. Says a writer:

> There is somewhat touching in the madness with
> which the passing age mischooses the object on which
> all candles shine, and all eyes are turned; the care
> with which it registers every trifle touching Queen
> Elizabeth, and King James, and the Essexes, Lei-
> cesters, Burleighs, and Buckinghams; and lets pass,
> without a single valuable note, the founder of another
> dynasty, which alone will cause the Tudor dynasty to
> be remembered, --the man who carries the Saxon
> race in him by the inspiration which feeds him, and
> on whose thoughts the foremost people of the world
> are now for some ages to be nourished, and minds
> to receive this and not another bias. A popular
> player, --nobody suspected he was the poet of the
> human race; and the secret was kept as faithfully
> from poets and intellectual men, as from courtiers
> and frivolous people. Bacon, who took the inventory
> of the human understanding for his times, never
> mentioned his name. Ben Jonson had no suspicion
> of the elastic fame whose first vibrations he was
> attempting. He no doubt thought the praise he has
> conceded to him generous, and esteemed himself,
> out of all question, the better poet of the two.

> If it need wit to know wit, according to the proverb,
> Shakespeare's time should be capable of recognizing
> it. ... Since the constellation of great men who
> appeared in Greece in the time of Pericles, there
> was never any such society;--yet their genius failed
> them to find out the best head in the universe. Our
> poet's mask was impenetrable. You cannot see the
> mountain near. It took a century to make it sus-
> pected; and not until two centuries had passed, after
> his death, did any criticism which we think adequate
> begin to appear. It was not possible to write the
> history of Shakespeare till now.

It is now almost fourteen years since Mr. Emerson
published his first book: Nature. A beautiful work it was,
and will be deemed for many a year to come. In this old

world of literature, with more memory than wit, with much
tradition and little invention, with more fear than love, and
a great deal of criticism upon very little poetry, there came
forward this young David, a shepherd, but to be a king,
"with his garlands and singing robes about him"; one note
upon his new and fresh-strung lyre was "worth a thousand
men." Men were looking for something original, they always
are; when it came some said it thundered, others that an
angel had spoke. How men wondered at the little book! It
took nearly twelve years to sell the five hundred copies of
Nature. Since that time Mr. Emerson has said much, and if
he has not printed many books, at least has printed much;
some things far surpassing the first essay, in richness of
material, in perfection of form, in continuity of thought; but
nothing which has the same youthful freshness, and the same
tender beauty as this early violet, blooming out of Unitarian
and Calvinistic sand or snow. Poems and Essays of a later
date are there, which show that he has had more time and
woven it into life; works which present us with thought deeper, wider, richer, and more complete, but not surpassing
the simplicity and loveliness of that maiden flower of his
poetic spring.

We know how true it is, that a man cannot criticise
what he cannot comprehend, nor comprehend either a man or
a work greater than himself. Let him get on a Quarterly
never so high, it avails him nothing; "pyramids are pyramids
in vales," and emmets are emmets even in a Review. Critics
often afford an involuntary proof of this adage, yet grow no
wiser by the experience. Few of our tribe can make the
simple shrift of the old Hebrew poet, and say, "we have not
exercised ourselves in great matters, nor in things too high
for us." Sundry Icarian critics have we seen, wending their
wearying way on waxen wing to overtake the eagle flight of
Emerson; some of them have we known getting near enough to
see a fault, to overtake a feather falling from his wing, and
with that tumbling to give name to a sea, if one cared to
notice to what depth they fell.

Some of the criticisms on Mr. Emerson, transatlantic
and cisatlantic, have been very remarkable, not to speak
more definitely. "What of this new book?" said Mr. Public
to the reviewer, who was not "seized and tied down to judge,"
but of his own free will stood up and answered: "Oh! 'tis out
of all plumb, my lord--quite an irregular thing! not one of
the angles at the four corners is a right angle. I had my
rule and compasses, my lord, in my pocket. And for the

poem, your lordship bid me look at it--upon taking the
length, breadth, height, and depth of it, and trying them at
home, upon an exact scale of Bossu's--they are out, my
lord, in every one of their dimensions. "

Oh, gentle reader, we have looked on these efforts of
our brother critics not without pity.   There is an excellent
bird, terrene, marine, and semi-aerial; a broad-footed bird,
broad-beaked, broad-backed, broad-tailed; a notable bird she
is, and a long-lived; a useful bird, once indispensable to
writers, as furnishing the pen, now frutiful in many a hint.
But when she undertakes to criticise the music of the thrush,
or the movement of the humming-bird, why, she oversteps
the modesty of her nature, and if she essays the flight of the
eagle--she is fortunate if she falls only upon the water. "No
man, " says the law, "may stultify himself. "   Does not this
canon apply to critics?   No, the critic may do so.   Suicide
is a felony, but if a critic only slay himself critically,
dooming himself to "hoise with his own petard, " why, 'tis to
be forgiven

> That in our aspirations to be great,
> Our destinies o'erleap our mortal state.

In a place where there were no Quarterly Journals,
the veracious historian, Sir Walter Scott, relates that Claud
Halcro, ambitious of fame, asked his fortune of an Orcadian
soothsayer:

> Tell me, shall my lays be sung.
> Like Hacon's of the golden tongue,
> Long after Halcro's dead and gone?
> Or shall Hialtland's minstrel own
> One note to rival glorious John?

She answers, that as things work after their kind, the
result is after the same kind:

> The eagle mounts the polar sky,
> The Imber-goose, unskill'd to fly,
> Must be content to glide along
> When seal and sea-dog list his song.

We are warned by the fate of our predecessors, when
their example does not guide us; we confess not only our in-
feriority to Mr. Emerson, but our consciousness of the fact,
and believe that they should "judge others who themselves

excel, " and that authors, like others on trial, should be
judged by their peers.   So we will not call this a criticism,
which we are about to write on Mr. Emerson, only an attempt at a contribution towards a criticism, hoping that, in
due time, some one will come and do faithfully and completely, what it is not yet time to accomplish, still less
within our power to do.

All of Mr. Emerson's literary works, with the exception of the Poems, were published before they were printed;
delivered by word of mouth to audiences.   In frequently
reading his pieces, he had an opportunity to see any defect
of form and amend it.   Mr. Emerson has won by his writings a more desirable reputation than any other man of
letters in America has yet attained.   It is not the reputation
which bring him money or academic honours, or membership
of learned societies; nor does it appear conspicuously in the
literary journals as yet.   But he has a high place among
thinking men, on both sides of the water; we think no man
who writes the English tongue has now so much influence in
forming the opinions and character of young men and women.
His audience steadily increases, at home and abroad, more
rapidly in England than America.   It is now with him as it
was, at first, with Dr. Channing; the fairest criticism has
come from the other side of the water; the reason is that he,
like his predecessor, offended the sectarian and party spirit,
the personal prejudices of the men about him; his life was a
reproach to them, his words an offence, or his doctrines
alarmed their sectarian, their party, or their personal
pride, and they accordingly condemned the man.   A writer
who should bear the same relation to the English mind as
Emerson to ours, for the same reason would be more acceptable here than at home.   Emerson is neither a sectarian
nor a partisan, no man less so; yet few men in America
have been visited with more hatred, --private personal
hatred, which the authors poorly endeavoured to conceal, and
perhaps did hide from themselves.   The spite we have heard
expressed against him, by men of the common morality,
would strike a stranger with amazement, especially when it
is remembered that his personal character and daily life are
of such extraordinary loveliness.   This hatred has not proceeded merely from ignorant men, in whom it could easily
be excused; but more often from men who have had opportunities of obtaining as good a culture as men commonly get
in this country.   Yet while he has been the theme of vulgar
abuse, of sneers and ridicule in public and in private; while
critics, more remarkable for the venom of their poison than

the strength of their bow, have shot at him their little shafts,
barbed more than pointed, he has also drawn about him some
of what old Drayton called "the idle smoke of praise." Let
us see what he has thrown into the public fire to cause this
incense; what he has done to provoke the immedicable rage
of certain other men; let us see what there is in his works,
of old or new, true or false, what American and what cosmopolitan; let us weigh his works with such imperfect scales
as we have, weigh them by the universal standard of beauty,
truth, and love, and make an attempt to see what he is
worth.

American literature may be distributed into two grand
divisions: namely, the permanent literature, consisting of
books not written for a special occasion, books which are
bound between hard covers; and the transient literature, written for some special occasion and not designed to last beyond
that.   Our permanent literature is almost wholly an imitation
of old models.   The substance is old, and the form old.
There is nothing American about it.   But as our writers are
commonly quite deficient in literary culture and scientific
discipline, their productions seem poor when compared with
the imitative portion of the permanent literature in older
countries, where the writers start with a better discipline
and a better acquaintance with letters and art.   This inferi-
ority of culture is one of the misfortunes incident to a new
country, especially to one where practical talent is so much
and so justly preferred to merely literary accomplishment
and skill.   This lack of culture is yet more apparent, in
general, in the transient literature which is produced mainly
by men who have had few advantages for intellectual discipline
in early life, and few to make acquaintance with books at a
later period.   That portion of our literature is commonly
stronger and more American, but it is often coarse and rude.
The permanent literature is imitative; the other is rowdy.
But we have now no time to dwell upon this theme, which
demands a separate paper.

Mr. Emerson is the most American of our writers.
The idea of America, which lies at the bottom of our original
institutions, appears in him with great prominence.   We
mean the idea of personal freedom, of the dignity and value
of human nature, the superiority of a man to the accidents
of a man.   Emerson is the most republican of republicans,
the most protestant of the dissenters.   Serene as a July sun,
he is equally fearless.   He looks everything in the face
modestly, but with earnest scrutiny, and passes judgment

upon its merits.   Nothing is too high for his examination;
nothing too sacred.   On earth only one thing he finds which
is thoroughly venerable, and that is the nature of man; not
the accidents, which make a man rich or famous, but the
substance, which makes him a man.   The man is before the
institutions of man; his nature superior to his history.   All
finite things are only appendages of man, useful, convenient,
or beautiful.   Man is master, and nature his slave, serving
for many a varied use.   The results of human experience--
the State, the Church, society, the family, business, literature, science, art--all of these are subordinate to man: if
they serve the individual, he is to foster them, if not, to
abandon them and seek better things.   He looks at all things,
the past and the present, the State and the Church, Christianity and the market-house, in the daylight of the intellect.
Nothing is allowed to stand between him and his manhood.
Hence there is an apparent irreverence; he does not bow to
any hat which Gessler has set up for public adoration, but
to every man, canonical or profane, who bears the mark of
native manliness.   He eats show-bread, if he is hungry.
While he is the most American, he is almost the most cosmopolitan of our writers, the least restrained and belittled
by the popular follies of the nation or the age.

In America, writers are commonly kept in awe and
subdued by fear of the richer class, or that of the mass of
men.   Mr. Emerson has small respect for either; would bow
as low to a lackey as a lord, to a clown as a scholar, to
one man as a million.   He spurns all constitutions but the
law of his own nature, rejecting them with manly scorn.
The traditions of the churches are no hindrances to his
thought; Jesus or Judas were the same to him, if either
stood in his way and hindered the proportionate development
of his individual life.   The forms of society and the ritual of
scholarship are no more effectual restraints.   His thought of
to-day is no barrier to freedom of thought tomorrow, for his
own nature is not to be subordinated, either to the history of
man, or his own history.   "Tomorrow to fresh fields and
pastures new, " is his motto.

Yet, with all this freedom, there is no willful display
of it.   He is so confident of his freedom, so perfectly possessed of his rights, that he does not talk of them.   They
appear, but are not spoken of.   With the hopefulness and
buoyant liberty of America, he has none of our ill-mannered
boasting.   He criticises America often; he always appreciates
it; he seldom praises, and never brags of our country.   The

most democratic of democrats, no disciple of the old régime
is better mannered, for it is only the vulgar democrat or
aristocrat who flings his follies in your face.   While it would
be difficult to find a writer so uncompromising in his ad-
hesion to just principles, there is not in all his works a
single jeer or ill-natured sarcasm.   None is less addicted to
the common forms of reverence, but who is more truly re-
verential?

          While his idea is American, the form of his literature
is not less so.   It is a form which suits the substance, and
is modified by the institutions and natural objects about him.
You see that the author lives in a land with free institutions,
with town-meetings and ballot-boxes; in the vicinity of a decaying church; amongst men whose terrible devils are poverty
and social neglect, the only devils whose damnation is much
cared for.   His geography is American.   Katskill and the
Alleghanies, Monadnock, Wachusett, and the uplands of New
Hampshire, appear in poetry or prose; Contocook and Agio-
chook are better than the Ilyssus, or Pactolus, or "smooth-
sliding Mincius, crowned with vocal reeds."   New York, Fall
River, and Lowell have a place in his writings, where a vulgar Yankee would put Thebes or Paestum.   His men and
women are American--John and Jane, not Coriolanus and
Persephone.   He tells of the rhodora, the club-moss, the
blooming clover, not of the hibiscus and the asphodel.   He
knows the humblebee, the blackbird, the bat, and the wren,
and is not ashamed to say or sing of the things under his own
eyes.   He illustrates his high thought by common things out
of our plain New-England life--the meeting in the church, the
Sunday school, the dancing-school, a huckleberry party, the
boys and girls hastening home from school, the youth in the
shop, beginning an unconscious courtship with his unheeding
customer, the farmers about their work in the fields, the
bustling trader in the city, the cattle, the new hay, the
voters at a town-meeting, the village brawler in a tavern full
of tipsy riot, the conservative who thinks the nation is lost
if his ticket chance to miscarry, the bigot worshipping the
knot hole through which a dusty beam of light has looked in
upon his darkness, the radical who declares that nothing is
good if established, and the patent reformer who screams in
your ears that he can finish the world with a single touch, --
and out of all these he makes his poetry, or illustrates his
philosophy.   Now and then he wanders off to other lands, reports what he has seen, but it is always an American report
of what an American eye saw.   Even Mr. Emerson's recent
exaggerated praise of England is such a panegyric as none

but an American could bestow.

We know an American artist who is full of American
scenery.   He makes good drawings of Tivoli and Subiaco,
but, to colour them, he dips his pencil in the tints of the
American heaven, and over his olive trees and sempervives,
his asses and his priests, he sheds the light only of his
native sky.   So is it with Mr. Emerson.   Give him the range
of the globe, it is still an American who travels.

Yet with this indomitable nationality, he has a culture
quite cosmopolitan and extraordinary in a young nation like
our own.   Here is a man familiar with books, not with many,
but the best books, which he knows intimately.   He has kept
good company.   Two things impress you powerfully and con-
tinually--the man has seen nature, and been familiar with
books.   His literary culture is not a varnish on the surface;
not a mere polish of the outside; it has penetrated deep into
his consciousness.   The salutary effect of literary culture is
more perceptible in Emerson than in any American that we
know, save one, a far younger man, and of great promise,
of whom we shall speak at some other time.

We just now mentioned that our writers were sorely
deficient in literary culture.   Most of them have only a
smattering of learning, but some have read enough, read
and remembered with ability to quote.   Here is one who has
evidently read much, his subject required it, or his disposition, or some accident in his history furnished the occasion;
but his reading appears only in his quotations, or references
in the margin.   His literature has not penetrated his soul
and got incorporated with his whole consciousness.   You see
that he has been on Parnassus, by the huge bouquet, pedantic
in its complexity, that he affronts you with; not by the odour
of the flowers he has trampled or gathered in his pilgrimage,
not by Parnassian dust clinging to his shoes, or mountain
vigour in his eye.   The rose gatherer smells of his sweets,
and needs not prick you with the thorn to apprize you of
what he has dealt in.

Here is another writer who has studied much in the
various literatures of the world, but has lost himself therein.   Books supersede things, art stands between him and
nature, his figures are from literature not from the green
world.   Nationality is gone.   A traveller on the ocean of
letters, he has a mistress in every port, and a lodging-place
where the night overtakes him; all flags are the same to him,

all climes; he has no wife, no home, no country. He has
dropped nationality, and in becoming a cosmopolitan, has
lost his citizenship everywhere. So, with all Christendom
and heathendom for his metropolis, he is an alien everywhere
in the wide world. He has no literary inhabitiveness. Now
he studies one author, and is the penumbra thereof for a
time; now another, with the same result. Trojan or Tyrian
is the same to him, and he is Trojan or Tyrian as occasion
demands. A thin vapoury comet, with small momentum of
its own, he is continually deflected from his natural course
by the attraction of other and more substantial bodies, till
he has forgotten that he ever had any orbit of his own, and
dangles in the literary sky, now this way drawn, now that,
his only certain movement an oscillation. With a chameleon
variability, he attaches himself to this or the other writer,
and for the time his own colour disappears and he along with
it.

　　With Emerson all is very different; his literary culture is of him, and not merely on him. His learning appears
not in his quotations, but in his talk. It is the wine itself,
and not the vintner's brand on the cask, which shows its
quality. In his reading and his study, he is still his own
master. He has not purchased his education with the loss
of his identity, not of his manhood; nay, he has not forgotten
his kindred in getting his culture. He is still the master of
himself; no man provokes him even into a momentary imitation. He keeps his individuality with maidenly asceticism,
and with a conscience rarely found amongst literary men.
Virgil Homerizes, Hesiodizes, and plays Theocritus now and
then. Emerson plays Emerson, always Emerson. He
honours Greece, and is not a stranger with her noblest sons;
he pauses as a learner before the lovely muse of Germany;
he bows low with exaggerating reverence before the practical
skill of England; but no one, nor all of these, have power to
subdue that serene and upright intellect. He rises from the
oracle he stooped to consult just as erect as before. His
reading gives a certain richness to his style, which is more
literary than that of any American writer that we remember;
as much so as that of Jeremy Taylor. He takes much for
granted in his reader, as if he were addressing men who
had read everything, and wished to be reminded of what they
had read. In classic times, there was no reading public,
only a select audience of highly cultivated men. It was so
in England once; the literature of that period, indicates the
fact. Only religious and dramatic works were designed for
pit, box, and gallery. Nobody can speak more clearly and

more plainly than Emerson, but take any one of his essays
or orations, and you see that he does not write in the language of the mass of men, more than Thucydides or Tacitus.
His style is allusive, as an ode of Horace or Pindar, and
the allusions are to literature which is known to but few.
Hence, while his thought is human in substance, and American in its modifications, and therefore easily grasped, comprehended, and welcomed by men of the commonest culture,
it is but few who understand the entire meaning of the sentences which he writes.   His style reflects American
scenery, and is dimpled into rare beauty as it flows by, and
so has a pleasing fascination, but it reflects also the literary
scenery of his own mind, and so half of his thought is lost
on half his readers.   Accordingly no writer or lecturer finds
a readier access for his thoughts to the mind of the people
at large, but no American author is less intelligible to the
people in all his manifold meaning and beauty of allusion.
He has not completely learned to think with the sagest sages
and then put his thoughts into the plain speech of plain men.
Every word is intelligible in the massive speech of Mr. Webster, and has its effect, while Emerson has still something
of the imbecility of the scholar, as compared to the power
of the man of action, whose words fall like the notes of the
wood-thrush, each in its time and place, yet without picking
and choosing.   "Blacksmiths and teamsters do not trip in
their speech, " says he, "it is a shower of bullets.   It is
Cambridge men who correct themselves, and begin again at
every half sentence; and moreover, will pun and refine too
much, and swerve from the matter to the expression. " But
of the peculiarities of his style we shall speak again.

Emerson's works do not betray any exact scholarship,
which has a certain totality, as well as method about it.   It
is plain to see that his favourite authors have been Plutarch,
especially that outpouring of his immense common-place book,
his Moral Writings, Montaigne, Shakspeare, George Herbert,
Milton Wordsworth, Coleridge, and Carlyle.   Of late years,
his works contain allusions to the ancient oriental literature,
from which he has borrowed some hard names and some valuable thoughts, but is occasionally led astray by its influence, for it is plain that he does not understand that curious
philosophy he quotes from.   Hence his oriental allies are
brought up to take a stand which no man dreamed of in their
time, and made to defend ideas not known to men till long
after these antediluvian sages were at rest in their graves.

In Emerson's writings you do not see indications of

exact mental discipline, so remarkable in Bacon, Milton,
Taylor, and South, in Schiller, Lessing, and Schleiermacher;
neither has he the wide range of mere literature noticeable
in all other men.   He works up scientific facts in his writings with great skill, often penetrating beyond the fact, and
discussing the idea out of which it and many other kindred
facts seem to have proceeded: this indicates not only a nice
eye for facts, but a mind singularly powerful to detect latent
analogies, and see the one in the many.   Yet there is nothing
to show any regular and systematic discipline in science
which appears so eminently in Schiller and Hegel.   He seems
to learn his science from occasional conversation, with men
of science, or from statements of remarkable discoveries in
the common Journals, not from a careful and regular study
of facts or treatises.

       With all his literary culture he has an intense love of
nature, a true sight and appreciation thereof; not the analytic
eye of the naturalist, but the synthetic vision of the poet. A
book never clouds his sky.   His figures are drawn from nature, he sees the fact.   No chart of nature hangs up in his
windows to shut out nature herself.   How well he says:

              If a man would be alone, let him look at the stars.
              The rays that come from those heavenly worlds,
              will separate between him and vulgar things.   One
              might think the atmosphere was made transparent
              with this design, to give man in the heavenly
              bodies, the perpetual presence of the sublime.
              Seen in the streets of cities, how great they are!
              If the stars should appear one night in a thousand
              years, how would men believe and adore; and pre-
              serve for many generations the remembrance of
              the city of God which had been shown!   But every
              night come out these preachers of beauty, and light
              the universe with their admonishing smile....

              To speak truly, few adult persons can see nature.
              Most persons do not see the sun.   At least they
              have a very superficial seeing.   The sun illuminates
              only the eye of the man, but shines into the eye
              and the heart of the child.   The lover of nature is
              he whose inward and outward senses are still truly
              adjusted to each other; who has retained the spirit
              of infancy even into the era of manhood.   His in-
              tercourse with heaven and earth becomes part of
              his daily food.   In the presence of nature, a wild

delight runs through the man, in spite of real sorrows. Nature says, --he is my creature, and
maugre all his impertinent griefs, he shall be glad
with me. Not the sun or the summer alone, but
every hour and season yields its tribute of delight;
for every hour and change corresponds to and
authorizes a different state of the mind, from
breathless noon to grimmest midnight. Nature is
a setting that fits equally well a comic or a mourn-
ing piece. In good health, the air is a cordial of
incredible virtue. Crossing a bare common, in
snow puddles, at twilight, under a clouded sky,
without having in my thoughts any occurrence of
special good fortune, I have enjoyed a perfect ex-
hilaration. Almost I fear to think how glad I am.
In the woods too, a man casts off his years, as
the snake his slough, and at what period soever of
life, is always a child. In the woods is perpetual
youth. Within these plantations of God a decorum
and sanctity reign, a perennial festival is dressed,
and the guest sees not how he should tire of them
in a thousand years. In the woods, we return to
reason and faith. There I feel that nothing can be-
fall me in life, --no disgrace, no calamity (leaving
me my eyes), which nature cannot repair. Standing on the bare ground, --my head bathed by the
blithe air, and uplifted into infinite space, --all
mean egotism vanishes. I become a transparent
eyeball. I am nothing. I see all. The currents
of the Universal Being circulate through me; I am
part or particle of God. The name of the nearest
friend sounds then foreign and accidental. To be
brothers, to be acquaintances, --master or servant,
is then a trifle and a disturbance. I am the lover
of uncontained and immortal beauty. In the wilderness, I find something more dear and connate
than in streets or villages. In the tranquil land-
scape, and especially in the distant line of the
horizon, man beholds somewhat as beautiful as his
own nature....

The tradesman, the attorney, comes out of the din
and craft of the street, and sees the sky and the
woods, and is a man again. In their eternal calm
he finds himself. The health of the eye seems to
demand a horizon. We are never tired, so long as
we can see far enough.

But in other hours nature satisfies the soul purely
by its loveliness, and without any mixture of cor-
poreal benefit.   I have seen the spectacle of morning from the hill-top over against my house, from
daybreak to sun-rise, with emotions which an angel
might share.   The long slender bars of cloud float
like fishes in the sea of crimson light.   From the
earth as a shore, I look out into that silent sea.
I seem to partake its rapid transformations: the
active enchantment reaches my dust, and I dilate
and conspire with the morning wind.   How does
nature deify us with a few and cheap elements!
Give me health and a day, and I will make the
pomp of emperors ridiculous.   The dawn is my
Assyria; the sunset and moon-rise my Paphos, and
unimaginable realms of faerie; broad noon shall be
my England of the senses and the understanding;
the night shall be my Germany of mystic philosophy
and dreams. --Nature, pp. 9-10, 11-13, 21-22.

Most writers are demonized or possessed by some
one truth, or perhaps some one whim.   Look where they
will, they see nothing but that.   Mr. Emerson holds himself
erect, and no one thing engrosses his attention, no one idea;
no one intellectual faculty domineers over the rest.   Sensation does not dim reflection, nor does his thought lend its
sickly hue to the things about him.   Even Goethe, with all
his boasted equilibrium, held his intellectual faculties less
perfectly in hand than Emerson.   He has no hobbies to ride;
even his fondness for the ideal and the beautiful, does not
hinder him from obstinately looking real and ugly things in
the face.   He carries the American idea of freedom into his
most intimate personality, and keeps his individuality safe
and sacred.   He cautions young men against stooping their
minds to other men.   He knows no master.   Sometimes this
is carried to an apparent excess, and he underrates the real
value of literature, afraid lest the youth become a bookworm, and not a man thinking.   But how well he says:

Meek young men grow up in libraries, believing it
their duty to accept the views which Cicero, which
Locke, which Bacon, have given, forgetful that
Cicero, Locke, and Bacon were only young men in
libraries, when they wrote these books.   Hence,
instead of man thinking, we have the bookworm.

Books are the best of things, well used; abused,

among the worst.   What is the right use?   What
is the one end, which all means go to effect? They
are for nothing but to inspire.   I had better never
see a book, than to be warped by its attraction
clean out of my own orbit, and made a satellite
instead of a system.   The one thing in the world,
of value, is the active soul.   This every man is
entitled to; this every man contains within him,
although, in almost all men, obstructed, and as
yet unborn.   The soul active sees absolute truth;
and utters truth, or creates...   The books, the
college, the school of art, the institution of any
kind, stop with some past utterance of genius.
This is good, say they, --let us hold by this. They
pin me down.   They look backward and not forward.   But genius looks forward: the eyes of man
are set in his forehead, not in his hindhead: man
hopes: genius creates.   Whatever talents may be,
if the man creates not, the pure efflux of the Deity
is not his;--cinders and smoke there may be, but
not yet flame. . . .

The world of any moment is the merest appearance.
Some great decorum, some fetish of a government,
some ephemeral trade, or war, or man, is cried
up by half mankind and cried down by the other
half, as if all depended on this particular up or
down.   The odds are that the whole question is not
worth the poorest thought which the scholar has
lost in listening to the controversy.   Let him not
quit his belief that a popgun is a popgun, though
the ancient and honourable of the earth affirm it to
be the crack of doom.   In silence, in steadiness,
in severe abstraction, let him hold by himself; add
observation to observation, patient of neglect,
patient of reproach, and bide his own time, --happy
enough, if he can satisfy himself alone, that this
day he has seen something truly.   Success treads
on every right step.   For the instinct is sure that
prompts him to tell his brother what he thinks.
He then learns, that in going down into the secrets
of his own mind, he has descended into the secrets
of all minds.   He learns that he who has mastered
any law in his private thoughts, is master to that
extent of all men whose language he speaks, and
of all into whose language his own can be translated.   The poet, in utter solitude remembering his

spontaneous thoughts and recording them, is found
to have recorded that which men in crowded cities
find true for them also. --<u>Nature, Addresses, Etc.</u>
pp. 85, 85-86, 98-99.

To us the effect of Emerson's writings is profoundly
religious; they stimulate to piety, the love of God, to goodness as the love of man.   We know no living writer, in any
language, who exercises so powerful a religious influence as
he.   Most young persons, not ecclesiastical, will confess
this.   We know he is often called hard names on pretence
that he is not religious.   We remember once being present
at a meeting of gentlemen, scholarly men some of them,
after the New-England standard of scholarship, who spent the
evening in debating "Whether Ralph Waldo Emerson was a
Christian. "   The opinion was quite generally entertained that
he was not: for "discipleship was necessary to Christianity. "
"And the essence of Christian discipleship" was thought to
consist in "sitting at the feet of our blessed Lord (pronounced Laawd!) and calling him Master, which Emerson
certainly does not do. "   We value Christianity as much as
most men, and the name Christian to us is very dear; but
when we remembered the character, the general tone and
conduct of the men who arrogate to themselves the name
Christian, and seem to think they have a right to monopolize
the Holy Spirit of Religion, and "shove away the worthy
bidden guest, " the whole thing reminded us of a funny story
related by an old writer: "It was once proposed in the
British House of Commons, that James Usher, afterward the
celebrated Archbishop of Armagh, but then a young man,
should be admitted to the assembly of the 'King's Divines. '
The proposition, if we remember rightly, gave rise to some
debate, upon which John Selden, a younger man than Usher,
but highly distinguished and much respected, rose and said,
"that it reminded him of a proposition which might be made,
that Inigo Jones, the famous architect, should be admitted
to the worshipful company of Mousetrap Makers!"

Mr. Emerson's writings are eminently religious;
Christian in the best sense of that word.   This has often
been denied for two reasons: because Mr. Emerson sets
little value on the mythology of the Christian sects, no more
perhaps than on the mythology of the Greeks and the Scandi-
navians, and also because his writings far transcend the
mechanical morality and formal pietism, commonly recommended by gentlemen in pulpits.   Highly religious, he is not
at all ecclesiastical or bigoted.   He has small reverence for

forms and traditions; a manly life is the only form of religion which he recognizes, and hence we do not wonder at all
that he also has been deemed an infidel.   It would be very
surprising if it were not so.   Still it is not religion that is
most conspicuous in these volumes; that is not to be looked
for except in the special religious literature, yet we must
confess that any one of Emerson's works seems far more
religious than what are commonly called "good books, " including the class of sermons.

To show what is in Mr. Emerson's books and what is
not, let us make a little more detailed examination thereof.
He is not a logical writer, not systematic; not what is commonly called philosophical; didactic to a great degree, but
never demonstrative.   So we are not to look for a scientific
plan, or for a system, of which the author is himself conscious.   Still, in all sane men, there must be a system,
though the man does not know it.   There are two ways of
reporting upon an author: one is to represent him by specimens, the other to describe him by analysis; one to show off
a finger or foot of the Venus de Medici, the other to give
the dimensions thereof.   We will attempt both, and will speak
of Mr. Emerson's starting point, his terminus a quo; then of
his method of procedure, his via in qua; then of the conclusion he arrives at, his terminus ad quem.   In giving the dimensions of his statue, we shall exhibit also some of the
parts described.

Most writers, knowingly or unconsciously, take as
their point of departure some special and finite thing.   This
man starts from a tradition, the philosophical tradition of
Aristotle, Plato, Leibnitz, or Locke, this from the theological tradition of the Protestants or the Catholics, and never
will dare get out of sight of his authorities; he takes the
bearing of everything from his tradition.   Such a man may
sail the sea for ages, he arrives nowhere at the last.   Our
traditionist must not outgo his tradition; the Catholic must
not get beyond his Church, nor the Protestant out-travel his
Bible.   Others start from some fixed fact, a sacrament, a
constitution, the public opinion, the public morality, or the
popular religion.   This they are to defend at all hazards; of
course they will retain all falsehood and injustice which
favour this institution, and reject all justice and truth which
oppose the same.   Others pretend to start from God, but in
reality do take their departure from a limited conception of
God, from the Hebrew notion of Him, or the Catholic notion,
from the Calvinistic or the Unitarian notion of God.   By and

by they are hindered and stopped in their progress.   The
philosophy of these three classes of men is always vitiated
by the prejudices they start with.

Mr. Emerson takes man for his point of departure,
he means to take the whole of man; man with his history,
man with his nature, his sensational, intellectual, moral,
affectional, and religious instincts and faculties.   With him
man is the measure of all things, of ideas and of facts; if
they fit man they are accepted, if not, thrown aside.   This
appears in his first book and in his last:

> The foregoing generations beheld God and nature
> face to face; we, through their eyes.   Why should
> not we also enjoy an original relation to the uni-
> verse?   Why should not we have a poetry and phi-
> losophy of insight and not of tradition, and a re-
> ligion by a revelation to us, and not the history of
> theirs?   Embosomed for a season in nature, whose
> floods of life stream around and through us, and
> invite us, by the powers they supply, to action pro-
> portioned to nature, why should we grope among
> the dry bones of the past, or put the living gen-
> eration into masquerade out of its faded wardrobe?
> The sun shines to-day also.   There is more wool
> and flax in the fields.   There are new lands, new
> men, new thoughts.   Let us demand our own works
> and laws and worship. --Nature, pp. 5-6.

Again he speaks in a higher mood of the same theme:

> That is always best which gives me to myself.
> The sublime is excited in me by the great stoical
> doctrine, Obey thyself.   That which shows God in
> me, fortifies me.   That which shows God out of
> me, makes me a wart and a wen.   There is no
> longer a necessary reason for my being.   Already
> the long shadows of untimely oblivion creep over
> me, and I shall decease for ever.
>
> Wherever a man comes, there comes revolution.
> The old is for slaves.   When a man comes, all
> books are legible, all things transparent, all reli-
> gions are forms.   He is religious.   Man is the
> wonder-worker.   He is seen amid miracles.   All
> men bless and curse.   He saith yea and nay only.
> The stationariness of religion; the assumption that

the age of inspiration is past, that the Bible is
closed; the fear of degrading the character of
Jesus by representing him as a man; indicate with
sufficient clearness the falsehood of our theology.
It is the office of a true teacher to show us that
God is, not was; that he speaketh, not spake.

Let me admonish you, first of all, to go alone; to
refuse the good models, even those which are
sacred in the imagination of men, and dare to love
God without mediator or veil.   Friends enough you
shall find who will hold up to your emulation Wes-
leys and Oberlins, Saints and Prophets.   Thank
God for these good men, but say, 'I also am a
man.'   Imitation cannot go above its model.   The
imitator dooms himself to hopeless mediocrity.
The inventor did it, because it was natural to him,
and so in him it has a charm.   In the imitator,
something else is natural, and he bereaves himself
of his own beauty, to come short of another man's.

Yourself a new-born bard of the Holy Ghost, --cast
behind you all conformity, and acquaint men at the
first hand with Deity.   Look to it first and only,
that fashion, custom, authority, pleasure, and
money, are nothing to you, --are not bandages over
your eyes, that you cannot see, --but live the privilege of the immeasurable mind. --Nature, Addresses,
Etc., pp. 127-128, 139-140, 141.

Let man then learn the revelation of all nature,
and all thought to his heart: this, namely; that the
Highest dwells with him; that the sources of nature
are in his own mind, if the sentiment of duty is
there.   But if he would know what the great God
speaketh, he must 'go into his closet and shut the
door,' as Jesus said.   God will not make Himself
manifest to cowards.   He must greatly listen to
himself, withdrawing himself from all the accents
of other men's devotion.   Their prayers even are
hurtful to him, until he has made his own.   The
soul makes no appeal from itself.   Our religion
vulgarly stands on numbers of believers.   Whenever the appeal is made, --no matter how indirectly,
--to numbers proclamation is then and there made,
that religion is not.   He that finds God a sweet,

enveloping thought to him, never counts his company.   When I sit in that presence, who shall dare
to come in?   When I rest in perfect humility, when
I burn with pure love, --what can Calvin or Swedenborg say?--Essays, p. 243.

And again in his latest publication:

The gods of fable are the shining moments of great
men.   We run all our vessels into one mould.   Our
colossal theologies of Judaism, Christism, Bud-
dhism, Mahometism, are the necessary and struc-
tural action of the human mind.

Man is that noble endogenous plant which grows,
like the palm, from within, outward.... I count
him a great man who inhabits a higher sphere of
thought, into which other men rise with labour and
difficulty; he has but to open his eyes to see things
in a true light, and in large relations; whilst they
must make painful corrections, and keep a vigilant
eye on many sources of error.

The genius of humanity is the right point of view
of history....   For a time our teachers serve us
personally, as metres or milestones of progress.
Once they were angels of knowledge, and their
figures touched the sky.   Then we drew near, saw
their means, culture, and limits; and they yielded
their place to other geniuses.   Happy, if a few
names remain so high, that we have not been able
to read them nearer, and age and comparison have
not robbed them of a ray.   But, at last, we shall
cease to look in men for completeness, and shall
content ourselves with their social and delegated
quality.

Yet, within the limits of human education and
agency, we may say, great men exist that there
may be greater men.   The destiny of organized
nature is amelioration, and who can tell its limits?
It is for man to tame the chaos; on every side,
whilst he lives, to scatter the seeds of science
and of song, that climate, corn, animals, men
may be milder, and the germs of love and benefit
may be multiplied.

The world is young? the former great men call to
us affectionately. We too must write Bibles, to
unite again the heavens and the earthly world. The
secret of genius is to suffer no fiction to exist for
us; to realize all that we know; in the high refinement of modern life, in arts, in sciences, in books,
in men, to exact good faith, reality, and a purpose; and first, last, midst, and without end, to
honour every truth by use.-- Representative Men,
pp. 10-11, 12, 38, 39-40, 284-285.

In this Emerson is more American than America herself --and is himself the highest exponent in literature of this
idea of human freedom and the value of man.   Channing talks
of the dignity of human nature, his great and brilliant theme;
but he commonly, perhaps always, subordinates the nature of
man to some of the accidents of his history.   This Emerson
never does; no, not once in all his works, nor in all his
life. Still we think it is not the whole of man from which
he starts, that he undervalues the logical, demonstrative,
and historical understanding, with the results thereof, and
also undervalues the affections.   Hence his man, who is the
measure of all things, is not the complete man.   This defect
appears in his ethics, which are a little cold, the ethics of
marble men; and in his religious teachings, the highest which
this age has furnished, full of reverence, full of faith, but
not proportionably rich in affection.

Mr. Emerson has a method of his own as plainly
marked as that of Lord Bacon or Descartes, and as rigidly
adhered to.   It is not the inductive method, by which you
arrive at a general fact from many particular facts, but
never reach a universal law; it is not the deductive method,
whereby a minor law is derived from a major, a special
from a general law; it is neither inductive nor deductive demonstration.   But Emerson proceeds by the way of intuition,
sensational or spiritual.   Go to the fact and look for yourself, is his command: a material fact you cannot always
verify, and so for that must depend on evidence; a spiritual
fact you can always legitimate for yourself.   Thus he says:

That which seems faintly possible--it is so refined,
is often faint and dim because it is deepest seated
in the mind among the eternal verities.   Empirical
science is apt to cloud the sight, and, by the very
knowledge of functions and processes, to bereave
the student of the manly contemplation of the whole.

The savant becomes unpoetic.   But the best naturalist, who lends an entire and devout attention
to truth, will see that there remains much to learn
of his relation to the world, and that it is not to
be learned by any addition or subtraction or other
comparison of known quantities, but is arrived at
by untaught sallies of the spirit, by continual self-
recovery, and by entire humility.   He will perceive
that there are far more excellent qualities in the
student than preciseness and infallibility; that a
guess is often more fruitful than an indisputable
affirmation, and that a dream may let us deeper
into the secret of nature than a hundred concerted
experiments.

Every surmise and vatication of the mind is entitled to a certain respect, and we learn to prefer
imperfect theories, and sentences which contain
glimpses of truth, to digested systems which have
no one valuable suggestion.   A wise writer will
feel that the ends of study and composition are best
answered by announcing undiscovered regions of
thought, and so communicating, through hope, new
activity to the torpid spirit. --Nature, pp. 82-83,
86-87.

And again:

Jesus astonishes and overpowers sensual people.
They cannot unite him to history or reconcile him
with themselves.   As they come to revere their
intuitions and aspire to live holily, their own piety
explains every fact, every word.

The inquiry leads us to that source, at once the
essence of genius, the essence of virtue, and the
essence of life, which we call spontaneity or instinct.   We denote this primary wisdom as intuition, whilst all later teachings are tuitions.   In
that deep force, the last fact behind which analysis
cannot go, all things find their common origin.   For
the sense of being which in calm hours rises, we
know not how, in the soul, is not diverse from
things, from space, from light, from time, from
man, but one with them, and proceedeth obviously
from the same source whence their life and being
also proceedeth.   We first share the life by which

things exist, and afterwards see them as appearances in nature, and forget that we have shared their cause. Here is the fountain of action and the fountain of thought. Here are the lungs of that inspiration which giveth man wisdom, of that inspiration of man which cannot be denied without impiety and atheism. We lie in the lap of immense intelligence, which makes us organs of its activity and receivers of its truth. When we discern justice, when we discern truth, we do nothing of ourselves, but allow a passage to its beams. If we ask whence this comes, if we seek to pry into the soul that causes, --all metaphysics, all philosophy is at fault. Its presence or its absence is all we can affirm.... Perception is not whimsical, but fatal. If I see a trait, my children will see it after me, and in course of time, all mankind, --although it may chance that no one has seen it before me. For my perception of it is as much a fact as the sun.

The relations of the soul to the Divine Spirit are so pure that it is profane to seek to interpose helps. It must be that when God speaketh, He should communicate not one thing but all things; should fill the world with His voice; should scatter forth light, nature, time, souls, from the centre of the present thought; and new-date and new-create the whole. Whenever a mind is simple, and receives a divine wisdom, then old things pass away, --means, teachers, texts, temples fall; it lives now and absorbs past and future into the present hour.

The soul is the perceiver and revealer of truth. We know truth when we see it, let sceptic and scoffer say what they choose. Foolish people ask you, when you have spoken what they do not wish to hear, 'how do you know it is the truth, and not an error of your own?' We know truth, when we see it, from opinion, as we know when we are awake that we are awake.

The great distinction between teachers, sacred or literary; between poets like Herbert and poets like Pope; between philosophers like Spinoza, Kant, and Coleridge, --and philosophers like Locke, Paley, Mackintosh, and Stewart; between men of the world

who are reckoned accomplished talkers, and here
and there a fervent mystic, prophesying half-insane
under the infinitude of his thought; is, that one
class speak from within, or from experience, as
parties and possessors of the fact; and the other
class, from without, as spectators merely, or perhaps as acquainted with the fact, on the evidence
of third persons.   It is of no use to preach to me
from without.   I can do that too easily myself.

The soul gives itself alone, original, and pure, to
the Lonely, Original, and Pure, who, on that condition, gladly inhabits, leads, and speaks through
it.   Then is it glad, young, and nimble.   It is not
wise, but it sees through all things.   It is not
called religious, but it is innocent.   It calls the
light its own, and feels that the grass grows and
the stone falls by a law inferior to, and dependent
on, its nature.   Behold, it saith, I am born into
the great, the universal mind.   I, the imperfect,
adore my own Perfect.   I am somehow receptive
of the Great Soul, and thereby I do overlook the
sun and the stars, and feel them to be but the fair
accidents and effects which change and pass.   More
and more the surges of everlasting nature enter
into me, and I become public and human in my regards and actions.   So come I to live in thoughts
and act with energies which are immortal. --Essays,
pp. 23, 52-53, 53-54, 231, 237, 245.

All your learning of all literatures would never enable you to anticipate one of its thoughts or expressions, and yet each is natural and familiar as
household words. --Nature, Addresses, Etc. , p. 209.

The same method in his last work is ascribed to
Plato:

Add to this, he believes that poetry, prophecy, and
the high insight, are from a wisdom of which man
is not master; that the gods never philosophize; but,
by a celestial mania, these miracles are accomplished. --Representative Men, p. 61.

Sometimes he exaggerates the value of this, and puts
the unconscious before the self-conscious state:

It is pitiful to be an artist, when, by forbearing
to be artists, we might be vessels filled with the
divine overflowings, enriched by the circulations of
omniscience and omnipresence. Are there not moments in the history of heaven when the human race
was not counted by individuals, but was only the
Influenced, was God in distribution, God rushing
into multiform benefit? It is sublime to receive,
sublime to love, but this lust of imparting as from
us, this desire to be loved, the wish to be recognized as individuals, --is finite, comes of a lower
strain. --Nature, Address, &c., pp. 201-202.

He is sometimes extravagant in the claims made for
his own method, and maintains that ecstasy is the natural
and exclusive mode of arriving at new truths, while it is
only one mode. Ecstasy is the state of intuition in which the
man loses his individual self-consciousness. Moments of
this character are few and rare even with men like the St.
Victors, like Tauler, and Böhme and Swedenborg. The writings of all these men, especially of the two last, who most
completely surrendered themselves to this mode of action,
show how poor and insufficient it is. All that mankind has
learned in this way is little, compared with the results of
reflection, of meditation, and careful, conscientious looking
after truth: all the great benefactors of the world have been
patient and continuous in their work;

Not from a vain and shallow thought
His awful Jove young Phidias brought.

Mr. Emerson says books are only for one's idle
hours; he discourages hard and continuous thought, conscious
modes of argument, of discipline. Here he exaggerates his
idiosyncracy into a universal law. The method of nature is
not ecstasy, but patient attention. Human nature avenges
herself for the slight he puts on her, by the irregular and
rambling character of his own productions. The vice appears more glaring in the Emersonidae, who have all the
agony without the inspiration; who affect the unconscious;
write even more ridiculous nonsense than their "genius" requires; are sometimes so child-like as to become mere
babies, and seem to forget that the unconscious state is
oftener below the conscious than above it, and that there is
an ecstasy of folly as well as of good sense.

Some of these imbeciles have been led astray by this

extravagant and one-sided statement.   What if books have
hurt Mr. Oldbuck, and many fine wits lie "sheathed to the
hilt in ponderous tomes, " sheathed and rusted in so that no
Orson could draw the blade, --we need not deny the real
value of books, still less the value of the serious and patient
study of thoughts and things.   Michael Angelo and Newton had
some genius; Socrates is thought not destitute of philosophical
power; but no dauber of canvas, no sportsman with marble,
ever worked like Angelo; the two philosophers wrought by
their genius, but with an attention, an order, a diligence,
and a terrible industry and method of thought, without which
their genius would have ended in nothing but guess-work.
Much comes by spontaneous intuition, which is to be got in
no other way; but much is to precede that, and much to follow it.   There are two things to be considered in the matter
of inspiration, one is the Infinite God from whom it comes,
the other the finite capacity which is to receive it.   If Newton had never studied, it would be as easy for God to reveal
the calculus to his dog Diamond as to Newton.   We once
heard of a man who thought everything was in the soul, and
so gave up all reading, all continuous thought.   Said another,
"if all is in the soul, it takes a man to find it. "

Here are some of the most important conclusions Mr.
Emerson has hitherto arrived at.

Man is above nature, the material world.   Last
winter, in his lectures, he was understood to affirm "the
identity of man with nature"; a doctrine which seems to have
come from his oriental reading before named, a doctrine
false as well as inconsistent with the first principles of his
philosophy.   But in his printed works he sees clearly the
distinction between the two, a fact not seen by the Hindoo
philosophers, but first by the Hebrew and Greek writers.
Emerson puts man far before nature:

> We are taught by great actions that the universe is
> the property of every individual in it.   Every ra-
> tional creature has all nature for his dowry and
> estate.   It is his if he will.   He may divest him-
> self of it; he may creep into a corner, and abdicate
> his kingdom, as most men do, but he is entitled to
> the world by his constitution.   In proportion to the
> energy of his thought and will, he takes up the
> world into himself.

Thus in art, does nature work through the will of

a man filled with the beauty of her first works.

> Nature is thoroughly mediate. It is made to serve.
> It receives the dominion of man as meekly as the
> ass on which the Saviour rode. It offers all its
> kingdoms to man as the raw material which he may
> mould into what is useful. --Nature, pp. 25, 30, 50-
> 51.

Nature is "an appendix to the soul."

Then the man is superior to the accidents of his past
history or present condition:

> No man ever prayed heartily, without learning
> something. --Nature, p. 92.

> The highest merit we ascribe to Moses, Plato, and
> Milton, is that they set at nought books and tradi-
> tions, and spoke not what men said but what they
> thought. A man should learn to detect and watch
> that gleam of light which flashes across his mind
> from within, more than the lustre of the firmament
> of bards and sages.

> Kingdom and lordship, power and estate, are a
> gaudier vocabulary than private John and Edward in
> a small house and common day's work; but the
> things of life are the same to both; the sum total
> of both is the same. Why all this deference to
> Alfred, and Scanderbeg, and Gustavus? Suppose
> they were virtuous; did they wear out virtue? As
> great a stake depends on your private act to-day,
> as followed their public and renowned steps. When
> private men shall act with vast views, the lustre
> will be transferred from the actions of kings to
> those of gentlemen. --Essays, pp. 37, 38, 51-52.

Hence a man must be true to his present conviction,
careless of consistency:

> A foolish consistency is the hobgoblin of little
> minds, adored by little statesmen and philosophers
> and divines. With consistency a great soul has
> simply nothing to do. He may as well concern him-
> self with his shadow on the wall. Out upon your
> guarded lips! Sew them up with packthread, do.

Else, if you would be a man, speak what you think
to-day in words as hard as cannon-balls, and tomorrow speak what to-morrow thinks in hard words
again, though it contradict everything you said to-
day. --Essays, p. 47.

The man must not be a slave to a single form of
thought:

How wearisome the grammarian, the phrenologist,
the political or religious fanatic, or indeed any
possessed mortal, whose balance is lost by the exaggeration of a single topic.   It is incipient in-
sanity. --Essays, p. 280.

Man is inferior to the great law of God, which over-
rides the world; "His wealth and greatness consist in his
being the channel through which heaven flows to earth"; "the
word of a poet is only the mouth of divine wisdom"; "the man
on whom the soul descends--alone can teach:" all nature
"from the sponge up to Hercules is to hint or to thunder man
the laws of right and wrong." This ethical character seems
the end of nature: "the moral law lies at the centre of nature
and radiates to the circumference.   It is the pith and mar-
row of every substance, every relation, every process. All
things with which we deal point to us.   What is a farm but
a mute gospel?" Yet he sometimes tells us that man is
identical with God under certain circumstances, an old Hindoo notion, a little favoured by some passages in the New
Testament, and revived by Hegel in modern times, in whom
it seems less inconsistent than in Emerson.

This moral law continually gives men their compensation.   "You cannot do wrong without suffering wrong."

And this law of laws which the pulpit, the senate,
and the college deny, is hourly preached in all
markets and all languages, by flights of proverbs,
whose teaching is as true and as omnipresent as
that of birds and flies.

All things are double, one against another. --Tit
for tat; an eye for an eye; a tooth for a tooth;
blood for blood; measure for measure; love for
love. --Give and it shall be given you. --He that
watereth shall be watered himself. --What will you
have? quoth God; pay for it and take it. --Nothing

venture, nothing have. --Thou shalt be paid exactly for what thou hast done, no more, no less. --
Who doth not work shall not eat. --Harm watch,
harm catch. --Curses always recoil on the head of
him who imprecates them. --If you put a chain
around the neck of a slave, the other end fastens
itself round your own. --Bad counsel confounds the
adviser. --The devil is an ass.

There is no den in the wild world to hide a rogue.
There is no such thing as concealment.   Commit a
crime, and the earth is made of glass.   Commit a
crime, and it seems as if a coat of snow fell on
the ground, such as reveals in the woods the track
of every partridge and fox and squirrel and mole.
You cannot recall the spoken word, you cannot wipe
out the foot-track, you cannot draw up the ladder,
so as to leave no inlet or clew.   Always some
damming circumstance transpires.   The laws and
substances of nature, water, snow, wind, gravitation, become penalties to the thief.

Neither can it be said, on the other hand, that the
gain of rectitude must be bought by any loss.
There is no penalty to virtue; no penalty to wisdom;
they are proper additions of being.   In a virtuous
action, I properly <u>am</u>; in a virtuous act, I add to
the world; I plant into deserts, conquered from
chaos and nothing, and see the darkness receding
on the limits of the horizon.   There can be no excess to love; none to knowledge; none to beauty,
when these attributes are considered in the purest
sense.   The soul refuses all limits.   It affirms in
man always an Optimism, never a Pessimism. --
<u>Essays</u>, pp. 90, 95-96, 100.

By virtue of obedience to this law great men are
great, and only so:

We do not yet see that virtue is height, and that a
man or a company of men plastic and permeable to
principles, by the law of nature must overpower
and ride all cities, nations, kings, rich men, poets,
who are not.

A true man belongs to no other time or place, but
is the centre of things.   Where he is, there is a

nature.   He measures you, and all men, and all
events.   You are constrained to accept his standard.   Ordinarily everybody in society reminds us
of somewhat else or some other person.   Character, reality, reminds you of nothing else.   It takes
place of the whole creation.   The man must be so
much that he must make all circumstances indifferent, --put all means into the shade.   This all
great men are and do.   Every true man is a cause,
a country, and an age; requires infinite spaces and
numbers and time fully to accomplish his thought;
--and posterity seem to follow his steps as a pro-
cession. --Essays, pp. 57, 50.

Through this any man has the power of all men:

Do that which is assigned thee, and thou canst not
hope too much or dare too much.   There is at this
moment, there is for me an utterance bare and
grand as that of the colossal chisel of Phidias, or
the trowel of the Egyptians, or the pen of Moses,
or Dante, but different from all these.   Not possibly will the soul, all rich, all eloquent, with
thousand-cloven tongue, deign to repeat itself; but
if I can hear what these patriarchs say, surely I
can reply to them in the same pitch of voice; for
the ear and the tongue are two organs of one nature.   Dwell up there in the simple and noble regions of thy life, obey thy heart, and thou shalt
reproduce the foreworld again.

The great poet makes us feel our own wealth, and
then we think less of his compositions.   His greatest communication to our mind, is, to teach us to
despise all he has done.   Shakespeare carries us
to such a lofty strain of intelligent activity, as to
suggest a wealth which beggars his own; and we
then feel that the splendid works which he has
created, and which in other hours we extol as a
sort of self-existent poetry, take no stronger hold
of real nature than the shadow of a passing traveller on the rock. --Essays, pp. 68-69, 239.

Yet he once says there is no progress of mankind;
"Society never advances. "

The civilized man has built a coach, but has lost

the use of his feet. He is supported on crutches,
but loses so much support of muscle. He has got
a fine Geneva watch, but he has lost the skill to
tell the hour by the sun. A Greenwich nautical
almanac he has, and so being sure of the informa-
tion when he wants it, the man in the street does
not know a star in the sky. The solstice he does
not observe; the equinox he knows as little; and the
whole bright calendar of the year is without a dial
in his mind. His note-books impair his memory;
his libraries overload his wit; the insurance office
increases the number of accidents; and it may be a
question whether machinery does not encumber;
whether we have not lost by refinement some
energy, by a Christianity entrenched in establish-
ments and forms, some vigour of wild virtue. For
every stoic was a stoic; but in Christendom where
is the Christian?--Essays, pp. 69-70.

But this is an exaggeration, which he elsewhere cor-
rects, and justly says that the great men of the nineteenth
century will one day be quoted to prove the barbarism of
their age.

He teaches an absolute trust in God:

Ineffable is the union of man and God in every act
of the soul. The simplest person, who in his in-
tegrity worships God, becomes God; yet for ever
and ever the influx of this better and universal
self is new and unsearchable. Ever it inspires
awe and astonishment.... When we have broken
our god of tradition, and ceased from our god of
rhetoric, then may God fire the heart with His
presence. It is the doubling of the heart itself,
nay, the infinite enlargement of the heart with a
power of growth to a new infinity on everyside. It
inspires in man an infallible trust. He has not the
conviction, but the sight that the best is the true,
and may in that thought easily dismiss all particular uncertainties and fears, and adjourn to the sure
revelation of time, the solution of his private rid-
dles. He is sure that his welfare is dear to the
heart of being. In the presence of law to his
mind, he is overflowed with a reliance so universal, that it sweeps away all cherished hopes and
the most stable projects of mortal condition in its

flood.   He believes that he cannot escape from his
good. --Essays, pp. 241-242.

In how many churches, by how many prophets, tell
me, is man made sensible that he is an infinite
soul; that the earth and heavens are passing into
his mind; that he is drinking for ever the soul of
God?   Where now sounds the persuasion, that by
its very melody imparadises my heart, and so affirms its own origin in heaven?   Where shall I hear
words such as in elder ages drew men to leave all
and follow--father and mother, house and land, wife
and child?   Where shall I hear these august laws of
moral being so pronounced, as to fill my ear, and
I feel ennobled by the offer of my uttermost action
and passion?   The test of the true faith, certainly,
should be its power to charm and command the
soul, as the laws of nature control the activity of
the hands, --so commanding that we find pleasure
and honour in obeying.   The faith should blend with
the light of rising and of setting suns, with the fly-
ing cloud, the singing bird, and the breath of
flowers.   But now the priest's Sabbath has lost the
splendour of nature; it is unlovely; we are glad
when it is done; we can make, we do make, even
sitting in our pews, a far better, holier, sweeter,
for ourselves. --Nature, &c., pp. 132-133.

God continually communicates Himself to man in various forms:

We distinguish the announcements of the soul, its
manifestations of its own nature, by the term Revelation.   These are always attended by the emotion
of the sublime.   For this communication is an influx of the Divine mind into our mind.   It is an ebb
of the individual rivulet before the flowing surges
of the sea of life.   Every distinct apprehension of
this central commandment agitates men with awe
and delight.   A thrill passes through all men at the
reception of new truth, or at the performance of a
great action, which comes out of the heart of nature.   In these communications, the power to see
is not separated from the will to do, but the insight proceeds from obedience, and the obedience
proceeds from a joyful perception.   Every moment
when the individual feels himself invaded by it, is
memorable. --Essays, pp. 232-233.

"The nature of these revelations is always the same: they are perceptions of the absolute law."

This energy does not descend into individual life, on any other condition than entire possession. It comes to the lowly and simple; it comes to whomsoever will put off what is foreign and proud; it comes as insight; it comes as serenity and grandeur. When we see those whom it inhabits, we are apprized of new degrees of greatness. From that inspiration the man comes back with a changed tone. He does not talk with men, with an eye to their opinion. He tries them. It requires of us to be plain and true.... The soul that ascendeth to worship the great God, is plain and true; has no rose-colour; no fine friends; no chivalry; no adventures; does not want admiration; dwells in the hour that now is, in the earnest experience of the common day, --by reason of the present moment, and the mere trifle having become porous to thought, and bibulous of the sea of light.

How dear, how soothing to man, arises the idea of God, peopling the lonely place, effacing the scars of our mistakes and disappointments!--Essays, pp. 239, 240, 241-242.

He says the same thing in yet more rhythmic notes:

Not from a vain or shallow thought
His awful Jove young Phidias brought;
Never from lips of cunning fell
The thrilling Delphic oracle;
Out from the heart of nature rolled
The burdens of the Bible old;
The litanies of nations came,
Like the volcano's tongue of flame,
Up from the burning core below, --
The canticles of love and woe:
The hand that rounded Peter's dome.
And groined the aisles of Christian Rome,
Wrought in a sad sincerity;
Himself from God he could not free;
He builded better than he knew;--
The conscious stone to beauty grew.

.   .   .   .   .

> The passive Master lent his hand
> To the vast soul that o'er him planned;
> And the same power that reared the shrine,
> Bestrode the tribes that knelt within.
> Ever the fiery Pentecost
> Girds with one flame the countless host.
> Trances the heart through chanting choirs,
> And through the priest the mind inspires. --<u>Poems</u>,
> pp. 17-18, 19.

If we put Emerson's conclusions into five great classes representing respectively his idea of man, of God, and of nature; his idea of self-rule, the relation of man's consciousness to his unconsciousness; his idea of religion, the relation of men to God; of ethics, the relation of man to man; and of economy, the relation of man to nature; we find him in the very first rank of modern science. No man in this age is before him. He demonstrates nothing, but assumes his position far in advance of mankind. This explains the treatment he has met with.

Then in his writings there appears a love of beauty in all its forms--in material nature, in art, literature, and above all, in human life. He finds it everywhere:

> The frailest leaf, the mossy bark,
> The acorn's cup, the raindrop's arc,
> The swinging spider's silver line,
> The ruby of the drop of wine,
> The shining pebble of the pond,
> Thou inscribest with a bond,
> In thy momentary play,
> Would bankrupt nature to repay.
>   .   .   .
> Oft, in streets or humblest places,
> I detect far-wandered graces,
> Which, from Eden wide astray,
> In lowly homes have lost their way. --<u>Poems</u>,
> pp. 137, 139.

Few men have had a keener sense for this in common life, or so nice an eye for it in inanimate nature. His writings do not disclose a very clear perception of the beauty of animated nature; it is still life that he describes, in water, plants, and the sky. He seldom refers to the great cosmic forces of the world, that are everywhere balanced into such systematic proportions, the perception of which makes the

writings of Alexander Von Humboldt so attractive and de-
lightful.

In all Emerson's works there appears a sublime confidence in man; a respect for human nature which we have
never seen surpassed--never equalled.   Man is only to be
true to his nature, to plant himself on his instincts, and all
will turn out well:

> Build, therefore, your own world.   As fast as you
> conform your life to the pure idea in your mind,
> that will unfold its great proportions.   A corres-
> pondent revolution in things will attend the influx
> of the spirit.   So fast will disagreeable appear-
> ances, swine, spiders, snakes, pests, mad-houses,
> prisons, enemies, vanish; they are temporary and
> shall be no more seen.   The sordor and filths of
> nature, the sun shall dry up, and the wind exhale.
> As when the summer comes from the south, the
> snow-banks melt, and the face of the earth becomes
> green before it, so shall the advancing spirit create
> its ornaments along its path, and carry with it the
> beauty it visits, and the song which enchants it; it
> shall draw beautiful faces, and warm hearts, and
> wise discourse, and heroic acts around its way,
> until evil is no more seen.   The kingdom of man
> over nature, which cometh not with observation, --
> a dominion such as now is beyong his dream of
> God, --he shall enter without more wonder than the
> blind man feels who is gradually restored to per-
> fect sight. --Nature, pp. 94-95.

> Foolish hands may mix and mar,
> Wise and sure the issues are.

He also has an absolute confidence in God.   He has
been foolishly accused of pantheism which sinks God in nature; but no man is further from it.   He never sinks God in
man, he does not stop with the law, in matter or morals,
but goes back to the Lawgiver; yet probably it would not be
so easy for him to give his definition of God as it would be
for most graduates at Andover or Cambridge.   With this
confidence in God he looks things fairly in the face, and
never dodges, never fears.   Toil, sorrow, pain, these are
things which it is impious to fear.   Boldly he faces every
fact, never retreating behind an institution or a great man.
In God his trust is complete; with the severest scrutiny he

joins the highest reverence.

Hence come his calmness and serenity. He is evenly
balanced and at repose. A more tranquil spirit cannot be
found in literature. Nothing seems to fret or jar him, and
all the tossings of the literary world never jostle him into
anger or impatience. He goes on like the stars above the
noise and dust of earth, as calm yet not so cold. No man
says things more terribly severe than he on many occasions;
few in America have encountered such abuse, but in all his
writings there is not a line which can be referred to ill-will.
Impudence and terror are wasted on him; "upstart wealth's
averted eye, " which blasts the hope of the politician, is
powerless on him as on the piles of granite in New Hampshire hills. Misconceived and misreported, he does not wait
to "unravel any man's blunders: he is again on his road,
adding new powers and honours to his domain, and new claims
on the heart. " He takes no notice of the criticism from
which nothing but warning is to be had, warning against
bigotry and impudence, and goes on his way, his only answer
a creative act. Many shafts has he shot, not an arrow in
self-defence; not a line betrays that he has been treated ill.
This is small praise, but rare; even cool egotistic Goethe
treated his "Philistine" critics with haughty scorn, comparing
them to dogs who bark in the court-yard when the master
mounts to ride:

> Es will der Spitz aus unserm Stall
>   Mit Bellen uns begleiten;
> Allein der Hundes lauter Schall
>   Beweist nur dass wir reiten.

He lacks the power of orderly arrangement to a remarkable degree. Not only is there no obvious logical order,
but there is no subtle psychological method by which the
several parts of an essay are joined together; his deep say-
ings are jewels strung wholly at random. This often con-
fuses the reader; this want appears the greatest defect of his
mind. Of late years there has been a marked effort to correct it, and in regard to mere order there is certainly a
great improvement in the first series of Essays on Nature,
a rather formless book.

Then he is not creative like Shakespeare and Goethe,
perhaps not inventive like many far inferior men; he seldom
or never undertakes to prove anything. He tells what he
sees, seeing things by glimpses, not by steady and continuous

looking, he often fails of seeing the whole object; he does
not always see all of its relations with other things.   Hence
comes an occasional exaggeration.   But this is commonly
corrected by some subsequent statement.   Thus he has seen
books imprison many a youth, and speaking to men, desirous
of warning them of their danger, he undervalues the worth
of books themselves.   But the use he makes of them in his
own writings shows that this statement was an exaggeration
which his practical judgment disapproves.   Speaking to men
whose chief danger was that they should be bookworms, or
mechanical grinders at a logic-mill, he says that ecstasy is
the method of nature, but himself never utters anything
"poor and extemporaneous"; what he gets in his ecstatic moments of inspiration, he examines carefully in his cool, reflective hours, and it is printed as reflection, never as the
simple result of ecstatic inspiration, having not only the
stamp of Divine truth, but the private mark of Emerson. He
is never demonized by his enthusiasm; he possesses the
spirit, it never possesses him; if "the God" comes into his
rapt soul "without bell, " it is only with due consideration
that he communicates to the world the message that was
brought.   Still he must regret that his extravagant estimate
of ecstasy, intuitive unconsciousness, has been made and has
led some youths and maids astray.

    This mode of looking at things, and this want of
logical order, make him appear inconsistent.   There are
actual and obvious contradictions in his works.   "Two sons
of Priam in one chariot ride. " Now he is all generosity and
nobleness, shining like the sun on things mean and low, and
then he says, with a good deal of truth but some exaggeration:

> Do not tell me of my obligation to put all poor men
> in good situations.   Are they my poor?   I tell
> thee, thou foolish philanthropist, that I grudge the
> dollar, the dime, the cent I give to such men as
> do not belong to me and to whom I do not belong.
> There is a class of persons to whom by all spiritual
> affinity I am bought and sold; for them I will go to
> prison, if need be; but your miscellaneous popular
> charities; the education at college of fools; the
> building of meeting-houses to the vain end to which
> many now stand; alms to sots; and the thousand-
> fold Relief Societies;--though I confess with shame
> I sometimes succumb and give the dollar, it is a
> wicked dollar which by-and-by I shall have the man-

hood to withhold. --<u>Essays</u>, p. 43.

Thus a certain twofoldness appears in his writings
here and there, but take them all together they form a whole
of marvellous consistency; take them in connection with his
private character and life--we may challenge the world to
furnish an example of a fairer and more consistent whole.

With the exceptions above stated, there is a remarkable balance of intellectual faculties, of creative and conservative, of the spontaneous and intuitive, and the voluntary and
reflective powers.   He is a slave to neither; all are balanced
into lovely proportions and intellectual harmony.   In many
things Goethe is superior to Emerson: in fertility of invention, in a wide acquaintance with men, in that intuitive perception of character which seems an instinct in some men,
in regular discipline of the understanding, in literary and
artistic culture; but in general harmony of the intellectual
powers, and the steadiness of purpose which comes thereof,
Emerson is incontestably the superior even of the many-sided
Goethe.   He never wastes his time on trifles; he is too
heavily fraught, and lies so deep in the sea that a little flaw
of wind never drives him from his course.   If we go a little
further and inquire how the other qualities are blended with
the intellectual, we find that the moral power a little out-
weighs the intellectual, and the religious is a little before the
moral, as it should be, but the affections seem to be less
developed than the intellect.   There is no total balance of all
the faculties to correspond with the harmony of his intellectual powers.   This seems to us the greatest defect in his
entire being, as lack of logical power is the chief defect in
his intellect; there is love enough for almost any man--not
enough to balance his intellect, hi conscience, and his faith
in God.   Hence there appears a c tain coldness in his
ethics.   He is a man running alone, and would lead others to
isolation, not society.   Notwithstanding his own intense individuality and his theoretic and practical respect for individuality, still persons seem of small value to him--of little
value except as they represent or help develope an idea of
the intellect.   In this respect, in his writings he is one-
sided, and while no one mental power has subdued another,
yet his intellect and conscience seem to enslave and belittle
the affections.   Yet, he never goes so far in this as Goethe,
who used men, and women too, as cattle to ride, as food to
eat.   In Emerson's religious writings there appears a worship of the infinite God, far transcending all we find in Taylor or Edwards, in Fénélon or Channing; it is reverence, it

is trust, the worship of the conscience, of the intellect; it is
obedience, the worship of the will; it is not love, the worship of the affections.

No writer in our language is more rich in ideas,
none more suggestive of noble thought and noble life.   We
will select the axioms which occur in a single essay,   which
we take at random, that on Self-reliance:

> It needs a divine man to exhibit anything divine.
> Nothing is at last sacred but the integrity of your
>   own mind.
> The virtue most in request is conformity.   Self-
>   reliance is its aversion.
> No law can be sacred to me but that of my nature,
>   the only wrong what is against it.
> Truth is handsomer than the affection of love.
> Your goodness must have some edge to it.
> Do your work and you shall reinforce yourself.
> A foolish consistency is the hobgoblin of little
>   minds.
> To be great is to be misunderstood.
> Character teaches above our wills.
> Greatness always appeals to the future.
> The centuries are conspirators against the sanity
>   and majesty of the soul.
> If we live truly we shall see truly.
> It is as easy for the strong to be strong as it is
>   for the weak to be weak.
> When a man lives with God, his voice shall be as
>   sweet as the murmur of the brook and the rustle
>   of the corn.
> Virtue is the governor.
> Welcome evermore to gods and men is the self-
>   helping man.
> Duty is our place, and the merry men of cir-
>   cumstance should follow as they may.
> My giant goes with me wherever I go.
> It was in his own mind that the artist sought his
>   model.
> That which each can do best none but his Maker
>   can teach him.
> Every great man is an unique.
> Nothing can bring you peace but the triumph of
>   principles.

His works abound also with the most genial wit; he

clearly sees and sharply states the halfnesses of things and
men, but his wit is never coarse, and wholly without that
grain of malice so often the accompaniment thereof.

Let us now say a word of the artistic style and
rhetorical form of these remarkable books.   Mr. Emerson
always gravitates towards first principles, but never sets
them in a row, groups them into a system, or makes of
them a whole.   Hence the form of all his prose writings is
very defective, and much of his rare power is lost.   He
never fires by companies, nor even by platoons, only man
by man; nay, his soldiers are never ranked into line, but
stand scattered, sundered and individual, each serving on his
own account, and "fighting on his own hook. "   Things are
huddled and lumped together; diamonds, pearls, bits of chalk
and cranberries, thrown pell-mell together.   You can

> No joints and no contexture find.
> Nor their loose parts to any method bring.

Here is a specimen of the Lucretian "fortuitous concourse of
atoms, " for things are joined by a casual connection, or else
by mere caprice.   This is so in the Orations, which were
designed to be heard, not read, where order is the more
needful.   His separate thoughts are each a growth.   Now and
then it is so with a sentence, seldom with a paragraph; but
his essay is always a piece of composition, carpentry, and
not growth.

Take any one of his volumes, the first series of Essays, for example, the book does not make an organic whole,
by itself, and so produce a certain totality of impression.
The separate essays are not arranged with reference to any
progress in the reader's mind, or any consecutive development of the author's ideas.   Here are the titles of the
several papers in their present order:--History, Self-Reliance,
Compensation, Spiritual Laws, Love, Friendship, Prudence,
Heroism, The Over-Soul, Circles, Intellect, Art.   In each
essay there is the same want of organic completeness and
orderly distribution of the parts.   There is no logical arrangement of the separate thoughts, which are subordinate to
the main idea of the piece.   They are shot together into a
curious and disorderly mass of beauty, like the colours in a
kaleidoscope, not laid together like the germs in a collection;
still less grown into a whole like the parts of a rose, where
beauty of form, fragrance, and colour make up one whole of
loveliness.   The lines he draws do not converge to one point;

there is no progress in his drama. Towards the end the interest deepens, not from an artistic arrangement of accumulated thoughts, but only because the author finds his heart
warmed by his efforts, and beating quicker. Some artists
produce their effect almost wholly by form and outline; they
sculpture with their pencil; the Parcae of Michael Angelo is
an example; so some writers discipline their pupils by the
severity of their intellectual method and scientific forms of
thought. Other artists have we known produce the effect almost wholly by their colouring; the drawing was bad, but the
colour of lip and eye, of neck and cheek, and hair, was
perfect; the likeness all men saw, and felt the impression.
But the perfect artist will be true to both, will keep the
forms of things, and only clothe them with appropriate hues.
We know some say that order belongs not to poetic minds,
but the saying is false. In all Milton's high poetic works,
the form is perfect as the colouring: this appears in the
grouping of the grand divisions of the Paradise Lost, and in
the arrangement of the smallest details in L'Allegro and Il
Penseroso, and then the appropriate hue of morning, of mid-
day, or of night is thrown upon the whole.

     His love of individuality has unconsciously deprived
him of the grace of order; his orations or essays are like a
natural field: here is common grass, only with him not so
common as wild roses and violets, for his common grasses
are flowers--and then rocks, then trees, brambles, thorns,
now flowers, now weeds, here a decaying log with raspberry-
bushes on the one side and strawberry-vines on the other,
and potentillas creeping among them all. There are emmets
and wood-worms, earth-worms, slugs, grasshoppers, and,
more obvious, sheep and oxen, and above and about them,
the brown thrasher, the hen-hawk, and the crow--making a
scene of beautiful and intricate confusion which belongs to
nature, not to human art.

     His marked love of individuality appears in his style.
His thoughts are seldom vague, all is distinct; the outlines
are sharply drawn, things are always discrete from one another. He loves to particularize. He talks not of flowers,
but of the violet, the clover, the cowslip and anemone; not
of birds, but the nuthatch, and the wren; not of insects, but
of the Volvex Globator; not of men and maids, but of Adam,
John, and Jane. Things are kept from things, each surrounded by its own atmosphere. This gives great distinct-
ness and animation to his works, though latterly he seems to
imitate himself a little in this respect. It is remarkable to

what an extent this individualization is carried. The essays
in his books are separate, and stand apart from one another,
only mechanically bound by the lids of the volume; his para-
graphs in each essay are distinct and disconnected, or but
loosely bound to one another; it is so with sentences in the
paragraph, and propositions in the sentence. Take for example his essay on Experience; it is distributed into seven
parts, which treat respectively of Illusion, Temperament,
Succession, Surface, Surprise, Reality, and Subjectiveness.
These seven brigadiers are put in one army with as little
unity of action as any seven Mexican officers; not subject to
one head, nor fighting on the same side. The subordinates
under these generals are in no better order and discipline;
sometimes the corporal commands the king. But this very
lack of order gives variety of form. You can never anticipate him. One half of the essay never suggests the rest. If
he have no order, he never sets his method a going, and
himself with his audience goes to sleep, trusting that he, they,
and the logical conclusion will all come out alive and waking
at the last. He trusts nothing to the discipline of his camp;
all to the fidelity of the individual soldiers.

     His style is one of the rarest beauty; there is no
affectation, no conceit, no effort at effect. He alludes to
everybody and imitates nobody. No writer that we remember,
except Jean Paul Richter, is so rich in beautiful imagery;
there are no blank walls in his building. But Richter's
temple of poesy is a Hindoo pagoda, rich, elaborate, of
costly stone, adorned with costly work, but as a whole,
rather grotesque than sublime, and more queer than beautiful; you wonder how any one could have brought such wealth
together, and still more that any one could combine things so
oddly together. Emerson builds a rambling Gothic church,
with an irregular outline, a chapel here, and a tower there,
you do not see why; but all parts are beautiful, and the whole
constrains the soul to love and trust. His manifold images
come from his own sight, not from the testimony of other
men. His words are pictures of the things daguerreotyped
from nature. Like Homer, Aristotle, and Tacitus, he describes the thing, and not the effect of the thing. This
quality he has in common with the great writers of classic
antiquity, while his wealth of sentiment puts him with the
classics of modern times. Like Burke he lays all literature
under contribution, and presses the facts of every-day life
into his service. He seems to keep the sun and moon as his
retainers, and levy black-mail on the cricket and the tit-
mouse, on the dawdling preacher and the snow-storm which

seemed to rebuke his unnatural whine.   His works teem with
beauty.   Take for example this:

> What do we wish to know of any worthy person so
> much as how he has sped in the history of this
> sentiment? [Love.]   What books in the circulating
> libraries circulate?   How we glow over these
> novels of passion when the story is told with any
> spark of truth and nature!   And what fastens atten-
> tion in the intercourse of life, like any passion be-
> traying affection between two parties?   Perhaps we
> never saw them before, and never shall meet them
> again.   But we see them exchange a glance, or be-
> tray a deep emotion, and we are no longer strang-
> ers.   We understand them, and take the warmest
> interest in the development of the romance.   All
> mankind love a lover.   The earliest demonstrations
> of complacency and kindness are nature's most
> winning pictures.   It is the dawn of civility and
> grace in the coarse and rustic.   The rude village
> boy teases the girls about the school-house door;--
> but to-day he comes running into the entry, and
> meets one fair child arranging her satchel: he holds
> her books to help her, and instantly it seems to
> him as if she removed herself from him infinitely,
> and was a sacred precinct.   Among the throng of
> girls he runs rudely enough, but one alone dis-
> tances him: and these two little neighbours that
> were so close just now, have learnt to respect each
> other's personality.   Or who can avert his eyes
> from the engaging, half-artful, half-artless ways of
> school girls who go into the country shops to buy a
> skein of silk or a sheet of paper, and talk half an
> hour about nothing with the broad-faced, good-na-
> tured shop-boy.   In the village they are on a per-
> fect equality, which love delights in, and without
> any coquetry the happy, affectionate nature of wo-
> man flows out in this pretty gossip.   The girls may
> have little beauty, yet plainly do they establish be-
> tween them and the good boy the most agreeable,
> confiding relations, what with their fun and their
> earnest, about Edgar, and Jonas, and Almira, and
> who was invited to the party, and who danced at the
> dancing-school, and when the singing-school would
> begin, and other nothings concerning which the
> parties cooed.   By-and-by that boy wants a wife,
> and very truly and heartily will he know where to

find a sincere and sweet mate, without any risk
such as Milton deplores as incident to scholars and
great men.

The passion re-makes the world for the youth.   It
makes all things alive and significant.   Nature
grows conscious.   Every bird on the boughs of the
tree sings now to his heart and soul.   Almost the
notes are articulate.   The clouds have faces as he
looks on them.   The trees of the forest, the wav-
ing grass and the peeping flowers have grown intelligent: and almost he fears to trust them with
the secret which they seem to invite.   Yet nature
soothes and sympathizes.   In the green solitude he
finds a dearer home than with men.

Behold there in the wood the fine madman!   He is
a palace of sweet sounds and sights; he dilates; he
is twice a man; he walks with arms akimbo; he
soliloquizes; he accosts the grass and the trees; he
feels the blood of the violet, the clover, and the
lily in his veins; and he talks with the brook that
wets his foot. --Essays, pp. 142-143, 145, 146.

Emerson is a great master of language; therewith he
sculptures, therewith he paints; he thunders and lightens in
his speech, and in his speech also he sings.   In Greece,
Plato and Aristophanes were mighty masters of the pen, and
have not left their equals in ancient literary art; so in Rome
were Virgil and Tacitus; four men so marked in individuality,
so unlike and withal so skilful in the use of speech, it were
not easy to find; four mighty masters of the art to write.
In later times there have been in England Shakespeare, Bacon, Milton, Taylor, Swift, and Carlyle; on the Continent,
Voltaire, Rousseau, and Goethe; all masters in this art,
skilful to work in human speech.   Each of them possessed
some qualities which Emerson has not.   In Bacon, Milton,
and Carlyle, there is a majesty, a dignity and giant strength,
not to be claimed for him.   Yet separating the beautiful from
what men call sublime, no one of all that we have named,
ancient or modern, has passages so beautiful as he.   From
what is called sublime if we separate what is simply vast, or
merely grand, or only wide, it is in vain that we seek in all
those men for anything to rival Emerson.

Take the following passage, and it is not possible, we
think, to find its equal for the beautiful and the sublime in

any tongue:

> The lovers delight in endearments, in avowals of
> love, in comparisons of their regards.   When alone,
> they solace themselves with the remembered image
> of the other.   Does that other see the same star,
> the same melting cloud, read the same book, feel
> the same emotion that now delight me?   They try
> and weigh their affection, and adding up all costly
> advantages, friends, opportunities, properties, ex-
> ult in discovering that willingly, joyfully, they
> would give all as a ransom for the beautiful, the
> beloved head, not one hair of which shall be
> harmed.   But the lot of humanity is on these
> children.   Danger, sorrow, and pain arrive to
> them as to all. Love prays.   It makes covenants
> with Eternal Power, in behalf of this dear mate.
> The union which is thus effected, and which adds
> a new value to every atom in nature, for it trans-
> mutes every thread throughout the whole web of
> relation into a golden ray, and bathes the soul in
> a new and sweeter element, is yet a temporary
> state.   Not always can flowers, pearls, poetry,
> protestations, nor even home in another heart, con-
> tent the awful soul that dwells in clay.   It arouses
> itself at last from these endearments, as toys, and
> puts on the harness, and aspires to vast and uni-
> versal aims.   The soul which is in the soul of
> each, craving for a perfect beatitude, detects in-
> congruities, defects, and disproportion in the be-
> haviour of the other.   Hence arise surprise, ex-
> postulation, and pain.   Yet that which drew them to
> each other was signs of loveliness, signs of virtue;
> and these virtues are there, however eclipsed.
> They appear and reappear, and continue to attract;
> but the regard changes, quits the sign, and attaches
> to the substance.   This repairs the wounded affec-
> tion.   Meantime, as life wears on, it proves a
> game of permutation and combination of all possible
> positions of the parties, to extort all the resources
> of each, and acquaint each with the whole strength
> and weakness of the other.   For it is the nature
> and end of this relation, that they should represent
> the human race to each other.   All that is in the
> world which is or ought to be known, is cunningly
> wrought into the texture of man, of woman.

> The person love does to us fit, ·
> Like manna, has the taste of all in it.

The world rolls; the circumstances vary, every
hour.   All the angels that inhabit this temple of
the body appear at the windows, and all the gnomes
and vices also.   By all the virtues, they are united.
If there be virtue, all the vices are known as such;
they confess and flee.   Their once flaming regard
is sobered by time in either breast, and losing in
violence what it gains in extent, it becomes a
thorough good understanding.   They resign each
other without complaint to the good offices which
man and woman are severally appointed to discharge
in time, and exchange the passion which once could
not lose sight of its object, for a cheerful disen-
gaged furtherance, whether present or absent, of
each other's designs.   At last they discover that
all which at first drew them together, --those once
sacred features, that magical play of charms, was
deciduous, had a prospective end, like the scaf-
folding by which the house was built; and the puri-
fication of the intellect and the heart, from year to
year, is the real marriage, foreseen and prepared
from the first, and wholly above their consciousness.   Looking at these aims with which two persons, a man and a woman, so variously and cor-
relatively gifted, are shut up in one house to spend
in the nuptial society forty or fifty years, I do not
wonder at the emphasis with which the heart pro-
phesies this crisis from early infancy, at the profuse beauty with which the instincts deck the nuptial
bower, and nature and intellect and art emulate
each other in the gifts and the melody they bring
to the epithalamium.

Thus are we put in training for a love that knows
not sex, nor person, nor partiality, but which
seeketh virtue and wisdom everywhere, to the end
of increasing virtue and wisdom.   We are by nature
observers, and thereby learners.   That is our
permanent state.   But we are often made to feel
that our affections are but tents of a night.   Though
slowly and with pain, the objects of the affections
change, as the objects of thought do.   There are
moments when the affections rule and absorb the
man, and make this happiness dependent on a

person or persons. But in health the mind is
presently seen again, its overarching vault, bright
with galaxies of immutable lights, and the warm
loves and fears that swept over us as clouds, must
lose their finite character, and blend with God, to
attain their own perfection. But we need not fear
that we can lose anything by the progress of the
soul. The soul may be trusted to the end. That
which is so beautiful and attractive as these relations, must be succeeded and supplanted only by
what is more beautiful, and so on for ever. --
Essays, pp. 152-155.

We can now only glance at the separate works named
above. His nature is more defective in form than any of his
pieces, but rich in beauty; a rare prose poem is it, a book
for one's bosom. The first series of Essays contain the
fairest blossoms and fruits of his genius. Here his wondrous
mind reveals itself in its purity, its simplicity, its strength,
and its beauty too. The second series of Essays is inferior
to the first; the style is perhaps clearer, but the water is
not so deep. He seems to let himself down to the capacity
of his hearers. Yet there is an attempt at order which is
seldom successful, and reminds one of the order in which
figures are tattooed upon the skin of a South Sea Islander,
rather than of the organic symmetry of limbs or bones. He
sets up a scaffold, not a living tree, a scaffold, too, on
which none but himself can walk.

Some of his Orations and Addresses are noble efforts:
old as the world is, and much and long as men are given to
speak, it is but rare in human history that such Sermons on
the Mount get spoken as the Address to the Students of Theology, and that before the Phi Beta Kappa, at Cambridge.
They are words of lofty cheer.

The last book, on Representative Men, does not come
up to the first Essays, neither in matter nor in manner. Yet
we know not a man, living and speaking English, that could
have written one so good. The lecture on Plato contains ex-
aggerations not usual with Emerson; it fails to describe the
man by genus or species. He gives you neither the principles nor the method of Plato, not even his conclusions. Nay,
he does not give you the specimens to judge by. The article
in the last classical dictionary, or the History of Philosophy
for the French Normal Schools gives you a better account of
the philosopher and the man. The lecture on Swedenborg is

a masterly appreciation of that great man, and to our way of
thinking, the best criticism that has yet appeared.   He appreciates but does not exaggerate him.   The same may be
said of that upon Montaigne; those on Shakespeare and Goethe
are adequate and worthy of the theme.   In the lecture on
Napoleon, it is surprising that not a word is said of his
greatest faculty, his legislative, organizing power, for we
cannot but think with Carlyle, that he "will be better known
for his laws than his battles. "   But the other talents of Napoleon are sketched with a faithful hand, and his faults justly
dealt with, not enlarged but not hid--though, on the whole, it
seems to us, no great admirers of Napoleon, that he is a
little undervalued.

    We must briefly notice Mr. Emerson's volume of
Poems.   He has himself given us the standard by which to
try him, for he thus defines and describes the poet:

> The sign and credentials of the poet are, that he
> announces that which no man foretold.   He is the
> true and only doctor: he knows and tells; he is the
> only teller of news, for he was present and privy
> to the appearance which he describes.   He is a be-
> holder of ideas, and an utterer of the necessary
> and causal.   For we do not speak now of men of
> poetical talents, or of industry and skill in metre,
> but of the true poet.   I took part in a conversation
> the other day, concerning a recent writer of lyrics,
> a man of subtle mind, whose head appeared to be
> a music box of delicate tunes and rhythms, and
> whose skill and command of language we could not
> sufficiently praise.   But when the question arose
> whether he was not only a lyrist, but a poet, we
> were obliged to confess that he is plainly a con-
> temporary, not an eternal man.   He does not stand
> out of our low limitations, like a Chimborazo under
> the line, running up from the torrid base through
> all the climates of the globe, with belts of the
> herbage of every latitude on its high and mottled
> sides; but this genius is the landscape-garden of a
> modern house, adorned with fountains and statues,
> with well-bred men and women standing and sitting
> in the walks and terraces.   We hear through all
> the varied music the ground tone of conventional
> life.   Our poets are men of talents who sing, and
> not the children of music.   The argument is

secondary, the finish of the verses is primary.

For it is not metres, but a metre-making argument, that makes a poem, --a thought so passionate
and alive, that, like the spirit of a plant or an
animal, it has an architecture of its own, and
adorns nature with a new thing.   The thought and
the form are equal in the order of time, but in the
order of genesis the thought is prior to the form.
The poet has a new thought: he has a whole new
experience to unfold; he will tell us how it was with
him, and all men will be the richer in his fortune.
--Essays, 2nd Series, pp. 9-11.

It is the office of the poet, he tells us, "by the beauty
of things" to announce "a new and higher beauty.   Nature
offers all her creatures to him as a picture language. "
"The poorest experience is rich enough for all the purposes
of expressing thought"; "the world being put under the mind
for verb and noun, the poet is he who can articulate it"; he
"turns the world to glass, and shows us all things in their
right series and proportions. "   For through that better perception he stands one step nearer things, and sees the flowing or metamorphosis, perceives that thought is multiform;
that within the form of every creature is a force impelling
it to ascend into a higher form, and, following with his eyes
the life, uses the forms which express that life, and so his
speech flows with the flowing of nature. "   "The poet alone
knows astronomy, chemistry, vegetation, and animation, for
he does not stop at these facts, but employs them as signs."

This insight, which expresses itself by what is
called imagination, is a very high sort of seeing,
which does not come by study, but by the intellect
being where and what it sees, by sharing the path
or circuit of things through forms, and so making
them translucid to others.   The path of things is
silent.   Will they suffer a speaker to go with
them?   A spy they will not suffer; a lover, a poet,
is the transcendency of their own nature, --him they
will suffer.   The condition of true naming, on the
poet's part, is his resigning himself to the divine
aura which breathes through forms, and accompany-
ing that.

It is a secret which every intellectual man quickly
learns, that, beyond the energy of his possessed

and conscious intellect, he is capable of a new
energy (as of an intellect doubled on itself), by
abandonment to the nature of things; that, besides
his privacy of power as an individual man, there
is a great public power, on which he can draw by
unlocking, at all risks, his human doors, and suffering the ethereal tides to roll and circulate
through him: then he is caught up into the life of
the Universe, his speech is thunder, his thought is
law, and his words are universally intelligible as
the plants and animals.   The poet knows that he
speaks adequately, then, only when he speaks somewhat wildly, or, 'with the flower of the mind;' not
with the intellect, used as an organ, but with the
intellect released from all service, and suffered to
take its direction from its celestial life; or, as the
ancients were wont to express themselves, not with
intellect alone, but with the intellect inebriated by
nectar.   As the traveller who has lost his way,
throws his reins on his horse's neck, and trusts to
the instinct of the animal to find his road, so we
must do with the divine animal who carries us
through this world.   For if in any manner we can
stimulate this instinct, new passages are opened
for us into nature, the mind flows into and through
things hardest and highest, and the metamorphosis
is possible. --Essays, 2nd Series, pp. 28-30.

In reading criticisms on Emerson's poetry, one is
sometimes reminded of a passage in Pepys' Diary, where
that worthy pronounces judgment on some of the works of
Shakspeare.   Perhaps it may be thought an appropriate introduction to some strictures of our own.

Aug. 20th, 1666.   To Deptford by water, reading
Othello, Moor of Venice, which I have heretofore
esteemed a mighty good play, but having so lately
read the Adventures of Five Hours, it seems a
mean thing.   Sept. 29th, 1662.   To the King's
Theatre, where we saw Midsummer Night's Dream,
which I had never seen before, nor shall ever
again, for it is the most insipid and ridiculous
play that ever I saw in my life.

Emerson is certainly one
        Quem tu, Melpomene, semel
            Nascentem placido lumine videris;

> Spissae nemorum comae
> Fingent Aeolio carmine nobilem.

Yet his best poetry is in his prose, and his poorest, thinnest, and least musical prose is in his poems.

The "Ode to Beauty" contains some beautiful thoughts in a fair form:

> Who gave thee, O Beauty,
>   The keys of this breast, --
> Too credulous lover
>   Of blest and unblest?
> Say, when in lapsed ages
>   Thee knew I of old?
> Or what was the service
>   For which I was sold?
> When first my eyes saw thee,
>   I found me thy thrall,
> By magical drawings,
>   Sweet tyrant of all!
> I drank at thy fountain
>   False waters of thirst;
> Thou intimate stranger,
>   Thou latest and first!
> Thy dangerous glances
>   Make women of men;
> New-born, we are melting
>   Into nature again. --Poems, pp. 136-137.

The three pieces which seem the most perfect poems, both in matter and form, are the "Problem," from which we have already given liberal extracts above; "Each in all," which, however, is certainly not a great poem, but simple, natural, and beautiful; and the "Sphinx," which has higher merits than the others, and is a poem of a good deal of beauty. The Sphinx is the creation of the old classic mythology. But her question is wholly modern, though she has been waiting so long for the seer to solve it, that she has become drowsy.

This is her problem:

> The fate of the man-child;
> The meaning of man.

All the material and animal world is at peace:

Erect as a sunbeam,
  Upspringeth the palm;
The elephant browses,
  Undaunted and calm;
In beautiful motion
  The thrush plies his wings;
King leaves of his covert,
  Your silence he sings.

     .   .   .   .

See, earth, air, sound, silence,
  Plant, quadruped, bird,
By one music enchanted,
  One deity stirred, --
Each the other adorning,
  Accompany still;
Night veileth the morning,
  The vapour the hill.

In his early age man shares the peace of the world:

The babe by its mother
  Lies bathed in joy;
Glide its hours uncounted, --
  The sun is its toy;
Shines the peace of all being,
  Without cloud, in its eyes;
And the sum of the world
  In soft miniature lies.

But when the child becomes a man he is ill at ease:

But man crouches and blushes,
  Absconds and conceals;
He creepeth and peepeth,
  He palters and steals;
Infirm, melancholy,
  Jealous glancing around,
An oaf, an accomplice,
  He poisons the ground.

Mother Nature complains of his condition:

Who has drugg'd my boy's cup?
  Who has mix'd my boy's bread?
Who, with sadness and madness,
  Has turn'd the man-child's head?

The Sphinx wishes to know the meaning of all this.
A poet answers that this is no mystery to him; man is superior to nature, and its unconscious and involuntary happiness is not enough for him; superior to the events of his own
history, so the joy which he has attained is always unsatisfactory:

> The fiend that man harries
>   Is love of the best;
> Yawns the pit of the dragon,
>   Lit by rays from the blest.
> The Lethe of nature
>   Can't trance him again,
> Whose soul sees the perfect,
>   Which his eyes seek in vain.
>
> Profounder, profounder,
>   Man's spirit must dive;
> To his aye-rolling orbit
>   No goal will arrive;
> The heavens that now draw him
>   With sweetness untold,
> Once found, --for new heavens
>   He spurneth the old.

Even sad things turn out well:

> Pride ruin'd the angels,
>   Their shame them restores;
> And the joy that is sweetest
>   Lurks in stings of remorse.

Thus the riddle is solved; then the Sphinx turns into
beautiful things:

> Uprose the merry Sphinx,
>   And crouch'd no more in stone;
> She melted into purple cloud,
>   She silver'd in the moon;
> She spired into a yellow flame;
>   She flower'd in blossoms red;
> She flow'd into a foaming wave;
>   She stood Monadnoc's head. --Poems, pp. 8-13.

We pass over the Threnody, where "well-sung woes"
might soothe a "pensive ghost. " The Dirge contains some
stanzas that are full of nature and well expressed:

Knows he who tills this lonely field,
   To reap its scanty corn,
What mystic fruit his acres yield
   At midnight and at morn?
         .   .   .   .

The winding Concord gleam'd below,
   Pouring as wide a flood
As when my brothers, long ago,
   Came with me to the wood.

But they are gone--the holy ones
   Who trod with me this lovely vale;
The strong, star-bright companions
   Are silent, low, and pale.

My good, my noble, in their prime,
   Who made this world the feast it was,
Who learn'd with me the lore of time,
   Who loved this dwelling-place!
      .   .   .   .   .

I touch this flower of silken leaf,
   Which once our childhood knew;
Its soft leaves wound me with a grief
   Whose balsam never grew.

Hearken to you pine-warbler
   Singing aloft in the tree!
Hearest thou, O traveller,
   What he singeth to me?

Not unless God made sharp thine ear
   With sorrow such as mine,
Out of that delicate lay could'st thou
   Its heavy tale divine.

'Go, lonely man,' it saith;
   'They loved thee from their birth;
Their hands were pure, and pure their faith, --
   There are no such hearts on earth.
      .   .   .   .   .

'Ye cannot unlock your heart,
   The key is gone with them;
The silent organ loudest chants
   the master's requiem.'--<u>Poems</u>, pp. 232-235.

Here is a little piece which has seldom been equalled
in depth and beauty of thought; yet it has sometimes been
complained of as obscure, we see not why:

TO RHEA.

Thee, dear friend, a brother soothes,
Not with flatteries, but truths,
Which tarnish not, but purify
To light which dims the morning's eye.
I have come from the spring-woods,
From the fragrant solitudes;
Listen what the poplar-tree
And murmuring waters counsell'd me.

If with love thy heart has burn'd;
If thy love is unreturn'd;
Hide thy grief within thy breast,
Though it tear thee unexpress'd;
For when love has once departed
From the eyes of the false-hearted,
And one by one has torn off quite
The bandages of purple light;
Though thou wert the loveliest
Form the soul had ever dress'd,
Thou shalt seem, in each reply,
A vixen to his alter'd eye;
Thy softest pleadings seem too bold,
Thy praying lute will seem to scold;
Though thou kept the straightest road,
Yet thou errest far and broad.

But thou shalt do as do the gods
In their cloudless periods;
For of this lore be thou sure, --
Though thou forget, the gods, secure,
Forget never their command,
But make the statute of this land.

As they lead, so follow all,
Ever have done, ever shall.
Warning to the blind and deaf,
'Tis written on the iron leaf,
Who drinks of Cupid's nectar cup
Loveth downward, and not up;
Therefore, who loves, of gods or men,
Shall not by the same be loved again;

His sweetheart's idolatry
Falls, in turn, a new degree.
When a god is once beguiled
By beauty of a mortal child,
And by her radiant youth delighted,
He is not fool'd, but warily knoweth
His love shall never be requited.
And thus the wise Immortal doeth. --
'Tis his study and delight
To bless that creature day and night;
From all evils to defend her;
In her lap to pour all splendour;
To ransack earth for riches rare,
And fetch her stars to deck her hair;
He mixes music with her thoughts,
And saddens her with heavenly doubts:
All grace, all good his great heart knows,
Profuse in love, the king bestows:
Saying, 'Hearken! earth, sea, air!
This monument of my despair
Build I to the All-Good, All-Fair.
Not for a private good,
But I, from my beatitude,
Albeit scorn'd as none was scorn'd,
Adorn her as was none adorn'd.
I make this maiden an ensample
To Nature, through her kingdoms ample,
Whereby to model newer races,
Statelier forms, and fairer faces;
To carry man to new degrees
Of power, and of comeliness.
These presents be the hostages
Which I pawn for my release.
See to thyself, O Universe!
Thou art better, and not worse. '--
And the god, having given all,
Is freed for ever from his thrall. --Poems, pp. 21-
24.

Several of the other pieces are poor; some are stiff
and rude, having no lofty thoughts to atone for their unlovely
forms. Some have quaint names, which seem given to them
out of mere caprice. Such are the following: Mithridates,
Hamatreya, Hermione, Merlin, Merops, &c. These names
are not more descriptive of the poems they are connected
with, than are Jonathan and Eleazer of the men thus baptized.
What have Astrea, Rhea, and Etienne de la Boéce to do with

the poems which bear their names?

We should think the following lines, from Hermione, were written by some of the youngest Emersonidae:

> Once I dwelt apart.
> Now I live with all;
> As shepherd's lamp on far hill-side
> Seems, by the traveller espied,
> A door into the mountain heart,
> So didst thou quarry and unlock
> Highways for me through the rock.
>
> Now, deceived, thou wanderest
> In strange lands unblest;
> And my kindred come to soothe me.
> Southward is my next of blood;
> He has come through fragrant wood,
> Drugg'd with spice from climates warm,
> And in every twinkling glade,
> And twilight nook,
> Unveils thy form.
> Out of the forest way
> Forth paced it yesterday;
> And when I sat by the watercourse,
> Watching the daylight fade,
> It throbb'd up from the brook. --Poems, pp. 153-154.

Such things are unworthy of such a master.

Here is a passage which we will not attempt to criticise. He is speaking of Love:

> He will preach like a friar,
> And jump like a harlequin;
> He will read like a crier,
> And fight like a Paladin, &c.

Good Homer sometimes nodded, they say; but when he went fast asleep, he did not write lines or print them.

Here is another specimen. It is Monadnoc that speaks:

> Anchor'd fast for many an age,
> I await the bard and sage,

> Who, in large thoughts, like fair pearl-seed,
> Shall string Monadnoc like a bead.

And yet another:

> For the present, hard
> Is the fortune of the bard.
>
> In the woods he travels glad,
> Without bitter fortune mad,
> Melancholy without bad.

We have seen imitations of this sort of poetry, which even surpassed the original. It does not seem possible that Emerson can write such stuff simply from "lacking the accomplishment of verse." Is it that he has a false theory, and so wilfully writes innumerous verse, and plays his harp, all jangling and thus out of tune? Certainly it seems so. In his poems he uses the old mythology, and in bad taste; talks of Gods, and not God; of Pan, the Oreads, Titan, Jove, and Mars, the Parcae and the Daemon.

There are three elaborate poems which demand a word of notice. The "Woodnotes" contains some good thoughts, and some pleasing lines, but on the whole a pine tree which should talk like Mr. Emerson's pine ought to be plucked up by the roots and cast into the depths of the sea. "Monadnoc" is the title of another piece which appears forced and unnatural, as well as poor and weak. The third is called "initial, daemonic, and celestial Love." It is not without good thoughts, and here and there a good line, but in every attribute of poetry it is far inferior to his majestic essay on Love. In his poetry Mr. Emerson often loses his command of language, metaphors fail him, and the magnificent images which adorn and beautify all his prose works, are gone.

From what has been said, notwithstanding the faults we have found in Emerson, it is plain that we assign him a very high rank in the literature of mankind. He is a very extraordinary man. To no English writer since Milton can we assign so high a place; even Milton himself, great genius though he was, and great architect of beauty, has not added so many thoughts to the treasury of the race; no, nor been the author of so much loveliness. Emerson is a man of genius such as does not often appear, such as has never appeared before in America, and but seldom in the world. He learns from all sorts of men, but no English writer, we

think, is so original. We sincerely lament the want of logic
in his method, and his exaggeration of the intuitive powers,
the unhappy consequences of which we see in some of his
followers and admirers. They will be more faithful than he
to the false principle which he lays down, and will think
themselves wise because they do not study, learned because
they are ignorant of books, and inspired because they say
what outrages common sense. In Emerson's poetry there is
often a ruggedness and want of finish which seems wilful in
a man like him. This fault is very obvious in those pieces
he has put before his several essays. Sometimes there is
a seed-corn of thought in the piece, but the piece itself
seems like a pile of rubbish shot out of a cart which hinders
the seed from germinating. His admirers and imitators not
unfrequently give us only the rubbish and probably justify
themselves by the example of their master. Spite of these
defects, Mr. Emerson, on the whole, speaks with a holy
power which no other man possesses who now writes the
English tongue. Others have more readers, are never
sneered at by respectable men, are oftener praised in the
journals, have greater weight in the pulpits, the cabinets,
and the councils of the nation; but there is none whose words
so sink into the mind and heart of young men and maids;
none who work so powerfully to fashion the character of the
coming age. Seeing the power which he exercises, and the
influence he is likely to have on generations to come, we
are jealous of any fault in his matter, or its form, and have
allowed no private and foolish friendship to hinder us from
speaking of his faults.

This is his source of strength: his intellectual and
moral sincerity. He looks after Truth, Justice, and Beauty.
He has not uttered a word that is false to his own mind or
conscience; has not suppressed a word because he thought it
too high for men's comprehension, and therefore dangerous
to the repose of men. He never compromises. He sees
the chasm between the ideas which come of man's nature and
the institutions which represent only his history; he does not
seek to cover up the chasm, which daily grows wider between Truth and Public Opinion, between Justice and the
State, between Christianity and the Church; he does not seek
to fill it up, but he asks men to step over and build institutions commensurate with their ideas. He trusts himself,
trusts man, and trusts God. He has confidence in all the
attributes of infinity. Hence he is serene; nothing disturbs
the even poise of his character, and he walks erect. Nothing impedes him in his search for the true, the lovely, and

the good; no private hope, no private fear, no love of wife
or child, or gold, or ease, or fame.   He never seeks his
own reputation; he takes care of his Being, and leaves his
seeming to take care of itself.   Fame may seek him; he
never goes out of his way a single inch for her.

He has not written a line which is not conceived in
the interest of mankind.   He never writes in the interest of
a section, of a party, of a church, of a man always in the
interest of mankind.   Hence comes the ennobling influence of
his works.   Most of the literary men of America, most of
the men of superior education, represent the ideas and interest of some party: in all that concerns the welfare of the
human race, they are proportionably behind the mass who
have only the common culture; so while the thought of the
people is democratic, putting man before the accidents of a
man, the literature of the nation is aristocratic, and opposed
to the welfare of mankind.   Emerson belongs to the exceptional literature of the times--and while his culture joins him
to the history of man, his ideas and his whole life enable
him to represent also the nature of man, and so to write for
the future.   He is one of the rare exceptions amongst our
educated men, and helps redeem American literature from
reproach of imitation, conformity, meanness of aim, and
hostility to the progress of mankind.   No faithful man is too
low for his approval and encouragement; no faithless man
too high and popular for his rebuke.

A good test of the comparative value of books, is the
state they leave you in.   Emerson leaves you tranquil, re-
solved on noble manhood, fearless of the consequences; he
gives men to mankind, and mankind to the laws of God.   His
position is a striking one.   Eminently a child of Christianity
and of the American idea, he is out of the Church and out of
the State.   In the midst of Calvinistic and Unitarian superstition, he does not fear God, but loves and trusts Him.   He
does not worship the idols of our time--wealth and respectability, the two calves set up by our modern Jeroboam.   He
fears not the damnation these idols have the power to inflict
--neither poverty nor social disgrace.   In busy and bustling
New England comes out this man serene and beautiful as a
star, and shining like "a good deed in a naughty world. "
Reproached as an idler, he is active as the sun, and pours
out his radiant truth on Lyceums at Chelmsford, at Waltham,
at Lowell, and all over the land.   Out of a cold Unitarian
Church rose this most lovely light.   Here is Boston, perhaps
the most humane city in America, with its few noble men

and women, its beautiful charities, its material vigour, and
its hardy enterprise; commercial Boston, where honour is
weighed in the public scales, and justice reckoned by the
dollars it brings; conservative Boston, the grave of the Revolution, wallowing in its wealth, yet grovelling for more,
seeking only money, careless of justice, stuffed with cotton
yet hungry for tariffs, sick with the greedy worm of ava-
rice, loving money as the end of life, and bigots as the
means of preserving it; Boston with toryism in its parlours,
toryism in its pulpits, toryism in its press, itself a tory
town, preferring the accidents of man to man himself--and
amidst it all there comes Emerson, graceful as Phoebus-
Apollo, fearless and tranquil as the sun he was supposed to
guide, and pours down the enchantment of his light, which
falls where'er it may, on dust, on diamonds, on decaying
heaps to hasten their rapid rot, on seeds new sown to
quicken their ambitious germ, on virgin minds of youths
and maids to waken the natural seed of nobleness therein,
and make it grow to beauty and to manliness. Such is the
beauty of his speech, such the majesty of his ideas, such
the power of the moral sentiment in men, and such the impression which his whole character makes on them, that they
lend him, everywhere, their ears, and thousands bless his
manly thoughts.

6.   A SERMON OF WAR*

"The Lord is a man of war, "   Exodus XV. 3.

"God is Love, "   1 John IV. 8.

I ask your attention to a Sermon of War.   I have
waited some time before treating this subject at length, till
the present hostilities should assume a definite form, and
the designs of the Government become more apparent.   I
wished to be able to speak coolly, and with knowledge of the
facts, that we might understand the comparative merits of
the present war.   Besides, I have waited for others in the
churches, of more experience to speak, before I ventured to
offer my counsel; but I have thus far waited almost in vain!
I did not wish to treat the matter last Sunday, for that was
the end of our week of Pentecost, when cloven tongues of
flame descend on the city, and some are thought to be full
of new wine, and others of the Holy Spirit.   The heat of the
meetings, good and bad, of that week, could not wholly have
passed away from you or me, and we ought to come coolly
and consider a subject like this.   So the last Sunday I only
sketched the background of the picture, to-day intending to
paint the horrors of war in front of that "Presence of Beauty
in Nature, " to which, with its "Meanings" and its "Lessons,"
I then asked you to attend.

It seems to me that an idea of God as the Infinite is
given to us in our nature itself.   But men create a more definite conception of God in their own image.   Thus a rude
savage man, who has learned only the presence of power in
Nature, conceives of God mainly as a force, and speaks of
Him as a God of power.   Such, though not without beautiful
exceptions, is the character ascribed to Jehovah in the Old
Testament.   "The Lord is a man of war. " He is "the Lord
of hosts. " He kills men, and their cattle.   If there is
trouble in the enemies' city, it is the Lord who hath caused
it.   He will "whet his glittering sword, and render vengeance

*Parker, Theodore.   Collected Works, ed.   F.   Cobbe
   (London: Trübner, 1863-79), IV, 1-31.

to his enemies. He will make his arrows drunk with blood,
and his sword shall devour flesh!" It is with the sword that
God pleads with all men. He encourages men to fight, and
says, "Cursed he be that keepeth back his sword from
blood. " He sends blood into the streets; he waters the land
with blood, and in blood he dissolves the mountains. He
brandishes his sword before kings, and they tremble at every
moment. He treads nations as grapes in a wine-press, and
his garments are stained with their life's blood. [1]

A man who has grown up to read the Older Testament
of God revealed in the beauty of the universe, and to feel
the goodness of God therein set forth, sees Him not as force
only, or in chief, but as love. He worships in love the God
of goodness and of peace. Such is the prevalent character
ascribed to God in the New Testament, except in the book of
"Revelation. " He is the "God of love and peace"; "our
Father, " "kind to the unthankful and the unmerciful. " In one
word, God is love. He loves us all, Jew and Gentile, bond
and free. All are His children, each of priceless value in
His sight. He is no God of battles; no Lord of hosts; no
man of war. He has no sword nor arrows; He does not
water the earth nor melt the mountains in blood, but "He
maketh His sun to rise on the evil and on the good, and
sendeth rain on the just and the unjust. " He has no garments dyed in blood; curses no man for refusing to fight.
He is spirit, to be worshipped in spirit and in truth! The
commandment is: Love one another; resist not evil with evil;
forgive seventy times seven; overcome evil with good; love
your enemies; bless them that curse you; do good to them
that hate you; pray for them that despitefully use you and
persecute you. [2] There is no nation to shut its ports against
another, all are men; no caste to curl its lip at inferiors;
all are brothers, members of one body, united in the Christ,
the ideal man and head of all. The most useful is the
greatest. No man is to be master, for the Christ is our
teacher. We are to fear no man, for God is our Father.

These precepts are undeniably the precepts of Christianity. Equally plain is it that they are the dictates of man's
nature, only developed and active; a part of God's universal
revelation; His law writ on the soul of man, established in
the nature of things; true after all experience, and true before all experience. The man of real insight into spiritual
things sees and knows them to be true.

Do not believe it the part of a coward to think so. I

have known many cowards; yes, a great many; some very
cowardly, pusillanimous, and faint-hearted cowards; but
never one who thought so, or pretended to think so. It requires very little courage to fight with sword and musket,
and that of a cheap kind. Men of that stamp are plenty as
grass in June. Beat your drum, and they will follow; offer
them but eight dollars a month, and they will come--fifty
thousand of them, to smite and kill. [3] Every male animal,
or reptile, will fight. It requires little courage to kill; but
it takes much to resist evil with good, holding obstinately
out, active or passive, till you overcome it. Call that non-
resistance, if you will; it is the stoutest kind of combat, de-
manding all the manhood of a man.

I will not deny that war is inseparable from a low
stage of civilization; so is polygamy, slavery, cannibalism.
Taking men as they were, savage and violent, there have
been times when war was unavoidable. I will not deny that
it has helped forward the civilization of the race, for God
often makes the folly and the sin of men contribute to the
progress of mankind. It is none the less a folly or a sin.
In a civilized nation like ourselves, it is far more heinous
than in the Ojibeways or the Camanches.

War is in utter violation of Christianity. If war be
right, then Christianity is wrong, false, a lie. But if
Christianity be true, if reason, conscience, the religious
sense, the highest faculties of man, are to be trusted, then
war is the wrong, the falsehood, the lie. I maintain that
aggressive war is a sin; that it is national infidelity, a
denial of Christianity and of God. Every man who under-
stands Christianity by heart, in its relations to man, to society, the nation, the world, knows that war is a wrong.
At this day, with all the enlightenment of our age, after the
long peace of the nations, war is easily avoided. Whenever
it occurs, the very fact of its occurrence convicts the rulers
of a nation either of entire incapacity as statesmen, or else
of the worst form of treason: treason to the people, to mankind, to God! There is no other alternative. The very fact
of an aggressive war shows that the men who cause it must
be either fools or traitors. I think lightly of what is called
treason against a government. That may be your duty to-
day, or mine. Certainly it was our fathers' duty not long
ago; now it is our boast and their title to honour. But treason against the people, against mankind, against God, is a
great sin, not lightly to be spoken of. The political authors
of the war on this continent, and at this day, are either

utterly incapable of a statesman's work, or else guilty of
that sin.   Fools they are, or traitors they must be.

Let me speak, and in detail, of the Evils of War. I
wish this were not necessary.   But we have found ourselves
in a war; the Congress has voted our money and our men to
carry it on; the Governors call for volunteers; the volunteers
come when they are called for.   No voice of indignation
goes forth from the heart of the eight hundred thousand souls
of Massachusetts; of the seventeen million freemen of the
land how few complain; only a man here and there!   The
Press is well-nigh silent.   And the Church, so far from
protesting against this infidelity in the name of Christ, is
little better than dead.   The man of blood shelters himself
behind its wall, silent, dark, dead and emblematic.   These
facts show that it is necessary to speak of the evils of war.
I am speaking in a city, whose fairest, firmest, most costly
buildings are warehouses and banks; a city whose most popular Idol is Mammon, the God of Gold; whose Trinity is a
Trinity of Coin!   I shall speak intelligibly, therefore, if I
begin by considering war as a waste of property.   It para-
lyzes industry.   The very fear of it is a mildew upon commerce.   Though the present war is but a skirmish, only a
few random shots between a squad of regulars and some
strolling battalions, a quarrel which in Europe would scarcely
frighten even the Pope--yet see the effect of it upon trade.
Though the fighting be thousands of miles from Boston, your
stocks fall in the market; the rate of insurance is altered;
your dealer in wood piles his boards and his timber on his
wharf, not finding a market.   There are few ships in the
great Southern mart to take the freight of many; exchange is
disturbed.   The clergyman is afraid to buy a book, lest his
children want bread.   It is so with all departments of industry and trade.   In war the capitalist is uncertain and slow
to venture, so the labourer's hand will be still, and his child
ill-clad and hungry.

In the late war with England, many of you remember
the condition of your fisheries, of your commerce; how the
ships lay rotting at the wharf.   The dearness of cloth, of
provisions, flour, sugar, tea, coffee, salt; the comparative
lowness of wages, the stagnation of business, the scarcity of
money, the universal sullenness and gloom--all this is well
remembered now.   So is the ruin it brought on many a man.

Yet but few weeks ago some men talked boastingly of
a war with England.   There are some men who seem to have

no eyes nor ears, only a mouth; whose chief function is talk.
Of their talk I will say nothing; we look for dust in dry
places. But some men thus talked of war, and seemed desirous to provoke it, who can scarce plead ignorance, and I
fear not folly, for their excuse.   I leave such to the just
resentment sure to fall on them from sober, serious men,
who dare to be so unpopular as to think before they speak,
and then say what comes of thinking.   Perhaps such a war
was never likely to take place, and now, thanks to a few
wise men, all danger thereof seems at an end.   But suppose
it had happened--what would become of your commerce, of
your fishing-smacks on the banks or along the shore? what
of your coasting vessels, doubling the headlands all the way
from the St. John's to the Nueces? what of your whale-ships
in the Pacific? what of your Indiamen, deep freighted with
oriental wealth? what of that fleet which crowds across the
Atlantic sea, trading with east and west, and north and
south?   I know some men care little for the rich, but when
the owners keep their craft in port, where can the "hands"
find work, or their mouths find bread?   The shipping of the
United States amounts nearly to 2, 500, 000 tons.   At $40 a
ton, its value is nearly $100, 000, 000.   This is the value
only of those sea-carriages; their cargoes I cannot compute.
Allowing one sailor for every twenty tons burden, here will
be 125, 000 seamen.   They and their families amount to
500, 000 souls.   In war, what will become of them?   A capital of more than $13, 000, 000 is invested in the fisheries of
Massachusetts alone.   More than 19, 000 men find profitable
employment therein.   If each man have but four others in
his family, a small number for that class, here are more
than 95, 000 persons in this State alone, whose daily bread
depends on this business.   They cannot fish in troubled
waters, for they are fishermen, not politicians.   Where
could they find bread or cloth in time of war?   In Dartmoor
prison?   Ask that of your demagogues who courted war!

   Then, too, the positive destruction of property in war
is monstrous.   A ship of the line costs from $500, 000 to
$1, 000, 000.   The loss of a fleet by capture, by fire, or by
decay, is a great loss.   You know at what cost a fort is
built, if you have counted the sums successively voted for
Fort Adams in Rhode Island, or those in our own harbour.
The destruction of forts is another item in the cost of war.
The capture or destruction of merchant ships with their
freight, creates a most formidable loss.   In 1812 the whole
tonnage of the United States was scarce half what it is now.
Yet the loss of ships and their freight, in "the late war, "

brief as it was, is estimated at $100,000,000. Then the
loss by plunder and military occupation is monstrous. The
soldier, like the savage, cuts down the tree to gather its
fruit. I cannot calculate the loss by burning towns and cities.
But suppose Boston were bombarded and laid in ashes. Calculate the loss if you can. You may say, "This could not
be," for it is as easy to say No, as Yes. But remember
what befell us in the last war; remember how recently the
best defended capitals of Europe, Vienna, Paris, Antwerp,
have fallen into hostile hands. Consider how often a strong
place, like Coblentz, Mentz, Malta, Gibraltar, St. Juan
d'Ulloa, has been declared impregnable, and then been taken;
calculate the force which might be brought against this town,
and you will see that in eight and forty hours, or half that
time, it might be left nothing but a heap of ruins smoking
in the sun! I doubt not the valour of American soldiers, the
skill of their engineers, nor the ability of their commanders.
I am ready to believe all this is greater than we are told.
Still, such are the contingencies of war. If some not very
ignorant men had their way, this would be a probability and
perhaps a fact. If we should burn every town from the
Tweed to the Thames, it would not rebuild our own city.

But, on the supposition that nothing is destroyed, see
the loss which comes from the misdirection of productive industry. Your fleets, forts, dockyards, arsenals, cannons,
muskets, swords, and the like, are provided at great cost,
and yet are unprofitable. They do not pay. They weave no
cloth; they bake no bread; they produce nothing. Yet, from
1791 to 1832, in forty-two years, we expended in these things
$303,242,576, namely, for the navy, &c., $112,703,933; for
the army, &c., $190,538,643. For the same time, all
other expenses of the nation came to but $37,158,047. More
than eight-ninths of the whole revenue of the nation was spent
for purposes of war. In four years from 1812 to 1815, we
paid in this way, $92,350,519.37. In six years, from 1835
to 1840, we paid annually on the average $21,328,903; in all,
$127,973,418. Our Congress has just voted $17,000,000, as
a special grant for the army alone. The 175,118 muskets at
Springfield are valued at $3,000,000; we pay annually
$200,000 to support that arsenal. The navy-yard at Charles-
ton, with its stores, &c., has cost $4,741,000. And, for
all profitable returns, this money might as well be sunk in
the bottom of the sea. In some countries it is yet worse.
There are towns and cities in which the fortifications have
cost more than all the houses, churches, shops, and other
property therein. This happens not among the Sacs and

Foxes, but in "Christian" Europe.

Then your soldier is the most unprofitable animal you can keep. He makes no railroads; clears no land, raises no corn. No, he can make neither cloth nor clocks! He does not raise his own bread, mend his own shoes, make his shoulder-knot of glory, nor hammer out his own sword. Yet he is a costly animal, though useless. If the President gets his fifty thousand volunteers, a thing likely to happen--for though Irish lumpers and hodmen want a dollar or a dollar and a half a day, your free American of Boston will enlist for twenty-seven cents, only having his livery, his feathers, and his "glory" thrown in--then at $8 a month, their wages amount to $400,000 a month. Suppose the present Government shall actually make advantageous contracts, and the subsistence of the soldier cost no more than in England, or $17 a month, this amounts to $850,000. Here are $1,250,000 a month to begin with. Then, if each man would be worth a dollar a day at any productive work, and there are 26 work-days in the month, here are $1,300,000 more to be added, making $2,550,000 a month for the new army of occupation. This is only for the rank and file of the army. The officers, the surgeons, and the chaplains, who teach the soldiers to wad their muskets with the leaves of the Bible, will perhaps cost as much more; or, in all, something more than $5,000,000 a month. This of course does not include the cost of their arms, tents, ammunition, baggage, horses, and hospital stores, nor the 65,000 gallons of whiskey which the Government has just advertised for! What do they give in return? They will give us three things, valour, glory, and--talk; which, as they are not in the price current, I must estimate as I can, and set them all down in one figure = 0; not worth the whiskey they cost.

New England is quite a new country. Seven generations ago it was a wilderness; now it contains about 2,500,000 souls. If you were to pay all the public debts of these States, and then, in fancy, divide all the property therein by the population, young as we are, I think you would find a larger amount of value for each man than in any other country in the world, not excepting England. The civilization of Europe is old; the nations old, England, France, Spain, Austria, Italy, Greece; but they have wasted their time, their labour, and their wealth in war, and so are poorer than we upstarts of a wilderness. We have fewer fleets, forts, cannon, and soldiers for the population, than any other "Christian" country in the world. This is one main reason why we

have no national debt; why the women need not toil in the
hardest labour of the fields, the quarries, and the mines;
this is the reason that we are well fed, well clad, well
housed; this is the reason that Massachusetts can afford to
spend $1,000,000 a year for her public schools! War, wast-
ing a nation's wealth, depresses the great mass of the
people, but serves to elevate a few to opulence and power.
Every despotism is established and sustained by war. This
is the foundation of all the aristocracies of the old world,
aristocracies of blood. Our famous men are often ashamed
that their wealth was honestly got by working, or peddling,
and foolishly copy the savage and bloody emblems of ancient
heraldry in their assumed coats of arms--industrious men
seeking to have a griffin on their seal! Nothing is so hostile
to a true democracy as war. It elevates a few, often bold,
bad men, at the expense of the many, who pay the money
and furnish the blood for war.

War is a most expensive folly. The revolutionary war
cost the general Government, directly and in specie,
$135,000,000. It is safe to estimate the direct cost to the
individual states also at the same sum, $135,000,000; making
a total of $270,000,000. Considering the interruption of
business, the waste of time, property and life, it is plain
that this could not have been a fourth part of the whole. But
suppose it was a third, then the whole pecuniary cost of the
war would be $810,000,000. At the beginning of the Revolu-
tion the population was about 3,000,000; so that war, lasting
about eight years, cost $270 for each person. To meet the
expenses of the war each year there would have been required
a tax of $33.75 on each man, woman, and child!

In the Florida war we spent between $30,000,000 and
$40,000,000, as an eminent statesman once said, in fighting
five hundred invisible Indians! It is estimated that the fortifications of the city of Paris, when completely furnished, will
cost more than the whole taxable property of Massachusetts,
with her 800,000 souls. Why this year our own grant for
the army is $17,000,000. The estimate for the navy is
$6,000,000 more; in all $23,000,000. Suppose, which is
most unlikely, that we should pay no more, why, that sum
alone would support public schools, as good and as costly as
those of Massachusetts, all over the United States, offering
each boy and girl, bond or free, as good a culture as they
get here in Boston, and then leave a balance of $3,000,000
in our hands! We pay more for ignorance than we need for
education! But $23,000,000 is not all we must pay this year.

A great statesman has said, in the Senate, that our war expenses at present are nearly $500,000 a day, and the President informs your Congress that $22,952,904 more will be wanted for the army and navy before next June!

For several years we spent directly more than $21,000,000 for war purposes, though in time of peace. If a railroad cost $30,000 a mile, then we might build 700 miles a year for that sum, and in five years could build a railroad therewith from Boston to the further side of Oregon. For the war money we paid in forty-two years, we could have had more than 10,000 miles of railroad, and, with dividends at seven per cent, a yearly income of $21,210,000. For military and naval affairs, in eight years, from 1835 to 1843, we paid $163,336,717. This alone would have made 5444 miles of railroad, and would produce, at seven per cent, an annual income of $11,433,569.19.

In Boston there are nineteen public grammar-schools, a Latin and English High school. The buildings for these schools, twenty in number, have cost $653,208. There are also 135 primary schools, in as many houses or rooms. I know not their value, as I think they are not all owned by the city. But suppose them to be worth $150,000, then all the school-houses of this city have cost $803,208. The cost of these 156 schools for this year is estimated at $172,000. The number of scholars in them is 16,479. Harvard University, the most expensive college in America, costs about $46,000 a year. Now the ship "Ohio," lying here in our harbour, has cost $834,845, and we pay for it each year $220,000 more. That is, it has cost $31,637 more than these 155 school-houses of this city, and costs every year $2000 more than Harvard University, and all the public schools of Boston!

The military academy at West Point contains two hundred and thirty-six cadets; the appropriation for it last year was $138,000, a sum greater, I think, than the cost of all the colleges in Maine, New Hampshire, Vermont, and Massachusetts, with their 1445 students.

The navy-yard at Charlestown, with its ordnance, stores, &c., cost $4,741,000. The cost of the 78 churches in Boston is $3,246,500; the whole property of Harvard University is $703,175; the 155 school-houses of Boston are worth $803,208; in all, $4,752,883. Thus the navy-yard at Charlestown has cost almost as much as the 78 churches and

the 155 school-houses of Boston, with Harvard College, its
halls, libraries, all its wealth, thrown in.   Yet what does
it teach?

Our country is singularly destitute of public libraries.
You must go across the ocean to read the history of the
Church or State; all the public libraries in America cannot
furnish the books referred to in Gibbon's Rome, or Giese-
ler's History of the Church.   I think there is no public library in Europe which has cost three dollars a volume.
There are six: the Vatican, at Rome; the Royal, at Paris;
the British Museum, at London; the Bodleian, at Oxford; the
University Libraries at Gottingen and Berlin--which contain,
it is said, about 4, 500, 000 volumes.   The recent grant of
$17, 000, 000 for the army is $3,500,000 more than the cost
of those magnificent collections!

There have been printed about 3, 000, 000 different
volumes, great and little, within the last 400 years.   If the
Florida war cost but $30, 000, 000, it is ten times more than
enough to have purchased one copy of each book ever printed,
at one dollar a volume, which is more than the average cost.

Now all these sums are to be paid by the people, "the
dear people, " whom our republican demagogues love so well,
and for whom they spend their lives, --rising early, toiling
late; those self-denying heroes, those sainted martyrs of the
Republic, eating the bread of carefulness for them alone!
But how are they to be paid?   By a direct tax levied on all
the property of the nation, so that the poor man pays according to his little, and the rich man in proportion to his much,
each knowing when he pays and what he pays for?   No such
thing; nothing like it.   The people must pay, and not know
it; must be deceived a little, or they would not pay after
this fashion!   You pay for it in every pound of sugar, copper,
coal, in every yard of cloth; and if the counsel of some
lovers of the people be followed, you will soon pay for it in
each pound of coffee and tea.   In this way the rich man
always pays relatively less than the poor; often a positively
smaller sum.   Even here I think that three-fourths of all the
property is owned by one-fourth of the people, yet that
three-fourths by no means pays a third of the national revenue.   The tax is laid on things men cannot do without, --
sugar, cloth, and the like.   The consumption of these articles
is not in proportion to wealth, but persons.   Now the poor
man, as a general rule, has more children than the rich;
and the tax being more in proportion to persons than property,

the poor man pays more than the rich. So a tax is really
laid on the poor man's children to pay for the war which
makes him poor and keeps him poor. I think your captains
and colonels, those sons of thunder and heirs of glory, will
not tell you so. They tell you so! They know it! Poor
brothers, how could they? I think your party newspapers,
penny or pound, will not tell you so; nor the demagogues,
all covered with glory and all forlorn, who tell the people
when to hurrah, and for what! But if you cipher the matter
out for yourself you will find it so, and not otherwise. Tell
the demagogues, whig or democrat, that. It was an old
Roman maxim, "The people wished to be deceived; let them."
Now it is only practised on; not repeated--in public.

Let us deal justly even with war, giving that its due.
There is one class of men who find their pecuniary advantage
in it. I mean army contractors, when they chance to be
favourites of the party in power; men who let steamboats to
lie idle at $500 a-day. This class of men rejoice in a war.
The country may become poor, they are sure to be rich.
Yet another class turn war to account, get the "glory," and
become important in song and sermon. I see it stated in a
newspaper that the Duke of Wellington has received, as gra-
tuities for his military services, $5,400,000, and $40,000
a-year in pensions!

But the waste of property is the smallest part of the
evil. The waste of life in war is yet more terrible. Human
life is a sacred thing. Go out into the lowest street of Boston; take the vilest and most squalid man in that miserable
lane, and he is dear to some one. He is called brother;
perhaps husband; it may be, father; at least, son. A human
heart, sadly joyful, beat over him before he was born. He
has been pressed fondly to his mother's arms. Her tears
and her smiles have been for him; perhaps also her prayers.
His blood may be counted mean and vile by the great men of
the earth, who love nothing so well as the dear people, for
he has no "coat of arms," no liveried servant to attend him,
but it has run down from the same first man. His family is
ancient as that of the most long-descended king. God made
him; made this splendid universe to wait on him and teach
him; sent His Christ to save him. He is an immortal soul.
Needlessly to spill that man's blood is an awful sin. It will
cry against you out of the ground--Cain! where is thy
brother? Now in war you bring together 50,000 men like
him on one side, and 50,000 of a different nation on the
other. They have no natural quarrel with one another. The

earth is wide enough for both; neither hinders the sun from
the other.   Many come unwillingly; many not knowing what
they fight for.   It is but accident that determines on which
side the man shall fight.   The cannons pour their shot--
round, grape, canister; the howitzers scatter their bursting
shells; the muskets rain their leaden death; the sword, the
bayonet, the horse's iron hoof, the wheels of the artillery,
grind the men down into trodden dust.   There they lie, the
two masses of burning valour, extinguished, quenched, and
grimly dead, each covering with his body the spot he defended with his arms.   They had no quarrel: yet they lie
there, slain by a brother's hand.   It is not old and decrepid
men, but men of the productive age, full of lusty life.

But it is only the smallest part that perish in battle.
Exposure to cold, wet, heat; unhealthy climates, unwhole-
some food, rum, and forced marches, bring on diseases
which mow down the poor soldiers worse than musketry and
grape.   Others languish of wounds, and slowly procrastinate
a dreadful and a tenfold death.   Far away, there are widows,
orphans, childless old fathers, who pore over the daily news
to learn at random the fate of a son, a father, or a husband!   They crowd disconsolate into the churches, seeking
of God the comfort men took from them, praying in the
bitterness of a broken heart, while the priest gives thanks
for "a famous victory, " and hangs up the bloody standard
over his pulpit!

When ordinary disease cuts off a man, when he dies
at his duty, there is some comfort in that loss.   "It was the
ordinance of God, " you say.   You minister to his wants; you
smooth down the pillow for the aching head; your love be-
guiles the torment of disease, and your own bosom gathers
half the darts of death.   He goes in his time, and God takes
him.   But when he dies in such a war, in battle, it is man
who has robbed him of life.   It is a murderer that is butchered.   Nothing alleviates that bitter, burning smart!

Others not slain are maimed for life.   This has no
eyes; that no hands; another no feet nor legs.   This has been
pierced by lances, and torn with the shot, till scarce anything human is left.   The wreck of a body is crazed with
pains God never meant for man.   The mother that bore him
would not know her child.   Count the orphan asylums in
Germany and Holland; go into the hospital at Greenwich, that
of the invalids in Paris, you see the "trophies" of Napoleon
and Wellington.   Go to the arsenal at Toulon, see the wooden

legs piled up there for men now active and whole, and you
will think a little of the physical horrors of war.

In Boston there are perhaps about 25, 000 able-bodied
men between eighteen and forty-five. Suppose them all slain
in battle, or mortally hurt, or mown down by the camp-
fever, vomito, or other diseases of war; and then fancy the
distress, the heart-sickness, amid wives, mothers, daughters, sons, and fathers, here! Yet 25, 000 is a small number to be murdered in "a famous victory"; a trifle for a
whole "glorious campaign" in a great war.   The men of
Boston are no better loved than the men of Tamaulipas.
There is scarce an old family, of the middle class, in all
New England, which did not thus smart in the Revolution;
many, which have not, to this day, recovered from the
bloody blow then falling on them.   Think, wives, of the
butchery of your husbands; think, mothers, of the murder
of your sons!

Here, too, the burden of battle falls mainly on the
humble class.   They pay the great tribute of money; they
pay also the horrid tax of blood.   It was not your rich men
who fought even the Revolution; not they.   Your men of property and standing were leaguing with the British, or fitting
out privateers when that offered a good investment, or buying
up the estates of more consistent tories; making money out
of the nation's dire distress.   True, there were most honourable exceptions; but such, I think, was the general rule.
Let this be distinctly remembered, that the burden of battle
is borne by the humble classes of men; they pay the vast
tribute of money; the awful tax of blood!   The "glory" is got
by a few; poverty, wounds, death, are for the people!

Military glory is the poorest kind of distinction, but
the most dangerous passion.   It is an honour to man to be
able to mould iron; to be skilful at working in cloth, wood,
clay, leather.   It is man's vocation to raise corn, to subdue
the rebellious fibre of cotton and convert it into beautiful
robes, full of comfort for the body.   They are the heroes of
the race who abridge the time of human toil and multiply its
results; they who win great truths from God, and send them
to a people's heart; they who balance the many and the one
into harmonious action, so that all are united and yet each
left free.   But the glory which comes of epaulets and feathers;
that strutting glory which is dyed in blood--what shall we say
of it?   In this day it is not heroism; it is an imitation of
barbarism long ago passed by.   Yet it is marvellous how

many men are taken with a red coat.   You expect it in
Europe, a land of soldiers and blood.   You are disappointed
to find that here the champions of force should be held in
honour, and that even the lowest should voluntarily enrol
themselves as butchers of men!

Yet more: aggressive war is a sin; a corruption of
the public morals.   It is a practical denial of Christianity;
a violation of God's eternal law of love.   This is so plain,
that I shall say little upon it to-day.   Your savagest and
most vulgar captain would confess he does not fight as a
Christian--but as a soldier; your magistrate calls for volun-
teers--not as a man loving Christianity, and loyal to God;
only as governor, under oath to keep the constitution, the
tradition of the elders; not under oath to keep the commandment of God.   In war the laws are suspended, violence and
cunning rule everywhere.   The battle of Yorktown was gained
by a lie, though a Washington told it.   As a soldier it was
his duty.   Men "emulate the tiger"; the hand is bloody, and
the heart hard.   Robbery and murder are the rule, the glory
of men.   "Good men look sad, but ruffians dance and leap. "
Men are systematically trained to burn towns, to murder
fathers and sons; taught to consider it "glory" to do so.
The Government collects ruffians and cut-throats.   It com-
pels better men to serve with these and become cut-throats.
It appoints chaplains to blaspheme Christianity; teaching the
ruffians how to pray for the destruction of the enemy, the
burning of his towns; to do this in the name of Christ and
God.   I do not censure all the men who serve: some of them
know no better; they have heard that a man would "perish
everlastingly" if he did not believe the Athanasian creed;
that if he questioned the story of Jonah, or the miraculous
birth of Jesus, he was in danger of hell-fire, and if he
doubted damnation was sure to be damned.   They never
heard that such a war was a sin; that to create a war was
treason, and to fight in it wrong.   They never thought of
thinking for themselves; their thinking was to read a newspaper, or sleep through a sermon.   They counted it their
duty to obey the Government, without thinking if that Government be right or wrong.   I deny not the noble, manly
character of many a soldier--his heroism, self-denial, and
personal sacrifice.

Still, after all proper allowance is made for a few
individuals, the whole system of war is unchristian and sin-
ful.   It lives only by evil passions.   It can be defended only
by what is low, selfish, and animal.   It absorbs the scum

of the cities--pirates, robbers, murderers. It makes them
worse, and better men like them. To take one man's life is
murder; what is it to practise killing as an art, a trade; to
do it by thousands? Yet I think better of the hands that do
the butchering than of the ambitious heads, the cold, re-
morseless hearts, which plunge the nation into war.

In war the State teaches men to lie, to steal, to kill.
It calls for privateers, who are commonly pirates with a
national charter, and pirates are privateers with only a personal charter. Every camp is a school of profanity, violence, licentiousness, and crimes too foul to name. It is so
without sixty-five thousand gallons of whisky. This is unavoidable. It was so with Washington's army, with Corn-
wallis's, with that of Gustavus Adolphus, perhaps the most
moral army the world ever saw. The soldier's life generally
unfits a man for the citizen's. When he returns from a
camp, from a war, back to his native village, he becomes a
curse to society and a shame to the mother that bore him.
Even the soldiers of the Revolution, who survived the war,
were mostly ruined for life--debauched, intemperate, vicious,
and vile. What loathsome creatures so many of them were!
They bore our burden: for such were the real martyrs of
that war, not the men who fell under the shot! How many
men of the rank and file in the late war have since become
respectable citizens?

To show how incompatible are War and Christianity,
suppose that he who is deemed the most Christian of Christ's
disciples, the well-beloved John, were made a navy-chaplain,
and some morning, when a battle is daily looked for, should
stand on the gun-deck, amid lockers of shot, his Bible resting on a cannon, and expound Christianity to men with cut-
lasses by their side! Let him read for the morning lesson
the Sermon on the Mount, and for text take words from his
own Epistle, so sweet, so beautiful, so true: "Every one
that loveth is born of God, and knoweth God, for God is
love." Suppose he tells his strange audience that all men
are brothers; that God is their common father; that Christ
loved us all, showing us how to live the life of love; and
then, when he had melted all those savage hearts by words
so winsome and so true, let him conclude, "Blessed are the
men-slayers! Seek first the glory which cometh of battle.
Be fierce as tigers. Mar God's image in which your brothers
are made. Be not like Christ, but Cain who slew his
brother! When you meet the enemy, fire into their bosoms;
kill them in the dear name of Christ; butcher them in the

spirit of God. Give them no quarter, for we ought not to
lay down our lives for the brethren; only the murderer hath
eternal life!"

Yet great as are these threefold evils, there are
times when the soberest men and the best men have welcomed war, coolly and in their better moments. Sometimes
a people, long oppressed, has "petitioned, remonstrated,
cast itself at the feet of the throne," with only insult for
answer to its prayer. Sometimes there is a contest between
a falsehood and a great truth; a self-protecting war for freedom of mind, heart, and soul; yes, a war for a man's body,
his wife's and children's body, for what is dearer to men
than life itself, for the unalienable rights of man, for the
idea that all are born free and equal. It was so in the
American Revolution; in the English, in the French Revolution. In such cases men say, "Let it come." They take
down the firelock in sorrow; with a prayer they go forth to
battle, asking that the right may triumph. Much as I hate
war, I cannot but honour such men. Were they better, yet
more heroic, even war of that character might be avoided.
Still, it is a colder heart than mine which does not honour
such men, though it believes them mistaken. Especially do
we honour them, when it is the few, the scattered, the
feeble, contending with the many and the mighty; the noble
fighting for a great idea, and against the base and tyrannical.
Then most men think the gain, the triumph of a great idea,
is worth the price it costs, the price of blood.

I will not stop to touch that question, If man may ever
shed the blood of man. But it is plain that an aggressive
war like this is wholly unchristian, and a reproach to the
nation and the age.

Now, to make the evils of war still clearer, and to
bring them home to your door, let us suppose there was war
between the counties of Suffolk, on the one side, and Middlesex on the other--this army at Boston, that at Cambridge.
Suppose the subject in dispute was the boundary line between
the two, Boston claiming a pitiful acre of flat land, which the
ocean at low-tide disdained to cover. To make sure of this,
Boston seizes whole miles of flats, unquestionably not its
own. The rulers on one side are fools, and traitors on the
other. The two commanders have issued their proclamations;
the money is borrowed; the whisky provided; the soldiers--
Americans, Negroes, Irishmen, all the able-bodied men--are
enlisted. Prayers are offered in all the churches, and ser-

mons preached, showing that God is a man of war, and Cain
his first saint--an early Christian, a Christian before Christ.
The Bostonians wish to seize Cambridge, burn the houses,
churches, college-halls, and plunder the library.   The men
of Cambridge wish to seize Boston, burn its houses and
ships, plundering its wares and its goods.   Martial law is
proclaimed on both sides.   The men of Cambridge cut
asunder the bridges, and make a huge breach in the mill-
dam, planting cannon to enfilade all those avenues.   Forts
crown the hill-tops, else so green.   Men, madder than
lunatics, are crowded into the asylum.   The Bostonians rebuild the old fortifications on the Neck; replace the forts on
Beacon-hill, Fort-hill, Copps-hill, levelling houses to make
room for redoubts and bastions.   The batteries are planted,
the mortars got ready; the furnaces and magazines are all
prepared.   The three hills are grim with war.   From
Copps-hill men look anxious to that memorable height the
other side of the water.   Provisions are cut off in Boston;
no man may pass the lines; the aqueduct refuses its genial
supply; children cry for their expected food.   The soldiers
parade, looking somewhat tremulous and pale; all the able-
bodied have come, the vilest most willingly; some are brought
by force of drink, some by force of arms.   Some are in
brilliant dresses, some in their working frocks.   The banners are consecrated by solemn words. [4]   Your church-
towers are military posts of observation.   There are Old
Testament prayers to the "God of Hosts" in all the churches
of Boston; prayers that God would curse the men of Cambridge, make their wives widows, their children fatherless,
their houses a ruin, the men corpses, meat for the beast of
the field and the bird of the air.   Last night the Bostonians
made a feint of attacking Charlestown, raining bombs and
red-hot cannon-balls from Copps-hill, till they have burnt a
thousand houses, where the British burnt not half so many.
Women and children fled screaming from the blazing rafters
of their homes.   The men of Middlesex crowd into Charlestown.

          In the meantime the Bostonians hastily repair a bridge
or two; some pass that way, some over the Neck; all stealthily by night; and while the foe expect them at Bunker's,
amid the blazing town, they have stolen a march and rush
upon Cambridge itself.   The Cambridge men turn back.   The
battle is fiercely joined.   You hear the cannon, the sharp
report of musketry.   You crowd the hills, the housetops; you
line the Common, you cover the shore, yet you see but little
in the sulphurous cloud.   Now the Bostonians yield a little,

a reinforcement goes over.   All the men are gone; even the
grey-headed who can shoulder a firelock.   They plunge into
battle, mad with rage, madder with rum.   The chaplains
loiter behind.

> Pious men, whom duty brought,
> To dubious verge of battle fought,
> To shrive the dying, bless the dead!

The battle hangs long in even scale.   At length it turns.
The Cambridge men retreat, they run, they fly.   The houses
burn.   You see the churches and the colleges go up, a
stream of fire.   That library--founded amid want and war,
and sad sectarian strife, slowly gathered by the saving of
two centuries; the hope of the poor scholar, the boast of the
rich one--is scattered to the winds and burnt with fire, for
the solid granite is blasted by powder, and the turrets fall.
Victory is ours.   Ten thousand men of Cambridge lie dead;
eight thousand of Boston.   There writhe the wounded; men
who but few hours before were poured over the battle-field
a lava flood of fiery valour--fathers, brothers, husbands,
sons.   There they lie, torn and mangled; black with powder;
red with blood; parched with thirst; cursing the load of life
they now must bear with bruised frames and mutilated limbs.
Gather them into hasty hospitals--let this man's daughter
come tomorrow and sit by him, fanning away the flies; he
shall linger out a life of wretched anguish, unspoken and un-
speakable, and when he dies his wife religiously will keep
the shot which tore his limbs.   There is the battle-field!
Here the horse charged; there the howitzers scattered their
shells, pregnant with death; here the murderous canister and
grape mowed down the crowded ranks; there the huge artillery, teeming with murder, was dragged o'er heaps of men
--wounded friends, who just now held its ropes, men yet
curling with anguish, like worms in the fire.   Hostile and
friendly, head and trunk are crushed beneath those dreadful
wheels.   Here the infantry showered their murdering shot.
That ghastly face was beautiful the day before--a sabre
hewed its half away.

> The earth is covered thick with other clay,
> Which her own clay must cover; heaped and pent,
> Rider and horse, friend, foe, in one red burial
> blent.

Again it is night.   Oh, what a night, and after what
a day!   Yet the pure tide of woman's love, which never ebbs

since earth began, flows on in spite of war and battle.
Stealthily, by the pale moonlight, a mother of Boston treads
the weary miles to reach that bloody spot; a widow she--
seeking among the slain her only son.   The arm of power
drove him forth reluctant to the fight.   A friendly soldier
guides her way.   Now she turns over this face, whose mouth
is full of purple dust, bit out of the ground in his extremest
agony, the last sacrament offered him by earth herself; now
she raises that form, cold, stiff, stony, and ghastly as a
dream of hell.   But, lo! another comes; she too a woman,
younger and fairer, yet not less bold, a maiden from the
hostile town to seek her lover.   They meet, two women
among the corpses; two angels come to Golgotha, seeking to
raise a man.   There he lies before them; they look.   Yes,
it is he you seek; the same dress, form, features, too; it
is he, the son, the lover.   Maid and mother could tell that
face in any light.   The grass is wet with his blood.   The
ground is muddy with the life of men.   The mother's innocent robe is drabbled in the blood her bosom bore.   Their
kisses, groans, and tears recall the wounded man.   He
knows the mother's voice; that voice yet more beloved. His
lips move only, for they cannot speak.   He dies!   The wax-
ing moon moves high in heaven, walking in beauty amid the
clouds, and murmurs soft her cradle-song unto the slumber-
ing earth.   The broken sword reflects her placid beams.   A
star looks down, and is imaged back in a pool of blood.   The
cool night wind plays in the branches of the trees shivered
with shot.   Nature is beautiful--that lovely grass underneath
their feet; those pendulous branches of the leafy elm; the
stars, and that romantic moon lining the clouds with silver
light!   A groan of agony, hopeless and prolonged, wails out
from that bloody ground.   But in yonder farm the whippoorwill sings to her lover all night long; the rising tide ripples
melodious against the shores.   So wears the night away, --
Nature, all sinless, round that field of woe.

> The morn is up again, the dewy morn,
>   With breath all incense and with cheek all bloom,
> Laughing the clouds away with playful scorn,
>   And living as if earth contained no tomb,
>   And glowing into day.

What a scene that morning looks upon!   I will not
turn again.   Let the dead bury their dead.   But their blood
cries out of the ground against the rulers who shed it, --
"Cain! where are thy brothers?"   What shall the fool answer;
what the traitor say?

Then comes thanksgiving in all the churches of Boston. The consecrated banners, stiff with blood and "glory, " are hung over the altar. The minister preaches and the singer sings: "The Lord hath been on our side. He treadeth the people under me. He teacheth my hands to war, my fingers to fight. Yea, He giveth me the necks of mine enemies; for the Lord is His name;" and "It was a famous victory!" Boston seizes miles square of land; but her houses are empty; her wives widows; her children fatherless. Rachel weeps for the murder of her innocents, yet dares not rebuke the rod.

I know there is no fighting across Charles River, as in this poor fiction; but there was once, and instead of Charles say Rio Grande; for Cambridge read Metamoras, and it is what your President recommended; what your Congress enacted; what your Governor issued his proclamation for; what your volunteers go to accomplish: yes, what they fired cannon for on Boston Common the other day. I wish that were a fiction of mine!

We are waging a most iniquitous war--so it seems to me. I know I may be wrong, but I am no partisan; and if I err, it is not wilfully, not rashly. I know the Mexicans are a wretched people; wretched in their origin, history, and character. I know but two good things of them as a people --they abolished negro slavery, not long ago; they do not covet the lands of their neighbors. True, they have not paid all their debts; but it is scarcely decent in a nation, with any repudiating States, to throw the first stone at Mexico for that!

I know the Mexicans cannot stand before this terrible Anglo-Saxon race, the most formidable and powerful the world ever saw; a race which has never turned back; which, though it number less than forty millions, yet holds the Indies, almost the whole of North America; which rules the commerce of the world; clutches at New Holland, China, New Zealand, Borneo, and seizes island after island in the furthest seas; the race which invented steam as its awful type. The poor, wretched Mexicans can never stand before us. How they perished in battle! They must melt away as the Indians before the white man. Considering how we acquired Louisiana, Florida, Oregon, I cannot forbear thinking that this people will possess the whole of the continent before many years; perhaps before the century ends. But this may be had fairly; with no injustice to any one; by the steady advance of a

superior race, with superior ideas and a better civilization;
by commerce, trade, arts; by being better than Mexico,
wiser, humaner, more free and manly. Is it not better to
acquire it by the schoolmaster than the cannon? by peddling
cloth, tin, anything rather than bullets? It may not all belong to this Government, and yet to this race. It would be
a gain to mankind if we could spread over that country the
idea of America--that all men are born free and equal in
rights, and establish there political, social, and individual
freedom. But to do that, we must first make real these
ideas at home.

     In the general issue between this race and that, we
are in the right. But in this special issue, and this particular war, it seems to me that we are wholly in the wrong;
that our invasion of Mexico is as bad as the partition of
Poland in the last century and in this. If I understand the
matter, the whole movement, the settlement of Texas, the
Texan revolution, the annexation of Texas, the invasion of
Mexico, has been a movement hostile to the American idea,
a movement to extend slavery. I do not say such was the
design on the part of the people, but on the part of the politicians who pulled the strings. I think the papers of the
Government and the debates of Congress prove that. The
annexation has been declared unconstitutional in its mode, a
virtual dissolution of the Union, and that by very high and
well-known authority. It was expressly brought about for
the purpose of extending slavery. An attempt is now made
to throw the shame of this on the democrats. I think the
democrats deserve the shame; but I could never see that the
whigs, on the whole, deserved it any less; only they were
not quite so open. Certainly, their leaders did not take
ground against it, never as against a modification of the
tariff! When we annexed Texas, we of course took her for
better or worse, debts and all, and annexed her war along
with her. I take it everybody knew that; though now some
seem to pretend a decent astonishment at the result. Now
one party is ready to fight for it as the other! The North
did not oppose the annexation of Texas. Why not? They
knew they could make money by it. The eyes of the North
are full of cotton; they see nothing else, for a web is before
them; their ears are full of cotton, and they hear nothing
but the buzz of their mills; their mouth is full of cotton, and
they can speak audibly but two words--Tariff, Tariff, Dividends, Dividends. The talent of the North is blinded,
deafened, gagged with its own cotton. The North clamoured
loudly when the nation's treasure was removed from the

United States Bank; it is almost silent at the annexation of a
slave territory big as the kingdom of France, encumbered
with debts, loaded with the entailment of war! Northern
governors call for soldiers; our men volunteer to fight in a
most infamous war for the extension of slavery! Tell it not
in Boston, whisper it not in Faneuil Hall, lest you waken
the slumbers of your fathers, and they curse you as cowards
and traitors unto men! Not satisfied with annexing Texas
and a war, we next invaded a territory which did not belong
to Texas, and built a fort on the Rio Grande, where, I take
it, we had no more right than the British, in 1841, had on
the Penobscot or the Saco. Now the Government and its
Congress would throw the blame on the innocent, and say
war exists "by the act of Mexico!" If a lie was ever told,
I think this is one. Then the "dear people" must be called
on for money and men, for "the soil of this free republic is
invaded"; and the Governor of Massachusetts, one of the men
who declared the annexation of Texas unconstitutional, recom-
mends the war he just now told us to pray against, and
appeals to our "patriotism," and "humanity," as arguments
for butchering the Mexicans, when they are in the right and
we in the wrong! The maxim is held up, "Our country,
right or wrong"; "Our country, howsoever bounded;" and it
might as well be "Our country, howsoever governed." It
seems popularly and politically forgotten that there is such a
thing as Right. The nation's neck invites a tyrant. I am
not at all astonished that northern representatives voted for
all this work of crime. They are no better than Southern
representatives; scarcely less in favour of slavery, and not
half so open. They say: Let the North make money, and
you may do what you please with the nation; and we will
choose governors that dare not oppose you, for, though we
are descended from the Puritans, we have but one article in
our creed we never flinch from following, and that is--to
make money; honestly, if we can; if not, as we can!

Look through the action of your Government, and your
Congress. You see that no reference has been had in this
affair to Christian ideas; none to justice and the eternal right.
Nay, none at all! In the churches, and among the people,
how feeble has been the protest against this great wrong.
How tamely the people yield their necks--and say: "Take our
sons for the war--we care not, right or wrong." England
butchers the Sikhs in India--her generals are elevated to the
peerage, and the head of her church writes a form of thanksgiving for the victory, to be read in all the churches of that
Christian land. [5] To make it still more abominable, the

blasphemy is enacted on Easter Sunday, the great holiday of
men who serve the Prince of Peace.   We have not had
prayers in the churches, for we have no political Archbishop.   But we fired cannon in joy that we had butchered a
few wretched men--half-starved, and forced into the ranks
by fear of death! Your peace-societies, and your churches,
what can they do? What dare they? Verily, we are a faithless and perverse generation.   God be merciful to us, sin-
ners as we are!

        But why talk for ever? What shall we do? In regard
to this present war, we can refuse to take any part in it; we
can encourage others to do the same; we can aid men, if
need be, who suffer because they refuse.   Men will call us
traitors: what then? That hurt nobody in '76! We are a
rebellious nation; our whole history is treason; our blood
was attainted before we were born; our creeds are infidelity
to the mother-church; our Constitution treason to our father-
land.   What of that? Though all the governors in the world
bid us commit treason against man, and set the example, let
us never submit.   Let God only be a master to control our
conscience!

        We can hold public meetings in favour of peace, in
which what is wrong shall be exposed and condemned.   It is
proof of our cowardice that this has not been done before
now.   We can show in what the infamy of a nation consists;
in what its real glory.   One of your own men, the last summer, startled the churches out of their sleep, [6] by his manly
trumpet, talking with us, and telling that the true grandeur
of a nation was justice, not glory; peace, not war.

        We can work now for future times, by taking pains to
spread abroad the sentiments of peace, the ideas of peace,
among the people in schools, churches--everywhere.   At
length we can diminish the power of the national Government,
so that the people alone shall have the power to declare war,
by a direct vote, the Congress only to recommend it.   We
can take from the Government the means of war, by raising
only revenue enough for the nation's actual wants, and raising that directly, so that each man knows what he pays, and
when he pays it, and then he will take care that it is not
paid to make him poor and keep him so.   We can diffuse a
real practical Christianity among the people, till the mass of
men have courage enough to overcome evil with good, and
look at aggressive war as the worst of treason and the foulest
infidelity!

Now is the time to push and be active. War itself
gives weight to words of peace. There will never be a
better time till we make the times better. It is not a day
for cowardice, but for heroism. Fear not that the "honour
of the nation" will suffer from Christian movements for
peace. What if your men of low degree are a vanity, and
your men of high degree are a lie? That is no new thing.
Let true men do their duty, and the lie and the vanity will
pass each to its reward. Wait not for the churches to
move, or the State to become Christian. Let us bear our
testimony like men, not fearing to be called traitors, infidels; fearing only to be such.

I would call on Americans, by their love of our
country, its great ideas, its real grandeur, its hopes, and
the memory of its fathers--to come and help to save that
country from infamy and ruin. I would call on Christians,
who believe that Christianity is a truth, to lift up their
voice, public and private, against the foulest violation of
God's law, this blasphemy of the Holy Spirit of Christ, this
worst form of infidelity to man and God. I would call on
all men, by the one nature that is in you, by the great human heart beating alike in all your bosoms, to protest manfully against this desecration of the earth, this high treason
against both man and God. Teach your rulers that you are
Americans, not slaves; Christians, not heathen; men, not
murderers, to kill for hire! You may effect little in this
generation, for its head seems crazed and its heart rotten.
But there will be a day after to-day. It is for you and me
to make it better: a day of peace, when nation shall no
longer lift up sword against nation; when all shall indeed be
brothers, and all blest. Do this, you shall be worthy to
dwell in this beautiful land; Christ will be near you; God
work with you, and bless you for ever!

This present trouble with Mexico may be very brief;
surely it might be even now brought to an end with no unusual manhood in your rulers. Can we say we have not deserved it? Let it end; but let us remember that war, horrid as it is, is not the worst calamity which ever befalls a
people. It is far worse for a people to lose all reverence
for right, for truth, all respect for man and God; to care
more for the freedom of trade than the freedom of men;
more for a tariff than millions of souls. This calamity
came upon us gradually, long before the present war, and
will last long after that has died away. Like people like
ruler, is a true word. Look at your rulers, representa-

tives, and see our own likeness! We reverence force, and
have forgot there is any right beyond the vote of a Congress
or a people; any good beside dollars; any God but majorities
and force. I think the present war, though it should cost
50,000 men and $50,000,000, the smallest part of our mis-
fortune. Abroad we are looked on as a nation of swindlers
and men-stealers! What can we say in our defence? Alas!
the nation is a traitor to its great idea, --that all men are
born equal, each with the same unalienable rights. We are
infidels to Christianity. We have paid the price of our
shame.

There have been dark days in this nation before now.
It was gloomy when Washington with his little army fled
through the Jerseys. It was a long dark day from '83 to
'89. It was not so dark as now; the nation never so false.
There was never a time when resistance to tyrants was so
rare a virtue; when the people so tamely submitted to a
wrong. Now you can feel the darkness. The sack of this
city and the butchery of its people were a far less evil than
the moral deadness of the nation. Men spring up again like
the mown grass; but to raise up saints and heroes in a dead
nation corrupting beside its golden tomb, what shall do that
for us? We must look not to the many for that, but to the
few who are faithful unto God and man.

I know the hardy vigour of our men, the stalwart intellect of this people. Would to God they could learn to love
the right and true. Then what a people should we be,
spreading from the Madawaska to the Sacramento, diffusing
our great idea, and living our religion, the Christianity of
Christ! O Lord! make the vision true; waken thy prophets
and stir thy people till righteousness exalt us! No wonders
will be wrought for that. But the voice of conscience speaks
to you and me, and all of us: the right shall prosper; the
wicked States shall die; and History responds her long amen.

What lessons come to us from the past! The Genius
of the old civilization, solemn and sad, sits there on the
Alps, his classic beard descending o'er his breast. Behind
him arise the new nations, bustling with romantic life. He
bends down over the midland sea, and counts up his children
--Assyria, Egypt, Tyre, Carthage, Troy, Etruria, Corinth,
Athens, Rome--once so renowned, now gathered with the
dead, their giant ghosts still lingering pensive o'er the spot.
He turns westward his face, too sad to weep, and raising
from his palsied knee his trembling hand, looks on his

brother genius of the new civilization. That young giant,
strong and mocking, sits there on the Alleghanies. Before
him lie the waters, covered with ships; behind him he hears
the roar of the Mississippi and the far distant Oregon--
rolling their riches to the sea. He bends down, and that far
ocean murmurs pacific in his ear. On his left are the har-
bours, shops, and mills of the East, and a fivefold gleam of
light goes up from Northern lakes. On his right spread out
the broad savannahs of the South, waiting to be blessed; and
far off that Mexique bay bends round her tropic shores. A
crown of stars is on that giant's head, some glorious with
flashing, many-coloured light; some bloody red; some pale
and faint, of most uncertain hue. His right hand lies folded
in his robe; the left rests on the Bible's opened page, and
holds these sacred words--All men are equal, born with
equal rights from God. The old says to the young, "Brother,
beware!" and Alps and Rocky Mountains say, "Beware!"
That stripling giant, ill-bred and scoffing, shouts amain:
"My feet are red with the Indian's blood; my hand has forged
the negro's chain. I am strong; who dares assail me? I
will drink his blood, for I have made my covenant of lies,
and leagued with hell for my support. There is no right,
no truth; Christianity is false, and God a name." His left
hand rends those sacred scrolls, casting his Bibles underneath his feet, and in his right he brandishes the negro-
driver's whip, crying again--"Say, who is God, and what is
Right!" And all his mountains echo--Right. But the old
genius sadly says again: "Though hand join in hand, the
wicked shall not prosper." The hollow tomb of Egypt,
Athens, Rome, of every ancient State, with all their wander-
ing ghosts, replies, "Amen."

Notes

1.   Isaiah lxiii. 1-6. --Noyes's Version.
The People.
    1.   Who is this that cometh from Edom?
In scarlet garments from Bozrah?
This, that is glorious in his apparel,
Proud in the greatness of his strength?

Jehovah.
I, that proclaim deliverance,
And am mighty to save.

The People.

2. Wherefore is thine apparel red,
   And thy garments like those of one that
   treadeth the wine-vat?

Jehovah.

3. I have trodden the wine-vat alone,
   And of the nations there was none with me.
   And I trod them in mine anger,
   And I trampled them in my fury,
   So that their life-blood was sprinkled upon
   my garments;
   And I have stained all my apparel.
4. For the day of vengeance was in my heart.
   And the year of my deliverance was come.
5. And I looked and there was none to help,
   And I wondered that there was none to uphold,
   Therefore my own arm wrought salvation for
   me,
   And my fury, it sustained me.
6. I trod down the nations in my anger:
   I crushed them in my fury,
   And spilled their blood upon the ground.

2. To show the differences between the Old and New Testament, and to serve as introduction to this discourse, the following passages were read as the morning lesson: Exodus xv. 1-6; 2 Sam. xxii. 32, 35-43, 48; xlv. 3-5; Isa. lxvi. 15, 16; Joel iii. 9-17; and Matt. v. 3-11, 38, 39, 43-45.

3. Such was the price offered, and such the number of soldiers then called for.

4. See the appropriate forms of prayer for that service by the present Bishop of Oxford, in Jay's Address before the American Peace Society, in 1845.

5. Form of Prayer and Thanksgiving to Almighty God.

O Lord God of Hosts, in whose hand is power and might irresistible, we, Thine unworthy servants, most humbly acknowledge Thy goodness in the victories lately vouchsafed to the armies of our Sovereign over a host of barbarous invaders, who sought to spread desolation over fruitful and populous provinces, enjoying the blessings of peace,

under the protection of the British Crown. We
bless Thee, O merciful Lord, for having brought
to a speedy and prosperous issue a war to which
no occasion had been given by injustice on our
part, or apprehension of injury at our hands! To
Thee, O Lord, we ascribe the glory! It was Thy
wisdom which guided the counsel! Thy power
which strengthened the hands of those whom it
pleased Thee to use as Thy instruments in the
discomfiture of the lawless aggressor, and the
frustration of his ambitious designs! From Thee
alone cometh the victory, and the spirit of mod-
eration and mercy in the day of success. Continue, we beseech Thee, to go forth with our
armies, whensoever they are called into battle in
a righteous cause; and dispose the hearts of their
leaders to exact nothing more from the vanquished
than is necessary for the maintenance of peace and
security against violence and rapine.

Above all, give Thy grace to those who preside in
the councils of our Sovereign, and administer the
concerns of her widely-extended dominions, that
they may apply all their endeavours to the purposes designed by Thy good Providence, in com-
mitting such power to their hands, the temporal
and spiritual benefit of the nations intrusted to
their care.

And whilst Thou preservest our distant posses-
sions from the horrors of war, give us peace and
plenty at home, that the earth may yield her increase, and that we, Thy servants, receiving Thy
blessings with thankfulness and gladness of heart,
may dwell together in unity, and faithfully serve
Thee, to Thy honour and glory, through Jesus
Christ our Lord, to whom with Thee and the Holy
Ghost, belong all dominion and power, both in
heaven and earth, now and for ever. Amen. --
See a defence of this prayer in the London Christian Observer for May, p. 319, et seq., and for
June, p. 346, et seq.

Would you know what he gave thanks for on Easter
Sunday? Here is the history of the battle:--

This battle had begun at six, and was over at

eleven o'clock; the hand-to-hand combat com-
menced at nine, and lasted scarcely two hours.
The river was full of sinking men. For two
hours, volley after volley was poured in upon
the human mass--the stream being literally red
with blood, and covered with the bodies of the
slain. At last, the musket ammunition becoming
exhausted, the infantry fell to the rear, the horse
artillery plying grape till not a man was visible
within range. No compassion was felt or mercy
shown. But, 'Twas a famous victory!'

6. Mr. Charles Sumner.

SELECTED BIBLIOGRAPHY

Works by Theodore Parker

Parker, Theodore. <u>Collected Works.</u> Edited by Frances
    P. Cobbe. 14 vols. London: Trübner, 1863-1879.

_____. <u>The Works of Theodore Parker.</u> "Centenary
    Edition. " 15 vols. Boston: American Unitarian
    Association, 1907-13.

_____. "The Previous Question between Mr. Andrews
    Norton and His Alumni. " The Levi Blodgett Letter.
    Contained in appendix of Dirks, John, <u>The Critical</u>
    <u>Theology of Theodore Parker.</u>

_____. <u>Theodore Parker: An Anthology.</u> Edited by H.
    S. Commager. Boston: Beacon, 1960.

Works about Theodore Parker

Bibliographies

The following works contain helpful bibliographies.

Albrecht, Robert C. <u>Theodore Parker.</u> New York: Twayne,
    1971.

Chadwick, John White. <u>Theodore Parker, Preacher and</u>
    <u>Reformer.</u> Boston: Houghton Mifflin Co. , 1900.

Commager, Henry Steele. <u>Theodore Parker, Yankee</u>
    <u>Crusader.</u> Boston: Little Brown and Co. , 1936.

Dirks, John E. <u>The Critical Theology of Theodore Parker.</u>
    Westport, Conn. : Greenwood, 1970.

Martin, John H. "Theodore Parker. " Unpublished Ph. D.

261

dissertation. Divinity School. University of Chicago, 1953.

Miller, Perry. Transcendentalists. Cambridge: Harvard
University Press, 1960.

Biographies

Albrecht, Robert C. Theodore Parker. New York: Twayne, 1971.

Chadwick, John White. Theodore Parker, Preacher and Reformer. Boston: Houghton Mifflin Co., 1900.

Commager, Henry Steele. Theodore Parker, Yankee Cru-
sader. Boston: Little Brown and Co., 1936.

Frothingham, Octavius B. Theodore Parker, A Biography.
New York: Putnam's Sons, 1874.

Martin, John H. "Theodore Parker." Unpublished Ph. D.
dissertation, Divinity School, University of Chicago,
1953.

Weiss, John. Life and Correspondence of Theodore Parker.
2 vols. New York: Bergman, 1969. This is a re-
print of the 1864 edition.

Studies

Aaron, Daniel. Men of Good Hope. New York: Oxford
University Press, 1951.

Bartlett, I. H. "Theodore Parker." Encyclopedia of Philosophy. Edited by Paul Edwards. 8 vols. New
York: Macmillan, 1967.

Commager, Henry Steele. "The Dilemma of Theodore
Parker," New England Quarterly, VI (1933), 257-77.

_____. "Tempest in a Boston Teacup," New England
Quarterly, VI (1933), 651-75.

_____. "Theodore Parker, Intellectual Gourmand,"
American Scholar, III (1934), 257-65.

Cooke, George W. Unitarianism in America. New York:
AMS Press, 1971.

Dirks, John E.   The Critical Theology of Theodore Parker.
     Westport, Conn. : Greenwood, 1970.

Faust, Clarence H.   "The Background of Unitarian Opposi-
     tion to Transcendentalism, " Modern Philology, XXV
     (1937), 297-324.

Frothingham, O. B.   Transcendentalism in New England.
     New York: Harper, 1959.

Goddard, Harold Clarke.   Studies in New England Transcen-
     dentalism.   New York: Columbia University Press,
     1908.

Gohdes, Clarence.   The Periodicals of American Transcen-
     dentalism.   Durham, N. C. : Duke University Press,
     1931.

Higginson, T. W.   "On Theodore Parker, "   Atlantic
     Monthly, VI (Oct. , 1860), 449-57.

Ladu, Arthur I.   "The Political Ideas of Theodore Parker, "
     Studies in Philology, XXXVIII (1941), 106-23.

Lewis, R. W. B.   The American Adam.   Chicago: University
     of Chicago Press, 1955.

Mead, David.   Yankee Eloquence in the Middle West: The
     Ohio Lyceum 1850-70.   East Lansing, Mich. : Michi-
     gan State College Press, 1951.

Mead, Edwin D.   The Influence of Emerson.   Boston:
     Beacon, 1903.

Miller, Perry.   Transcendentalists.   Cambridge: Harvard
     University Press, 1960.

Nelson, Truman.   The Sin of the Prophet.   Boston: Little,
     Brown, 1952.

Newbrough, George F.   "Reason and Understanding in the
     Works of Theodore Parker, " South Atlantic Quarterly,
     XLVII (Jan. , 1948), 64-75.

Parrington, V. L.   Main Currents in American Thought.
     2 vols.   New York: Harcourt, Brace, 1954.

Pochmann, Henry A.   German Culture in America: Philosophical and Literary Influences, 1600-1900. Madison, Wis.: University of Wisconsin Press, 1957.

Riback, William H. "Theodore Parker of Boston: Social Reformer," Social Service Review, XXII (1948), 451-60.

Schneider, Herbert W. A History of American Philosophy. New York: Columbia University Press, 1963.

Smith, H. Shelton. "Was Theodore Parker a Transcendentalist?" New England Quarterly, XXIII (1950), 351-64.

Tyler, Alice. Freedom's Ferment. New York: Harper, 1962.

Welleck, René. "The Minor Transcendentalists and German Philosophy," New England Quarterly, XV (1942), 652-80.

Whicher, George F. (ed.) Transcendentalist Revolt Against Materialism. Boston: Heath, 1949.

INDEX

Adams, John Quincy   3
America, amusements of   157
America, chief characteristics   143-144; secondary charac-
    teristics   144-158, 161-166; impatience with authority
    144-148; philosophical tendency   148-151; lack of first
    principles 151-155; intensity of life and purpose,   155-
    158; materialism,   161-166
America, ideal of   167-169
American Church, the ideal   168
American literature   See   Parker, literature.
American politics   See   Emerson, politics; Parker, politics.
Aristotle   51
Arius   24, 25, 83
Athanasius   24, 25, 83

Bacon, Francis   54, 73
Bentham, Jeremy   59, 63
Berkeley, George   16, 18, 63, 65, 73
Bible   See Emerson, Bible; Parker, religion.
bibliolatry   22, 85, 87
Bowditch, Nathaniel   39, 163
Brown, John   19

Calhoun, John   3, 58
Channing, William Ellery   175, 191, 208
characteristics, of America   See   America, characteristics.
Christ   See   Emerson, Christ; Parker, religion.
Christianity   See   Emerson, religion; Parker, religion.
Church, American, ideal   168; role of true   8-9
Condillac, Etienne   63
conscience   16, 66, 68
consciousness, facts of   64
Constitution   67

Parker on politics 2-4; American, appraisal 35-38, 40;
Emerson, comparison with 33-41; goal of 33-34, 41,
167; means to goal 34-35, 40-41, 167; philosophic
party 149-150; and sensationalist philosophy 18, 55-58;
and transcendentalism 16, 66-68
Parker on religion 7-9; abuses, solution for 22, 23-24, 99-
102; Bible 92, Bible, origin and authority 85-87; bibliolatry 22, 85, 87; Christ 88-94; Christ as ideal 92-
93; Christ, nature and authority 88-89; Christianity 95-
98; Christianity, the permanent in 77-79, 80; Christianity, transient, in general 79-80; Christianity, transient, doctrine 81-95; Christianity, transient, doctrine on
origin and authority of Bible 85-87; Christianity, transient, doctrine on Trinity 83; Christianity, transient,
forms and rites 80-81; Christianity, transient, theology
82-84; Church, American, ideal 168; Church, role of
true 8-9; Emerson, comparison 21-25; false 21-22,
23-24, 84-95; God, existence of and sensationalist philosophy 60-62; God, existence and character of and
transcendentalism 71-72; God and man, no mediator
needed 96-97; God, view of 232-233; and sensationalist
philosophy 60-63; and transcendentalism 70-73; true
8-9, 21, 23, 95-98
Parker on scholarship, scholar, his debt 103-108; scholar,
his duty 115-116; scholar, self-made 104; scholar,
service owed 108-109; scholarship, American, appraisal
26, 29-31, 121-136; scholarship, American, cultural
setting 26-27, 31, 109, 111-116; scholarship, American,
comparison with Emerson 26-33; scholarship, American,
opportunity 29, 32, 111-115, 136-137; scholarship,
American, purpose 28-29, 108-109; scholarship, American, science 30, 121-122; scholarship and the American
mind 116; scholarship, German 28, 31, 109-111;
scholarship, true 28-29, 31-32, 124-125
Parker on sensationalist philosophy 13, 53; and ethics 58-
60; freedom of will 63; God, existence of 60-62; good
of 20, 73; immortality 62-63; and physics 17-18, 53-
55; and politics 18-19, 55-58; and religion 60-63
Parker on transcendentalism, transcendental-mad 19-20, 65-
66, 68, 70, 73; definition 12-13, 15, 64; Emerson,
comparison with 12-21; and ethics 68-70; God, existence
and character of 71-72; immortality 72; and physics 15-
16, 65-66; and politics 16, 66-68; and religion 70-73;
its work 74
Parker on war, aggressive 234, 245, 247, 254; army 238;
and Christianity 234, 245, 246-247, 255; and the Church
235; commerce, destruction of 235-236; corruption it
brings 245-246; cost 237, 239-242; cost to poor 241-